RADICAL ACCEPTANCE

THE SECRET TO HAPPY, LASTING LOVE

ANDREA MILLER

ATRIA BOOKS

NEW YORK   LONDON   TORONTO   SYDNEY   NEW DELHI

ATRIA BOOKS

An Imprint of Simon & Schuster, Inc.
1230 Avenue of the Americas
New York, NY 10020

First Atria Books hardcover edition March 2017

ATRIA BOOKS and colophon are trademarks of Simon & Schuster, Inc.

For information about special discounts for bulk purchases,
please contact Simon & Schuster Special Sales at 1-866-506-1949
or business@simonandschuster.com.

The Simon & Schuster Speakers Bureau can bring authors to your live event. For
more information or to book an event, contact the Simon & Schuster Speakers
Bureau at 1-866-248-3049 or visit our website at www.simonspeakers.com.

Interior design by Dana Sloan

Manufactured in the United States of America

10 9 8 7 6 5 4 3 2 1

Library of Congress Cataloging-in-Publication Data

Names: Miller, Andrea, author.
Title: Radical acceptance : the secret to happy, lasting love / Andrea Miller.
Description: First Atria Books hardcover edition. | New York : Atria Books, 2017.
Identifiers: LCCN 2016039291 (print) | LCCN 2016049169 (ebook) | ISBN
    9781501139208 (hardback) | ISBN 9781501139215 (paperback) | ISBN
    9781501139222 (ebook)
Subjects: LCSH: Love. | Self-acceptance. | Interpersonal relations. | BISAC:
    FAMILY & RELATIONSHIPS / Marriage. | SELF-HELP / Personal Growth /
    Self-Esteem.
Classification: LCC BF575.L8 M46 2017 (print) | LCC BF575.L8 (ebook) | DDC
    306.7—dc23
LC record available at https://lccn.loc.gov/2016039291

ISBN 978-1-5011-3920-8
ISBN 978-1-5011-3922-2 (ebook)

To Sanjay, the love of my life.

CONTENTS

AUTHOR'S NOTE

THIS BOOK IS for everyone who wants to achieve happy, lasting love; to feel more confident and compassionate; to have greater emotional resilience; and to be more connected to friends and family. I hope my message will appeal to you regardless of your age, gender, sexual orientation, race, or religion.

That said, my perspective is largely informed by my own experiences as a married, heterosexual woman. After considerable deliberation, I decided to narrate this book in a conversational "girlfriend-to-girlfriend" tone to avoid subjecting you to a bevy of pronouns in an effort to make the voice as neutral as possible. (I tried, I promise.) This would have only made for tiresome writing and even more tiresome reading.

Instead, I interviewed and observed people with very different backgrounds, and have incorporated their stories and insights to create as inclusive an environment as possible. As you'll see in this book, Radical Acceptance transcends labels. Love is paramount, no matter what form it takes. Please remember that I am here for you, regardless of how you identify yourself.

Speaking of identities: I have carefully concealed the identity of the individuals referenced in this book. With the exception of Sanjay and me, along with a handful of references to friends and family whose stories offer positive examples for this book, virtually all other names and identifying features have been changed.

This book is for people at every stage of love they may find themselves in. Whether you are single, dating, engaged, married, living together, nursing a broken heart, going through a divorce or breakup, or describe your situation as "complicated," Radical Acceptance is for you. You'll see references to and stories about people in all stages of love throughout the book.

I have laid this book out very deliberately to ease you into the Radical Acceptance mind-set and help you build a strong foundation for it. In part 1, we begin with an overview of Radical Acceptance and address different scenarios you may find yourself in. By the time you enter part 2, which features the five steps to Radical Acceptance, my goal is for your heart and mind to be open and engaged to ensure you get the most out of this book.

I have peppered all sections with entertaining and informative morsels. While they may not all apply to you at exactly this moment, many of them, I suspect, will be relatable nevertheless, and may be helpful to you in the future or may offer insights for you to share with a friend. For instance, there are many insights and anecdotes in part 1 that are targeted to people who are single or dating, but a number of them are likely to prove useful to you even if you're in a long-term relationship or married. From flirting to fighting to infidelity to building trust in your relationship and learning to manage expectations, these chapters are filled with material that I hope you find interesting and useful, no matter what love stage you are in.

My wish is that you'll read the entire text from beginning to end, perhaps make notes in the margins, your e-reader, or your journal, and then return to the parts that resonated with you, challenged you, or inspired you. You'll find that this book is packed to the gills with wisdom, thoughtful advice, illuminating anecdotes, scientific research, inspiring quotes, cameo appearances from popular cultural icons, and so much more. It may be tough to take it all in at once, even for you ultra-careful readers. In any event, I hope you love it.

Finally! I would truly love if you were to share feedback with me during your Radical Acceptance journey via social media and through my website. Together, we can spark a Radical Acceptance movement, leading to much more love, compassion, and happiness in our world.

Now, let's get started!

INTRODUCTION

ONE NIGHT, AFTER years of living with my boyfriend Sanjay, one of our disagreements became too much. *"You are impossible!"* I shouted at him. "I love you, but I can't keep doing this." I bolted out of the apartment we shared on the Upper West Side and, shaking with anger, stormed down Broadway and stopped at a hotel to inquire about a room. I wound up instead sitting in a dark, dingy Irish pub nearby drinking tea and reading a book until three a.m.

Walking back home late that night, and in the days following, I thought a lot about my relationship with Sanjay, whom I had fallen for the instant I laid eyes on him. He was the most brilliant man I'd ever met, and I loved him dearly. But our relationship was riddled with conflict. We had chemistry galore and were committed to each other, yet we sustained a lot of frustration that never seemed to get resolved. This wasn't because either of us had fatal flaws. In fact, we were very much alike: well-educated, ambitious, hard-working professionals who had a lot of fun together, who endeavored to have a family and share a rewarding, love- and joy-filled life.

And yet. There was pain. And fighting. And blame. We had them in spades. Oh—and endless discussions about what each of us could do better that stretched into the wee hours of the night. He needed me to work less and prioritize him more. I needed him to be less critical of

1

me and to learn to express his frustrations and criticisms much more constructively. He needed me to always have his back—even in public situations where I disagreed with him. And he needed me to be less defensive. I needed him to appreciate me more and understand me better. Despite how much we cared for each other, we did not feel loved enough by each other, which led to a vicious cycle of defensiveness and withholding. Looking back now, it was obvious that we both needed to listen better, judge each other a lot less, and find more constructive ways to manage our differences and disappointments.

Shortly after the night at the Irish pub, I recounted the challenges Sanjay and I were experiencing to Lorell, an old family friend, someone very wise whom I had known for years. She had surprising advice. Profound advice, in fact. She said, simply, "Andrea, just love him."

That stopped me dead in my tracks. What she said was spot on. Moreover, hearing it was such a relief, so liberating. I will always recall that conversation with Lorell—it was such a pivotal moment in my life. I was on the phone with her, standing in the bedroom of the New York City apartment where Sanjay and I had lived together for a few years. I had been wringing my hands and ruminating endlessly about what to do, about how we could make it work. We weren't married yet, but we were planning to be. And suddenly, upon hearing Lorell's three simple words, any nagging sense of fear and anxiety that had been eating away at me evaporated.

Her words offered me a powerful path forward. Upon deciding to "just love him," I was finally, *really* making a commitment to him and to our relationship. While we had been together for a handful of years, and though I loved him very much, our differences sometimes seemed intractable, to the point where I had been nursing an exit strategy in the back of my mind. During these challenging phases I would think about how I could extricate myself from our relationship without falling apart. Where would I live? How would Sanjay handle it? How would *I* handle it? I'd convince myself that I'd feel heartbroken, but that we would both be better off. I now know that planning for the worst will inevitably result in a failed relationship. There was a better way.

The immense, binary power of commitment became clear to me. I say binary because it is on or it is off. You can't kind of be committed. I realized that when I vowed to simply love Sanjay, a profound shift had occurred in my heart and in my mind. My thoughts, actions, intentions, and words all aligned to communicate and achieve this commitment. Previously, the signals I had unwittingly been sending were along the lines of: *Well, maybe I will be there for you as long as you behave and we are getting along. Or maybe I can't always be there for you. My work is my top priority.*

Now, rather than withdraw, brood, and ruminate, I would extend compassion and approach any disagreements more constructively. I would obsess less about my current annoyance and instead focus more on the long run—together. This series of related insights not only changed my relationship dramatically, but it planted one of two crucial seeds for what would eventually blossom into Radical Acceptance.

· · ·

In the meantime, the other crucial seed had already taken root. I had been pursuing my MBA at Columbia Business School, where I was the managing editor of the student newspaper, *The Bottom Line.* My background was in finance and engineering, but this position gave me a taste of media. I loved it. I had just concluded a terrific summer internship at Goldman Sachs, but I returned to my second year at Columbia determined to do something I was truly passionate about. I hail from a family of entrepreneurs and entered B-school thinking about starting my own business one day.

Based on my and Sanjay's experiences, I had been reflecting on relationships. I thought about the doubts and fights in the love lives of many of the people I was close to, including the painful divorce one of my best friends went through. I realized that every person, every couple, does a dance of sorts to connect and try to get close. But many times they only end up creating distance from one another.

I thought a lot about a couple I know who have been married for nearly twenty years, Vinod and Priya. They were high school sweethearts. They have a ton of chemistry and clearly love each other very much. But he is incredibly critical and judgmental of her, and she is ready to implode with resentment and hurt. She makes a noble effort to placate him, to minimize creating any waves, to try to protect herself and not upset him. But while she's done this out of love, she has also disconnected from him, creating a horrendous cycle: he perceives her distance, which makes him feel bad, which he responds to with anger. Somehow he doesn't connect the dots that she's put up walls because of him. And thus the cycle of hurt continues. Vinod and Priya's relationship is a classic example of how often loneliness or disappointment in a relationship translates into anger. It's something I had experienced for far too long. It's incredibly painful and can be very destructive: the common pattern where we punish those who hurt us where it hurts the most. It's some of the worst kind of pain and suffering that can be experienced. Unfortunately, it's also some of the most common.

I realized that everyone can relate to love's heart-soaring triumphs and its unparalleled ability to bring them to their knees. My experience was a testament to how maintaining a loving relationship is often the hardest but most rewarding experience in life. Then, early in my second year in B-school, as I was sitting in Professor Feiner's high-performance leadership class, I had an epiphany.

Earlier that week I had read an excerpt of the book *Soul Mates: Honoring the Mystery of Love and Relationships* out loud to Sanjay, which led to a lively and endearing conversation. During Professor Feiner's class, I started thinking about how the incredibly crowded media landscape tended to cover the topic of love and relationships—and then suddenly the moon and stars aligned. I was floored by how simplistic, and often downright superficial, this coverage was. "59 Ways to Please Your Man,"

"17 Sneaky Ways to Get Him to Propose," and "Just Lose 10 lbs. and You'll Be Happy!" are representative of the kinds of headlines that have dominated this subject area, especially by some of the most popular women's magazine brands. Of course, these articles often cause women to feel even worse about themselves: disillusioned, self-conscious, and alone.

Love was just one element in a much broader editorial mix among the traditional women's media outlets, along with sections dedicated to hair, shoes, shopping, celebrities, dieting, and so on. Across the media and publishing landscape there were magazines and websites devoted to sports, beauty, fashion, architecture, cooking, home décor, celebrities, computers—the list goes on and on—but there was not one solely dedicated to love. It struck me that any really good, compelling information on love and relationships was primarily acquired through books. *The Truth about Love; Men Are from Mars, Women Are from Venus; Getting the Love You Want*—I had read and been inspired by them all.

Love permeates pop culture: it has a major or minor presence in nearly every story ever sold, from *The Good Wife* and *Friends* to *Gone with the Wind* and *Titanic*. When you think about it, most superhero movies even have romance as a key plot line! Yet, despite all of its power and importance in our lives, I realized that no media company had laid claim to this topic in a truly substantive, affirming way. I knew that love in all of its forms was the root of happiness and so much more; it's the most powerful, important thing in the world—and typically the most difficult to get right.

Sitting there in class, I managed to find monumental "white space" in the overcrowded media landscape. Having identified this enormous opportunity, I decided to leave my lucrative, promising career in finance and start a media company focused on love and relationships.

Given what a wonderful metaphor dance is to love, my cousin Elise suggested I call it Tango. I was hesitant at first: Wouldn't people think it was dedicated to the famous Argentinian dance? But finding and sustaining true love is nothing if not an ever-dynamic dance. Indeed, it takes two to tango! After a day or two, I decided her idea was brilliant. The name I gave to my company was Tango Publishing, which led to the eventual creation of YourTango.com, where we passionately believe that helping people love better and connect more meaningfully is key to increasing their happiness, confidence, and sense of belonging. An abundance of data fuels our passion, including the epic Harvard Grant Study. After seventy-five years and $20 million, this research, which attempted to determine what variables promote a fulfilling life, reported its number-one most important conclusion: "Happiness is Love. Full Stop."

YourTango focuses on what's happening inside women's hearts and minds—and at its core, YourTango is based on my belief that truly accepting ourselves and the ones we love is the key to success in love.

My vision for YourTango is to be to love what ESPN is to sports. For over ten years I have been on a personal mission to help millions of people across the globe love more deeply and more successfully, to help them feel more connected and more confident, and to help them achieve life's ultimate prize: unconditional love and belonging. My conviction only grows with each passing day, especially when we receive messages from readers thanking our writers and editors for the beautiful stories and insightful advice we post. My team and I feel enormously proud to know we have improved countless lives and, based on some emotional missives from readers, that we have even saved some.

YourTango has succeeded in creating a community for people to be inspired and entertained by validating stories, approachable experts, and thought-provoking perspectives. We have built a unique marketing platform called YourTango Experts, which hosts nearly a thousand dating coaches, family therapists, mediators, relationship counselors, and other relationship and mental-health experts, including: John Gray, Harville Hendrix, Helen LaKelly Hunt, Pat Love, Stan Tatkin, Esther Perel, Sue Johnson, Mary Morrissey, Marty Klein, Charles J. Orlando, Bernie Siegel, John Gottman, Paul Brunson, Nick Ortner, Helen Fisher,

Ian Kerner, and many more of the foremost thought leaders in this space.

. . .

As I immersed myself in building YourTango and analyzed what was happening in my own relationship, it eventually became clear to me that I had been perpetuating the turmoil in my relationship by continuing to focus on our conflicts, my disappointment, and my habit of running away from pain and frustration. Rather than looking at disappointments and differences as a chance to grow closer (and wiser!), I allowed them to severely strain our relationship.

Sanjay had his flaws. I had mine. But he was a truly good man and we loved each other deeply. Going one big step beyond "just love him," I determined that fully accepting Sanjay, and fully accepting myself, was a powerful idea. In fact, it was a radical one. This powerful new approach is what I call *Radical Acceptance*. Radical Acceptance is the key to making a relationship not only work, but thrive. It's been the key to making my relationship with Sanjay deep and rewarding. And it changed the way I view love forever.

And now, I want to share it with you.

Just think for a moment how it would feel if you knew your significant other fully accepted you—*all* of you. Wouldn't that be the most liberating and empowering feeling imaginable? No matter your flaws or shortcomings, you are okay; you are loved. In my observations, only a very lucky few have achieved such a status—but it is my belief that almost anyone can. I say "almost" because Radical Acceptance requires a degree of fortitude, self-awareness, and maturity. These can be challenging traits for some to nurture. But for those of us who do manage to develop them, we can become practically bulletproof. It's worth every ounce of effort you are willing to make.

So, what is Radical Acceptance? It is loving without judgment. It is replacing judgment with compassion and empathy. It is loving your partner fully for who he really is—flaws, shortcomings, insecurities, and all. Radical Acceptance creates such a feeling of safety, security, and trust in the relationship that you both can truly be yourselves. To radically accept someone means: "I love you right here, right now. I have your back, no matter what. I know your flaws, failures, and shortcomings—and I still love you. I will not resent or resist them. Instead, I will extend tenderness to them."

Now, here's the beautiful, uber-powerful secret of Radical Acceptance. You will find that this process is actually often less about loving his unlovable parts and more about loving *your* unlovable parts. It's about loving yourself fully for who you really are—insecurities, flaws, and all. As you practice Radical Acceptance "on him," your perceptions shift and you are more readily able to quit sweating the small stuff; to let go of your tendency to control, blame, and be defensive; and to extend more empathy and compassion to yourself. You will be more loving and confident. Love and abundance beget further love and abundance. That said, it's not a walk in the park. This takes plenty of inner work and brutal honesty. Radical Acceptance is often less about his shortcomings, flaws, failures, and annoyances than your *reaction* to them.

There is something "kabbalah-esque" in this core component of Radical Acceptance. (Kabbalah is an ancient tradition tied to the Jewish faith that endeavors to help people find fulfillment in their lives.) A wonderful mentor of mine, David Bell, who has studied kabbalah, once quipped, "The opponent is not the person with whom you are in a relationship. The opponent is your reaction to this person and what arises in the relationship." *Bingo!* (Get ready. We're going to see this phrase again during this book.)

My friend and renowned biological anthropologist Dr. Helen Fisher has extensively studied the impact of love on the brain, which she details in multiple brilliant TED Talks, numerous *New York Times* bestselling books, and in speeches around the globe. Helen has discovered compelling insights[1] among couples who remain happy over many years together. For example, after putting more than one hundred people into MRI machines and studying brain activity, she unequivocally asserts that the top three physiological traits—traits revealed by the activity in their brain—which long-term happy couples exhibit are as follows: they are empathetic, they have strong emotional control (i.e., they don't freak out easily), and they maintain "positive illusions" about their partners over the long run, which means these couples focus on one another's desirable traits while overlooking the negative traits. Fortunately, these observations align perfectly with Radical Acceptance, and as we'll see again and again in this book, the science backs it up every time.

By the way, even the most secure couples still occasionally fight and feel hurt by each other. During your Radical Acceptance journey, your partner is bound to say something critical to you, lose his temper, flake out on your anniversary, or do any number of things that upset or annoy you. But Radical Acceptance will reduce friction and negativity in a big way, and it will provide you and your partner with a powerful new framework to manage disagreements and disappointments.

Radical Acceptance does NOT give license for you to be a doormat, nor does it mean you should be passive or lazy in your relationship. It is not about taking the path of least resistance. It offers a means to proactively and positively manage your perceptions of and reactions to your partner's normal shortcomings and flaws. It's about preventing the quest for perfection from becoming the enemy of what is good or great about your partner.

Radical Acceptance makes you stronger and more powerful because of how much it asks of you and what it gives back to you, like after you have been doing some serious yoga, running, or any training that is physically demanding. It may be tough to get started but after a while you feel soooo good and strong. And I am not just talking about your emotions! I could go on and on (and on) here about the physical benefits you derive from a healthy, active love (and sex!) life. If you care about your physical health, add Radical Acceptance to your routine.

Radical Acceptance also does not mean your partner has license to take advantage of you. It does not make allowances for behaviors and traits that are patently unacceptable, including acute character flaws (e.g., he seriously lies, cheats, or steals); verbal, emotional, or physical abuse; or any behavior that is threatening or dangerous. There are gray areas, of course, that are best managed case by case—naturally, all relationships are different. Radical Acceptance can be a salve for some difficult emotional issues, such as a bad temper, melancholy, or low self-esteem. It's a call only you can make. You may be able to handle one or more of these challenging tendencies. But if you can't, you can't. Any issues that skirt the line between unfortunate shortcomings and fatal flaws may require more than Radical Acceptance, including professional or medical help.

And, yes—in some cases, Radical Acceptance may lead you to terminate the relationship. If this happens, you will do it with confidence. Breaking up is a heart-wrenching decision, one that typically leads to self-doubt and what-ifs: *What if he is just about to turn himself around? What if he just needed time to learn he could really trust me? What if I'm ending this too soon? What if I'm making the wrong decision?* Radical Acceptance helps you minimize these doubts by instilling a sense of calm confidence that you made the right decision.

As in any venture, success is never guaranteed. A relationship can still fail no matter how much work you put into it. However, if your partner recognizes your efforts, the good man in him—the man you are trying to love—should reciprocate. If he does not—if he takes advantage of you, or he exploits your efforts—then you are in a deal-breaker scenario and it will be time for you to move on. Ideally this won't happen, of course, but Radical Acceptance provides you with the tools to confront almost any situation, no matter how painful it can be, and ensures that you will emerge stronger and more confident than ever before.

This is a great segue to explain the connection between feminism and Radical Acceptance. For the purposes of this book, I identify *femi-*

nism as an extremely positive term, and believe its primary purpose is to empower women to achieve our full potential—personally, professionally, financially, and spiritually.

I consider myself an ardent feminist and actively support feminist causes. YourTango is a bastion of what I call happy, positive, productive feminism, the kind that builds women up instead of callously judging and tearing them down. I have crafted Radical Acceptance to be pro-feminist—even if some of my writing may seem counter to certain stereotypical feminist principles. I prefer to call these ideas *pro-humanist.* It's important to note that while I have written this book in a hetero girlfriend-to-girlfriend, conversational narrative, *all aspects of Radical Acceptance apply equally to men* and the LGBTQ community. When I say something like "Make him a priority," if you happen to be a heterosexual male, or a homosexual female, you should interpret this as "Make *her* a priority."

Radical Acceptance is *not* about subjugating readers to their male partners. It is about making anyone who reads this book stronger, more confident, and more empowered as individuals and as romantic partners. Moreover, Radical Acceptance is not about keeping score—you cannot measure your worth by what he does or doesn't do, moment by moment, tit for tat. It is okay to take the initiative, and it is okay to be the one who "gives more"—at least until Radical Acceptance starts to really take root in your relationship.

When Radical Acceptance seems to be asking too much of you, reflect on these ancient wise words from Lao Tzu: "Being deeply loved by someone gives you strength, while loving someone deeply gives you courage." Yup. Pretty much.

. . .

Looking around, I see an endless slew of people trying to evolve and transform themselves. But the truth is, people do not self-actualize in isolation. In other words, people who transform themselves positively do so with others. Throughout this book, I provide considerable evidence that experiencing love and belonging is a biological imperative. While we are emotionally and biologically wired for connection, many of us lack the wherewithal to truly love ourselves and our significant others, especially past the honeymoon phase. People who self-actualize can be truly seen and loved for who they really are—including the scary, shameful parts. As our egos stand down, our hearts can open to others and ourselves.

"Self" only exists within the context of "others"—they are inextricably linked. Improving yourself means improving your relationship with the people around you.

> **"Love is not a contract between two narcissists.**
> **It's more than that. It's a construction that**
> **compels the participants to go beyond**
> **narcissism. In order that love lasts, one has to**
> **reinvent oneself."**
>
> —ALAIN BADIOU, FRENCH PHILOSOPHER

If everyone had the wisdom and the ability to offer unconditional love, the failure rate of marriage would be much lower. Meanwhile, among marriages that ostensibly remain intact—which, in many instances should be characterized less as "successful" than an effective cycle of détente—many more would be genuinely healthy and fulfilling. Instead, far too many people merely muddle through life feeling love for their spouse but also feeling a lot of resentment, boredom, hurt, loneliness, and anger—while simultaneously feeling endlessly judged and criticized. Too many people do not feel enough love coming back at them. They hold back, they judge, they resist, they blame, they nag, they keep score, they withdraw. Thus fueling the vicious cycle. Does this sound familiar?

These are experiences I know far too well. I had to learn the hard way. I knew I wanted to spend the rest of my life with Sanjay very early in our relationship. We've been together through seventeen years of joy and pain, we now have two young children, and we both run our own companies. Even now, we still find there's room for practice. The difference is that we have the Radical Acceptance framework and insights to draw upon, again and again.

I want to help you experience the transformative power of Radical Acceptance. By committing to this journey, you may well realize that you are with Mr. Right already. For others, Radical Acceptance will place you in a better position to recognize when you have finally found him or her. After all, soul mates are *made*—they are not born. Nicholas Sparks may be amazing, but don't let *The Notebook* lead you to believe that you just have to keep waiting for the One. Instead, I have laid out the path for you to proactively forge happy, lasting love. Most crucially, *you* will become stronger by practicing Radical Acceptance. *You* will become happier. *You* will become more compassionate. *You* will become more confident and emotionally resilient.

. . .

We have a lot to cover! After a more in-depth primer of how Radical Acceptance is the best gift ever in part 1, we're going to proceed with a short but critically important caveat: when *not* to practice Radical Acceptance. Radical Acceptance isn't a cure-all for a bad relationship, nor is it the fix to a relationship in which a major difference or disconnect will prevent long-term compatibility. There are times when it's best—or imperative—to walk away from a relationship and to not attempt Radical Acceptance. Next, rather than the bright red flags, we will address various shades of orange that may be harder to discern, which may in fact be deal-breakers or merely manageable differences. We will explore why most long-lasting relationships evolve into a phase demanding more than romance and chemistry. We will face a common, heartbreaking scenario: when you are at the end of the rope in your marriage. And we will dive deeply into the question that plagues many women: Am I settling?

Then comes the exciting, challenging, rewarding parts! This is heart of the book: the five steps to Radical Acceptance. They are:

STEP 1: Just Love Him (or Just Dump Him). You will identify his unlovable parts, and then you will commit to just loving him, no matter what. If you can't commit to loving him, then it's time to move on. Without this crucial, binary step, Radical Acceptance cannot happen.

STEP 2: Stop, Reflect, Introspect. You will explore what happens when you inevitably want to reject something, maybe several things, about him. You will want to make him stop doing *that extremely annoying thing he does.* Perhaps you'll mutter, "Oh my God, I'm going to *kill* him," under your breath. That's okay—who hasn't felt these excruciating pangs of anger and hurt? Stop, Reflect, Introspect is a powerful technique that allows you to get outside your emotional reactions. Not only will this help prevent blowups, but you will understand what occurs internally for you that enables so much pain and hurt. Empathy and compassion play a leading role in this chapter.

STEP 3: Radical Communication. We will discuss proven methods for creating safety in your relationship. Safety and trust are essential ingredients for successful communication. Creating a safe space for vulnerability is crucial for Radical Acceptance to fully take root, and I will help you get there. We will delve into techniques to facilitate better communication, including being very mindful of body language (both yours and his).

STEP 4: Love *All* of Him—Even the "Unlovable" Parts. There is no such thing as meeting him halfway when it comes to Radical Acceptance. Radical Acceptance means you always have his back—even when he is wrong. Radical Acceptance is unconditional love—even when it feels unbearably difficult, when you feel deeply hurt or disappointed, or when you feel he is at fault. Step 4 is the bread and butter of Radical Acceptance. How do you love the unlovable parts of someone? Or at the very least make peace with them? I will show you.

STEP 5: Apply the Platinum Rule and Make Him Your Priority. Yup, we're going one past the golden rule! In this section, we'll practice how to express your affection in ways that are most meaningful to him, and how to train yourself to become more in tune with his wants and needs without becoming a feminist's nightmare! We'll also delve into how crucial it is to make sure he's a priority to you—and that he knows it!

Next, we'll focus on the amazing, glorious *you*. It is just as important to *be* the right person as it is to find the right person. From taking care of yourself physically to nurturing those traits and interpersonal skills that make you feel special and lovable, your relationship will benefit from you being healthy, happy, and empowered. Finally, we'll look beyond Radical Acceptance at great ways for making your relationship last and making it more fun!

Each section will feature real-life stories from couples who have dramatically improved their relationships, plus many more insights gleaned from my years of developing Radical Acceptance. I'll show you how to bring your intimacy and communication to the next level. I will share in-depth guidelines for when *not* to commit, and how to differentiate between annoying habits and outright deal-breakers. Sometimes you simply cannot accept someone's flaws. He tends to be impatient, is a little bit of a cheapskate, and has no fashion sense? We can work with that, assuming he has plenty of other redeeming traits. He's an extreme narcissist prone to excessively passive-aggressive behavior? Nope, probably not.

This book will serve as your definitive guide for not only when to love him or leave him, but more importantly how to *truly* love him—and yourself. That's because radically accepting someone requires radically accepting yourself. It means being brutally honest. It means taking ownership of your own vulnerabilities and insecurities. You will find the process immensely liberating and empowering—and yes, at times, pretty tough.

> **"Trying to change someone else is**
> **an act of aggression. Trying to change yourself is**
> **an act of love."**
>
> —DAVID BELL

. . .

Radical Acceptance is about recalibrating the importance and value of love—for ourselves and for others. It is a call to action to elevate love and togetherness to their rightful high-priority status in all people's lives. The value to individuals, families, and society of doing so is truly inestimable. Not only does vast data bear this out, but think of the historical figures that have achieved near-universal respect and admiration: Martin Luther King Jr., Gandhi, Jesus, the Buddha, Nelson Mandela, and Mother Teresa, among other individuals who galvanized the masses with their messages of love, compassion, and inclusivity.

I have channeled my passion and knowledge of Radical Acceptance into a book that taps into this immense power, one that can transform your life. I am relentlessly committed to planting Radical Acceptance into the hearts and homes of people across the globe, spawning an army of happy, loving "Radical Acceptors." Please join me!

PART 1

PREPARING FOR RADICAL ACCEPTANCE

COMMIT TO RADICAL ACCEPTANCE: THE BEST GIFT EVER

I'T'S EASY TO complain that your partner isn't living up to your expectations. But what's actually effective—what puts the energy of love in motion—is seeing someone who has flaws, yes, but realizing you can help this person become the best version of himself through unconditional love. This is Radical Acceptance.

A friend of mine once described Radical Acceptance as the "EpiPen of relationships." I love that metaphor, but it needs a very big caveat. What she meant was how unbelievably helpful Radical Acceptance can be in a flash—that is, when things are about to spiral out of control and you are about to react badly to some dumb little thing. In that regard, Radical Acceptance is an instant, ready-made injection that can stave off toxic, avoidable outcomes. When my blood is boiling after Sanjay says something irritating, I always try to ask myself, "Are you practicing Radical Acceptance right now?" Instead of reacting badly, I try exercising restraint and extending tenderness to him. As we'll explore later in the book, controlling our emotional reactions is key to Radical Acceptance.

But here's where the metaphor breaks down: Unlike an actual EpiPen, which is merely a temporary fix and is unable to permanently rid the body of life-threatening allergies, Radical Acceptance effects profound, lasting change. It's built to work for the long haul—and while it can work wonders in a pinch, significant effort is required for it to truly take root in a transformative, healing way. I will provide you with a ton of data and offer many suggestions for how to make your journey easier, but the absolutely essential key is that you *have to practice Radical Acceptance for it to really work.*

I know. Buzzkill. Barely three paragraphs in and we're already talking about hard work.

But here's the good news: Radical Acceptance can introduce (or re-introduce) healing, grace, confidence, and, ultimately, tremendous love, into your relationship. You will replace that vicious cycle of negativity with a virtuous cycle of positivity. Yes, you will face resistance and setbacks during your journey, and you will slip up from time to time. That's okay. The key is not to be discouraged. Radical Acceptance will only remain a great idea and an interesting theory if you do not make the regular, daily effort to practice it. After all, fundamentally changing your habits and your way of thinking doesn't happen overnight. By consciously choosing to accept his unlovable parts (and your own!), by focusing on the positive and overlooking the negative, you will actually establish new neural pathways. Thankfully, our brains are more than capable of changing in positive, profound ways, even well into adulthood. This is called neuroplasticity, and we'll revisit this and related concepts regularly in this book.

> *Not long ago, I received a message on Facebook from Kevin, a very old friend who had read some of my early writing on Radical Acceptance. He wrote:*

I think the last we talked I was showing my appreciation for your take on Radical Acceptance. I must tell you, I try to put it into practice as often as I can. Accepting those that I love for who they are . . . not what I want them to be. It's been life changing. I am the happiest I have ever been.

I have had so many people share their praise for Radical Acceptance, but Kevin's note is powerful in part due to its brevity. It's incredibly rewarding to hear testimonials of how the simple idea of Radical Acceptance can lead to what we all seek: lasting love and happiness.

I want to raise some foundational points before we progress further the heart of the program. The first are the most burning concerns people have about Radical Acceptance: "What if I practice Radical Acceptance but he never gets it? What if he never reciprocates? Won't this put me in a position of weakness?" I touch on reciprocation, along with how Radical Acceptance makes you stronger, below, and address these themes in depth throughout this book.

Next we'll take a look at trust in a relationship and why it is so crucially important to establish in your Radical Acceptance journey. Loving and being loved unconditionally means taking a leap of faith. It means feeling safe in your relationship and making room for vulnerability. It means taking off your mask and enabling him to do the same, so that you can both be truly seen for who you are. This level of security may take time to develop, but I will hold your hand as you learn this process.

RECIPROCATION

Just loving him fully without expecting immediate reciprocation . . . that sounds tough. Will it work? Will opening your heart actually make you feel stronger and more confident in your relationship and in your life?

You can't possibly know unless you try. And what you will get, no matter what, is clarity. Clarity on whether you should stay in the relationship or if you should end it. After you have done everything you can to love and radically accept him, if the relationship still isn't working or if his behavior just proves too challenging, you know it's time to say good-bye. You've tried everything. The what-ifs—*What if I tried harder? What if he wasn't seeing the real me? What if I needed to give him a chance?*—will evaporate. You may be sad and angry for a time, but you will harbor much less—if any—uncertainty or doubt. Because of that, you will find how much easier it is for you to move on.

Understandably, most people want to ensure their efforts aren't "wasted." To those I say: love is never wasted. When it comes to love, there are never guarantees of success. All you can do in the relationship is your part, which is why I always urge each partner to initially quit worrying about how the other is reciprocating. It rarely works to go halfway and expect him to immediately meet you there, fifty-fifty, even-steven. In fact, when I offer advice to people who want to improve their relationship, I always encourage them to each go all in, to each give 150 percent. This might feel scary for a little while, but it's a winning long-run approach.

> "There is no safe investment.[2] To love at all is to
> be vulnerable. Love anything, and your heart
> will certainly be wrung and possibly be broken.
> If you want to make sure of keeping it intact, you

**must give your heart to no one, not even to an
animal. Wrap it carefully round with hobbies and
little luxuries; avoid all entanglements; lock it up
safe in the casket or coffin of your selfishness.
But in that casket—safe, dark, motionless,
airless—it will change. It will not be broken;
it will become unbreakable, impenetrable,
irredeemable. The alternative to tragedy, or
at least to the risk of tragedy, is damnation.
The only place outside Heaven where you can
be perfectly safe from all the dangers and
perturbations of love is Hell."**

—C. S. LEWIS, *THE FOUR LOVES*

But won't you look desperate if you offer your undivided love and affection to your partner without knowing if you'll get something in return? Won't you just be a doormat? And shouldn't the guy always love the girl just a *tiny* bit more?

Nope, definitely not, and heck no!

Radical Acceptance requires radical giving—giving more, giving your all, and doing it all again, over and over. I know this may be a different way of thinking about love and life than you're used to. We live in an instant-gratification world in which we are conditioned to get what we pay for, stat. Radical Acceptance requires a fundamental recalibration of your relationship expectations. It's about not expecting someone else to "make you happy," but thinking much more about what you have to offer your partner. The *relationship* has to make you happy. As Katharine Hepburn once said, "Love has nothing to do with what you are expecting to get, only with what you are expecting to give, which is everything."

While you will ultimately need and deserve reciprocation, giving love to others is still self-serving. At the same time, it's about remembering that you are worthy of tremendous love from others and yourself.

Far too often, we are our own worst enemies. We think shitty, defeating thoughts about ourselves as often as pop radio stations play Taylor Swift—again and again and again. We beat ourselves up and refuse to give ourselves a break. And then we expect someone else to magically treat us as rock stars.

Um, do you see the paradox here? I always say that love starts with you. It is the opposite of selfish to love yourself, to know your worth, and to claim your beauty. As we will discuss in part 3, even the most successful women fall prey to a very debilitating "confidence gap" in which they are mired in self-doubt. No one can stop this debilitating cycle but you. You have to believe that you are worthy of love, praise, sacrifice, tenderness, and, yes, because we are all flawed, that you are worthy of forgiveness and compassion. As my wise big sis Maria says, "It's an inside job!"

Practicing Radical Acceptance is the ultimate inside job—it's doing that crucial inner work that leads to personal transformation and your ability to be a far better partner (and friend, parent, son or daughter, etc.).

Friend: I am here to tell you that YOU. ARE. WORTHY. You are worthy of love. You are worthy of respect. You are worthy of admiration. Believe it.

As we all know, it's a common fallacy to "just put a ring on it" and expect that we will live happily ever after. My close friend Kimberly's experience in her marriage exemplifies this problem. She wrote to me,

I had all sorts of fantasies about "happily ever after" that I was not aware of when my boyfriend Phillip and I decided to marry. What I was aware of was that Phillip possessed many qualities I found attractive and important in a lifelong partner. However, over the years,

I found myself developing resentment, as my needs—ones that I was not even aware of—went unmet.

I blamed my husband.

In the deep emotional recess of my heart, I really, really thought that marriage (and raising a family) would make me feel fulfilled: I thought this was supposed to make me happy. What made it harder was my resistance to the truth of my marriage. I looked to my husband to give me validation, affirmation, help (on my timetable), attention, and friendship. If I'm rigorously honest, I demanded that Phillip give me what I wanted or I'd feel let down by him.

Basically what I wanted from him was what I imagined was a male version of myself. Naturally, that is not who he is! Although I didn't ask him to "change," I did measure his behavior against an internalized image of how I thought he "should" be. And when I wanted to talk about us, what I really wanted to do was point fingers and dwell on what he was doing wrong.

As I have started to practice Radical Acceptance, I can't help but see how I am in our way. I realize that one of our biggest challenges is my expectations of Phillip. And that's not going to change by coming up with rules or making suggestions on how we can "improve" or "do it differently."

What I'm now much more tuned into is that my husband truly means well and loves me dearly. If he drops the ball, it's not because he doesn't care about or love me. In loving without judgment, I am reminded that Phillip is who he is and how he is. We have areas of similarity and areas of complete differentness. Frankly, when I really allow myself to see him, I thoroughly value who he is. And when I do, magic happens!

Our life together now is a pleasure. I realize blaming him never ever fixes me or helps us. It simply doesn't. When I am "blaming," Radical Acceptance helps me bring my focus back to me. For me, Radical Acceptance is tuning into Grace.

I love this beautiful testimonial because Kimberly is so honest about ex-periences that are incredibly common in relationships. She blamed and judged her husband and projected her own insecurities onto him. She clung to an idealized version of her partner—essentially, a man that was her flawless mirror image—instead of loving him for who he was, right there in front of her. We will delve into these common traps in greater detail throughout this book.

Kimberly's experience encapsulates a crucial but simple insight, one that should be self-evident but often isn't. I said it above and I am going to say it again here, but more emphatically.

LOVE STARTS WITH YOU.

You must be prepared to give it and not be obsessed with a pre-conceived, perfect version coming right back to you. Why aren't we taught this in school as, like, a basic life lesson? I suppose Paul and John tried when they sang that "the love you take is equal to the love you make." But seriously, it's time for some government-sponsored PSAs and billboards.

I suspect some Christians (and others of faith) might tell me, "Girl, we've been saying that for a long time. Get with the program!" Maybe my haphazard Catholic upbringing failed to sufficiently educate me on this, but I also don't think love is the exclusive province of the church. This should be social doctrine rooted in science, medicine, and cultural norms. Let love and kindness start with you. Let loving without judg-ment start with you.

I had a fascinating conversation with Dr. Dan Siegel, a clinical pro-fessor of psychiatry at the UCLA School of Medicine and bestsell-ing author of *Mindsight*, among many other brilliant books. Based on his groundbreaking research in interpersonal neurobiology, Dan has reached a provocative conclusion: "Rather than relationships *shaping* people,[3] my research shows that relationships *make* people." The impli-cation is that relationships have vastly more impact on individual devel-opment and well-being than is commonly believed.

"Take South Africans, for example," Dan told me. "Many communities subscribe to a philosophy known as Ubuntu, which means that you as an individual exist in the response of someone else." Among the Zulu people of South Africa, a customary greeting has two parts. The first, *Sikhona*, means, "I am here to be seen." The second, *Sawubona*, means, "I see you." This same idea of being seen is also the core of Radical Acceptance. Being truly seen allows vulnerability to take root, creating fertile ground for intimacy and connection to flourish. See, and be seen.

Ubuntu has roots in pluralism—community and togetherness is emphasized over the individual. In Ubuntu culture, Dan told me, "Yelling at another person and yelling at yourself are literally synonyms for the same thing. You exist within the connections to others and because of them." (For more about Dan's exploration into the mysteries of the human mind, I urge you to pick up his latest book, *Mind: A Journey to the Heart of Being Human.*) In the same spirit, Radical Acceptance urges couples to see themselves as one self-supporting unit. Negativity and hurt directed at one partner is directed at the relationship as a whole, while joy for one partner should be joy for both.

Dan advocates passionately for a new definition of self, one that is not determined by "you" and "me." Given the crucial role our relationships play in every aspect of our being, self is really a version of "we." There was a famous antidrug PSA[4] during the 1980s that showed a rat alone in a cage with two water bottles. One bottle was filled with pure water and the other was laced with cocaine. Unsurprisingly, the rat became addicted to the cocaine water. The ad ominously warned: "Nine out of ten laboratory rats[5] will use it . . . and use it . . . and use it . . . until they are dead."

But here's the catch: These tests were done in isolation. Each rat was by itself, alone in a cage for a prolonged period of time. The experiment was repeated a second time, but the rats were now living together. This time, the rats mostly ignored the cocaine water. They didn't like it, and no rats died. Community and togetherness, it turns out, can often overpower the most self-destructive threats. Like many people, these rats were less interested in getting high than in escaping a profound sense of loneliness.

Human beings are fundamentally wired for connection—physiologically, emotionally, sexually, and in so many other ways. There's even evidence of this in the mystical realm! Lorell Frysh, who has a doctorate in East-West psychology and was a key catalyst for this book, emphatically agrees with me. (She's the one who told me to "just love" Sanjay, as you may recall from the introduction.) Lorell has spent over forty-five years exploring, studying, and receiving initiation in many of the great spiritual, mystical, and healing traditions of the world.

"From a mystical perspective,[6] relationships are seen in the context of a greater wholeness," she told me. "Mystics understand that we are all connected as the fabric and expression of One Being. People feel complete when every aspect of themselves can show up, be seen, and loved. Very often problems occur in relationships when we feel unseen, unheard, and unacknowledged. But in truth, as we ease our own barriers and defenses, we become better equipped to serve each other. As we release pain and disconnection from ourselves and our past trauma, it becomes easier to find a deeper home in love." The primacy of our connectedness offers an existential truth that we should all act upon.

This is why I am incredibly motivated to spur Radical Acceptance into a beautiful, powerful movement. A sense of belonging and being seen are paramount to our well-being. But this mutuality doesn't happen by itself. It must start somewhere. Why not let it start with you?

LOVE IS A BIOLOGICAL IMPERATIVE

I had the great fortune of interviewing Dr. C. Sue Carter and her husband, Dr. Stephen Porges. They are both brilliant scientists who have performed groundbreaking work in neurophysiol-

ogy, biology, behavioral neuroendocrinology, and psychophysiology.

A biologist and behavioral neurobiologist, Dr. Carter is the director of the Kinsey Institute and Rudy Professor of Biology at Indiana University, and she was the first person to identify the physiological mechanisms responsible for social monogamy. Dr. Porges is a Distinguished University Scientist at the Kinsey Institute and research professor in the Department of Psychiatry at the University of North Carolina at Chapel Hill, and he is responsible for the Polyvagal Theory, which I touch upon later in the book. In 2013 they cowrote an article in European Molecular Biology Organization Reports entitled "The Biochemistry of Love: An Oxytocin Hypothesis," which truly stopped me in my tracks. One big Ah Ha after another!

The article makes a compelling case for the crucial role love plays on a physiological as well as emotional level: how it not only impacts the circuitry of our brains and the physiological health of our hearts, but how love even affects the expression of our genes, potentially impacting future generations. Based on Sue's research, we now know that oxytocin, an important hormone that serves as a neurotransmitter and is known as "the cuddle drug," plays a crucial role in this phenomenon.

I have excerpted some of my favorite portions of the text, but will start with a bit of commentary to clarify key points. (I know for some readers this may be a bit tough to grasp. It's powerful, fascinating stuff that helps clarify why love and loss impact us so deeply, but please don't stress if a lot of it reads like a foreign language to you!)

The vagus nerve is the tenth cranial nerve, originating in the brain's medulla, and it has two branches, the dorsal and ventral. The ventral vagus connects the brain to our heart, middle ears, *eyes, larynx, and pharynx, among other places in our bodies and is affiliated with how we communicate with others. For this reason, it is often referred to as the "social vagus," and in addition to assisting with how we communicate and socialize with others, it plays a key role in how we self-soothe and calm ourselves. Oxytocin is often activated by the presence of infants, and it's heightened in new and nursing mothers, as well as in positive social interactions. Oxytocin assists with attachment from early life to old age. Highlights of the article are as follows:*

The biology of love originates in the primitive parts of the brain—the emotional core of the human nervous system—that evolved long before the cerebral cortex. The brain of a human "in love" is flooded with sensations, often transmitted by the (ventral) vagus nerve, creating much of what we experience as emotion.

Love is an epigenetic phenomenon: social behaviors, emotional attachment to others and long-lasting reciprocal relationships are plastic and adaptive and so is the biology on which they are based. Infants of traumatized or highly stressed parents might be chronically exposed to vasopressin (also a neuropeptide and close cousin to oxytocin), either through their own increased production of the peptide, or through higher levels of vasopressin in maternal milk. Such increased exposure could sensitize the infant to defensive behaviors or create a life-long tendency to overreact to threat.

Both parental care and exposure to oxytocin in early life can permanently modify hormonal systems, altering the capacity to form relationships and influence the expression of love across the lifespan.

Given the power of positive social experiences, it is not surprising that a lack of social relationships might also lead to alterations in behavior and concurrently changes in oxytocin and vasopressin pathways.

Although research has only begun to examine the physiological effects of these peptides beyond social behavior, there is a wealth of new evidence indicating that oxytocin influences physiological responses to stress and injury. Thus, oxytocin exposure early in life not only regulates our ability to love and form social bonds; it also has an impact on our health and well-being.

In "modern" societies humans can survive, at least after childhood, with little or no human contact. Communication technology, social media, electronic parenting and many other technological advances of the past century might place both children and adults at risk for social isolation and disorders of the autonomic nervous system, including deficits in their capacity for social engagement and love.

Social engagement actually helps us to cope with stress. The same hormones and areas of the brain that increase the capacity of the body to survive stress also enable us to better adapt to an ever-changing social and physical environment. Individuals with strong emotional support and relationships are more resilient in the face of stressors than those who feel isolated or lonely. Lesions in bodily tissues, including the brain, heal more quickly in animals that are living socially compared with those in isolation. The protective effects of positive sociality seem to rely on the same cocktail of hormones that carry a biological message of "love" throughout the body.

Oxytocin receptors are expressed in the heart, and precursors for oxytocin seem to be crucial for the development of the fetal heart. Oxytocin exerts protective and restorative effects in part through its capacity to convert undifferentiated stem cells into cardiac muscle cells. Oxytocin can facilitate adult neurogenesis and tissue repair, especially after a stressful experience. We know that oxytocin has direct anti-inflammatory and antioxidant properties in in vitro models of heart disease. The heart seems to rely on oxytocin as part of a normal process of protection and self-healing.

Although research into mechanisms through which love protects us against stress and disease is in its infancy, this knowledge will ultimately increase our understanding of the way that our emotions have an impact on health and disease. We have much to learn about love and much to learn from love."

In other words, love is a biological imperative and so much more! Loving, healthy relationships contribute significantly to your heart health, specifically, as well as to your overall health and well-being. We simply cannot thrive as human beings in the absence of healthy relationships.

We have such a powerful opportunity as sisters, mothers, daughters, friends, wives, girlfriends, and caregivers to provide these healing benefits to those we love.

TRUST

Let's talk a little more about trust, an indispensable ingredient of Radical Acceptance. Simply put: you must trust yourself and your partner—I cannot underscore this strongly enough. After all, loving your partner without judgment is only possible, of course, if you truly trust him. Otherwise, how do you know that he won't take advantage of you?

Trust can be a bit of a fickle mistress, even for those people in strong, secure relationships. It's good to hold your own feet to the fire when he irritates you and your trust in him suddenly feels a bit illusive.

When your partner does something stupid, how often do you throw trust out the window and assume he is being deliberately hurtful toward you? Do you regularly assume the worst about his motives? You may feel these pangs of doubt on your Radical Acceptance journey. Trust means offering your partner the benefit of the doubt, even when you are not sure whether he deserves it. That said, if you find yourself frequently making excuses for him, or if you're seeing red flags, have confidence in yourself to determine whether your trust in him is misplaced.

You may think that your ability to trust someone resets with every new person you meet. This is not true. The ability to develop a high degree of trust for other people typically begins during infancy. Based on the care and attention we did or did not receive from our parents or another caregiver as babies and young children, our brains became neurologically wired in a way that either facilitates trust throughout or lives—or inhibits it. The brilliant clinician and author Dr. Stan Tatkin corroborated the above and added, "The ability to trust another person[7] has everything to do with our earliest experiences." Stan explains this process beautifully in his book *Wired for Love*:

> *Ideally, all babies have a parent[8] or other caregiver who puts their relationship before all other matters. The baby feels loved and secure, and the adult also enjoys the feeling of being loved and of being with and caring for the baby. These two are in it together. We call this a primary attachment relationship, because the baby and caregiver are bonded, or attached, to one another.*
>
> *. . . This baby bubble sets the stage for enjoyable relationships with others later in life.*

. . .

As I've observed over the years, and as research has proven, individuals who experienced less-than-secure relationships with their caregivers during childhood are much more likely to be insecure in adulthood.

Their brains have not yet learned to form the neurological connections necessary to develop deep trust for another person. Thankfully, due to the neuroplastic nature of the brain—meaning that with effort, it can be changed in meaningful ways as we age, causing us to feel and think differently—most people who didn't receive secure attachment from their parents or caregivers can, effectively, rewire their brains to facilitate trust, attachment, and intimacy as adults. Granted, this is not easy. We have all heard endless bitching and moaning from individuals who blame their parents for this and that. It's tempting to merely tell them, "Get over it already! You're an adult now!" Unfortunately, for many people, it's not that simple. But with a concerted effort, there's reason to be optimistic.

Stan likens a strong relationship to being in a foxhole: You have your partner's back and he has yours. No matter what happens, you deal with problems together and with unwavering security and trust in one another. But how do you build it?

We're going to talk about this in depth throughout this book, but here's a quick exercise you can start practicing right now. Practice graciously and sincerely saying things like, "You were right. I was wrong" (only when this is true, of course), and "I am sorry." Rather than being defensive and deflecting blame back to him, be willing to admit when you are wrong—whether your mistake was intentional or not. The effect is instantly disarming. Using these techniques is a powerful way to build trust and foster connection, provided they're said with sincerity. Being able to admit you are wrong and being apologetic makes you stronger, not weaker, and it gives you more power. *You* are offering a hand and choosing to move the relationship forward as opposed to retreating and putting up walls.

That said, do not make a habit of apologizing for every tiny thing. Don't let this technique fuel a self-sabotaging situation. Don't put yourself on trial. Trust yourself to understand when you are at fault and when you are not. An ex-boyfriend of mine—to whom I am forever grateful—used to say during our fights, exasperated: "Andrea, I am in your corner! We are on the same team." *Oh Jesus*, I'd think. *Of course we are.* Why is that so easy to forget? I always try to remember that now, and you should, too. Even when you feel like he deserves the Pain in the Ass of the Year Award, even when he is so incredibly, obviously, *maddeningly* wrong, just remember: You are on the same team. You both want the same thing. Even if you "win" the fight, what have you gained?

I know this can all be hard but it is a key means to fortify trust in your relationship. It used to be *extremely* hard for me, I will admit. Here was a common dynamic for Sanjay and myself: I don't like criticism and I get defensive pretty easily, while Sanjay is naturally critical. Add some stress, two young kids, and sprinkle in a few primeval hurt feelings, and BAM! A full-blown fight has ensued. (I partly blame my aversion to criticism on my star sign. This is a common issue for Aries. In fact, Virgos—which is Sanjay's star sign—tend to be critical. I felt weirdly overjoyed to discover this.)

We survived this pattern for many painful years, but since we discovered Radical Acceptance this cycle has become much less prevalent. I am better able to say, "I'm sorry," or "I was wrong." I know I can trust Sanjay, and he knows he can trust me. As a result, we've trained ourselves to not be so defensive. A little anecdote comes to mind: We were getting ready to renovate our apartment and we had been looking at photos of potential interiors. Then Sanjay made a semi-mocking, critical comment about the flooring I had liked. It was a light moment. I mentioned to him what I had learned about Virgos being critical. He chuckled, and then I said: "So, in other words, it's you, not me!" We laughed and high-fived. While it was lighthearted, it was also very meta. For so long I had reacted poorly to his critical commentary. I used to take it so personally! But I have learned to restrain myself and accept that being critical is part of who he is. It makes Sanjay a shrewd businessman in the boardroom, but it can also make him a difficult husband in the living room. I must emphasize: as Radical Acceptance has taken root, he has become considerably less critical.

While prepping for your Radical Acceptance journey, take this to heart: similar to Ubuntu culture, how you treat your partner is, effectively, how you treat yourself. The amazing author and activist Dr. Helen LaKelly Hunt concurs, and further explains that this requirement is rooted in neurobiology—activating upper and lower regions of the brain. The upper region gets most of the sexy research and publicity. It's divided into the logical and analytical "left" side, and the creative and imaginative "right" side. But the more primitive "lower" region, which includes the thalamus, hypothalamus, and the hippocampus, controls most of our emotional processes.

As Helen explained,[9] if you give your partner a gift, your upper brain registers whom you're giving it to and why. But your lower brain does not recognize the recipient or even the source of this kindness—it merely registers kindness and processes pleasure hormones. Helen notes that because the lower brain cannot make this differentiation, "Being kind to others is being kind to yourself." The same goes when you are expressing anger and negativity. Your lower brain cannot differentiate between being angry or being the recipient of anger. So if you yell at your partner (or at that crazy driver ahead of you), your lower brain registers anger and pumps out the same stress hormones as if he were yelling at you.

In short, by being kind and loving toward him, by minimizing or even eliminating negativity and criticism, you not only strengthen your relationship and make him feel better, *you treat yourself better.*

**"The less you open your heart to others, the
more your heart suffers."**

—DEEPAK CHOPRA

. . .

When friends would ask what this book is about while I was writing it, Sanjay would quip with a smile, "She's writing a book about me! It's about how to make your marriage work despite your husband." It was always a light-hearted statement—Sanjay is incredibly generous in his support of this book, even though it reveals a lot about our personal lives—but my reply would always be, "Yes, you're a key character, but the book is as much about my desire for Radical Acceptance and my own journey about loving myself, being seen, and being able to both love, and be loved, fully."

A dozen years ago, Sanjay gave me a card inscribed with a quote by the Bengali polymath Rabindranath Tagore: "Love's gift cannot be given. It waits to be accepted." I kept it on my bedside table until it was yellow and faded, to the point of being illegible, as a reminder that Sanjay's love for me is always there—even if I sometimes had trouble accepting the form it was taking.

We have always had a lot of love for one another—despite how we suffered and struggled with how to successfully express it. It took me a while to understand and to be able to fully accept his love, in large part because of my own trust and vulnerability issues, as well as my fierce independence. I regret how my instinct was to push him away when our conflict seemed insurmountable. My marriage brought me to my knees: I loved this man dearly, yet we fought so much and experienced so much hurt. The deep, painful sadness and anger were often like open wounds. Finally, though, there was a point at which I realized that I couldn't live with him and I couldn't live without him.

I came to the last possible conclusion: I had to change for the sake of the relationship. I had to take the lead.

Before I go any further, I am eager to take a moment to share why I was willing to go to such lengths for the sake of our relationship.

Like many other couples, Sanjay and I met at work. He was overseeing a very large team undertaking a massive project in India, where he is from. I had previously been to India, where I was taken in by its cultural richness and the kindness of its people, and I was extremely interested in Eastern philosophy, so I leapt at the first opportunity to join Sanjay's team.

I had heard a lot about Sanjay before we met. Everyone said that he was an incredible leader and that he was one of the smartest guys in the room—as evidenced by his master's degree in engineering from Stanford and MBA with distinction from Harvard Business School, along with the fact that he graduated with distinction from India's vaunted Indian Institute of Technology. His intense drive and work ethic were the stuff of legend.

I couldn't wait to learn from him. But I never expected that I would fall head over heels in love within minutes of meeting him. I remember calling my friend Brenda after that initial encounter and confessing I had a big problem. As the consummate professional, I knew I had to ignore this huge crush and focus on my work. Besides, he had a serious girlfriend at the time.

We continued to work together very closely. Our team stayed at the Oberoi Hotel in Mumbai for weeks and sometimes months on end, living and breathing the project. My infatuation with Sanjay only increased. It was like classic teenage love, butterflies and all, even though I was in my late twenties. I would daydream about him endlessly. I would get nervous and excited any time we were in a meeting together. I loved his confidence and his sense of humor. He was handsome and totally sexy.

Eventually, he and his girlfriend broke up. We started to date. I left the company and moved to New York to attend Columbia Business School. I remember standing in the shower counting the weeks and then months that we were together. Our chemistry was ridiculous. I wrote him poems that he devoured like a dehydrated man gulps down cold, fresh water.

We always felt heartbroken to be apart for any extended length of time. In the fall of my first year, I remember sitting with Sanjay in a restaurant on Columbus Avenue several hours before his flight back to India and lamenting his impending departure. We sat, sadly holding hands. I asked him if he could delay it by just one more day, but he could not.

Even in our early dating phase, Sanjay would give me these incredible, long-lasting, full-body hugs. I remember thinking, *He must really love me to hug me like this.* As the months and eventually years wore on, he would periodically hug me this way, communicating to me just how deeply he felt about me. It was the best feeling in the world. I felt so treasured, so loved.

As time has gone on, while the intense magnetism has worn off, we still have a chemistry that energizes and feeds our relationship. We continue to learn about each other as we grow and change.

Of course, there is so much that draws us together. I love his powerful mind and his big heart. I love that he knows so much about virtually every topic. I love to learn from him, ski with him, and discuss political and social issues. Knowing that we are on the same team, that he always has my back is beyond invaluable.

Naturally, Sanjay has his challenging parts. But I know now that my Radical Acceptance journey has been as much about my need to be seen and accepted for who I really am—imperfect, flawed, and in some ways deeply inadequate—as it was to see and accept Sanjay for who he really is. Tired of grappling with my hurt and doubt, I wanted Sanjay to love me even as I went to the ends of the earth, down into an endless abyss, to fix my broken parts and reclaim that essential part of me that had long felt lost. I had shouldered these defeating, sometimes even devastating, feelings for so long. I wanted someone to make them go away, to convince me that they were no longer true.

This is why I connect so deeply with the work of Brené Brown, the brilliant researcher and bestselling author of *Daring Greatly, Rising*

Strong and *The Gifts of Imperfection*, which I will talk about at greater length later in this book. I think often about her prophetic first TED Talks in which she revealed powerful, relatable insights about shame and vulnerability. Her talk reached a crescendo when she revealed what so many people who suffer simply need to hear: "You are enough," she said. That's it. This is something that I have long struggled with. I know so many others have, too.

In my case, something missing inside prevented me from feeling a strong sense of belonging. It's a weird paradox. I have many spectacular friends and family members who love me and who would do anything for me. I know this and am grateful for it. And yet, I still needed to prove myself; to ingratiate myself, even. I was a people-pleaser. I felt that I was not enough, that I was on the outside looking in. I would go to great lengths to be liked and avoid conflict. Conflict was very threatening to me, probably because I erroneously equated it with rejection.

This is my seriously warped truth. I am smart, have strong moral fiber, and I have accomplished quite a lot. But deep down, and sometimes not so deep down, it was just not enough. It didn't occur to me that the answer to this would be found on the other side of the crucible with my husband. Ha! Looking back, there was a time when such an idea would have been laughable. Then, the only possible antidote, in my mind, was to forge my own path and work tirelessly to prove my worth.

I knew I could rely on myself and I was comfortable being alone. I wore my independence like a badge of honor. It had served me well. But it has its shadowy side. Independence has made me immensely capable, yes, but in some ways it's like a shell: strong on the outside but empty on the inside.

In retrospect, I can see why my deep-seated propensity was to go solo and why conflict with Sanjay was so painful and so threatening to me. Isolating myself emotionally and minimizing my reliance on others was my adaptive behavior. It is a self-destructive coping method.

Instead of trying to work through challenging differences, my instinct had been to assert my independence by putting up walls or simply by doing my own thing. When our conflict was especially intractable, I would punish him for the hurt I felt by retreating even further. Sanjay, who grew up in a super interdependent, close-knit culture, would always accuse me of "having no idea what togetherness is about."

My logic amounted to: Why always compromise and do things together? Why bother arguing or feeling bad about it? Let's just do our own thing when we are not in alignment, and then connect where we are. It made sense to me, but I was rejecting what Sanjay needed. My MO of doing things on my own was painful and foreign to him, just like ceding control and striving to be in lockstep as a couple was equally painful and foreign to me. Just as I was unable to extend compassion or tenderness to my own weaknesses, I was a harsh judge of Sanjay and his shortcomings. Making matters worse, as our relationship fractured and split, I retreated into the safety of work—my proudly crafted and preserved fortress of independence. But all this did was isolate us from one another, both physically and emotionally.

Our worst disagreements triggered intense, irrational reactions for me. I didn't know how to manage these overwhelming feelings. I frequently felt consumed by rage or completely depleted, compounded by feeling I had no control. For someone who prided herself on her ability to keep it together, who otherwise kept her emotions close to the vest, these feelings were incredibly frustrating and confounding to me.

I felt "so not understood." Whatever Sanjay said to me, all I heard was: *YOUR FEELINGS DON'T MATTER. YOU'RE WRONG. YOU'RE NOT ENOUGH. YOU ARE UNLOVABLE.*

Which meant being alone. Once again on the outside.

As I look back, I know that he, too, was in pain. I don't think he understood that I was so fragile, nor that it would sometimes take me weeks to recover from our blowouts. I know now that we were equally at fault for what was going on, even though at the time I blamed him. If I were to be brutally honest, I would have to admit that I wanted him to change. Sometimes, I even wanted him to come and rescue me. I eventually concluded that I needed to radically accept myself and break the vicious cycle that was tearing us apart. While I hoped that Sanjay would eventually see those lonely, desperate fragments that skulked behind my brave mask of independence, that he would tenderly reach in, and quietly embrace them, I refused to let him in, continuing to try and work it out on my own.

What I finally figured out—*FINALLY!*—is that I needed to do these things for myself, and that I needed to give Sanjay what I so desperately sought. I realized that I needed to tenderly reach for those broken parts of him and quietly embrace them as opposed to rebelling and feeling hurt that he couldn't or wouldn't do this for me.

Inadvertently, by withdrawing from him and rejecting the parts of him that I did not like, I unwittingly bred and fed the exact opposite of what I deeply desired and—go figure!—we both, along with our relationship, suffered greatly.

Through Radical Acceptance I have now managed to bring out the best in my husband. This didn't happen by denying his challenging parts or by insisting that he change. Instead, I have extended more tenderness to him and to myself. I have practiced and practiced. I have learned to take the high road and I have stretched myself in ways that I never thought possible.

> **"Go and love someone exactly as they are. And then watch how quickly they transform into the greatest, truest version of themselves. When one feels seen and appreciated in their own essence, one is instantly empowered."**
>
> —WES ANGELOZZI[10]

I have become brutally honest with myself so that I can challenge the painful feelings that used to haunt me. I don't let them ride roughshod like they once did. I have developed much more empathy for myself and for others. I am less reactive and more emotionally mature and resilient.

I am super blessed to have a partner as loving, generous, supportive, wise, and wonderful as Sanjay is. As individuals and as a couple, we have benefitted enormously from Radical Acceptance. It has created a beautiful cycle wherein love and understanding beget more love and understanding. As a result, we have built an incredible relationship. Thanks to how much we have opened our hearts and let go of our egos, we have given each other the best gift ever. Our marriage has become brilliantly transformed over the years.

I want to do the same for you and your relationship. I want you to learn from my experiences so you can reverse the negative habits that are preventing lasting love from taking root and that are causing you to be awash in doubt.

Gandhi-ji said, "Be the change you want to see in the world." I say, "Give the love you want to feel in the world." Love is more than a feeling, though. Nearly twenty years ago, my friend Dahl told me, "Love is an action word." I have adopted that as my mantra. It's millions of actions, words, and intentions. It's actively exercising compassion, empathy, and nonjudgment—especially when it's hard. It's exercising restraint. It's exhibiting kindness and generosity. It's extending yourself in the spirit of love, even when it's the hardest thing you've ever done, even when you have to beat back your ego, your anger, and your fear. And it's finding serenity and bliss on the other side. This is why I say that committing to Radical Acceptance is truly the greatest gift ever—both for him and yourself.

And so, while I will talk a lot about your partner in this book, Radical Acceptance begins with you. We expect our partners to gaze deeply into our eyes and profess that we complete them. We expect someone to magically understand and sponge up all those hurts that haunt us.

We expect to get swept off our feet by Prince Charming and live happily ever after. Well, it doesn't work that way. You only get to live happily ever after if you put in the work. Of course, there are times when you may decide not to, and that is what we will discuss next.

. . .

- When you're with someone you love or who has real potential, get ready to go ALL IN. Go 150% of the way and don't expect him to meet you halfway, 50/50, every step of the way—especially in the beginning.

- To practice Radical Acceptance successfully, you'll need to trust yourself and your partner. It may take some time to develop, but it's imperative to do so. This includes extending him the benefit of the doubt, even when you're inclined to assume the worst of his intentions or his abilities.

- Do not expect instant reciprocation when you begin to practice Radical Acceptance. Give your partner time to step it up. If Radical Acceptance doesn't eventually come back to you, you may be in an untenable relationship.

RED FLAGS

BEFORE WE BEGIN discussing how to practice Radical Acceptance, we need to discuss when not to practice it. Radical Acceptance is not a magic pill, and it's certainly not a one-size-fits-all cure for a bad relationship. Radical Acceptance cannot fix a relationship in which there is abuse, nor one in which a major difference or problem will prevent long-term compatibility. This chapter and the next will address various categories of red flags and total deal-breakers ranging from serious differences to bona fide threats. Sometimes these hurdles are significant but manageable; other times they are simply insurmountable and spell the end of the relationship.

Deep breath, now. This might happen. But the key is not to view this potential outcome as a failure. If the relationship fails because you cannot radically accept your partner's challenging behavior, I hope you can walk away knowing that you did the right thing. So many women stay in crappy or even abusive relationships for the wrong reasons. Too afraid to leave. Hoping he'll change. Uncertain she can find someone better. The reasons go on and on. We've all had doubts and struggles in our relationships, but what happens when these doubts and struggles truly signal that a relationship is doomed?

Sometimes it's best, or even imperative, to leave a relationship and not attempt Radical Acceptance. I am a strong advocate of using Radical Acceptance to solidify a relationship that is worth pursuing, but I'm an equally strong advocate of calling it quits when the relationship is not worth pursuing. Some of these red flags are undisputable deal-breakers. (We'll discuss lesser deal-breakers at length in the next chapter, e.g., he's a Republican and you're a Democrat, or when he lacks ambition and you're ready to colonize Mars single-handedly. These manageable differences are subjective and we can typically get past them with some work, along with an open heart and mind.) In this chapter, we'll broadly address three forms of red flags. The first has to do with serious threats, the second has to do with potential dysfunction, and the third has to do with significant differences.

I cannot communicate this vehemently enough: Radical Acceptance is *NOT* meant to be a convenient excuse nor a justification to accept behavior or conditions that are unacceptable or possibly even dangerous. If you feel threatened, if you feel like you're in a deeply unhealthy relationship, or if you wonder whether he's just bad news, he probably is and you should not attempt Radical Acceptance. I will delve more deeply into different scenarios below, but the last thing I want is for anyone to use Radical Acceptance as justification to stay in an abusive or unhealthy, untenable relationship.

When I refer to serious threats, I don't mean nail-biting, leaving dirty dishes in the sink, or other minor offenses that can be addressed with a bit of kindness and patience. I mean genuine bright red flags with sirens blazing, such as a partner who is verbally, emotionally, or physically abusive; who is manipulative, oppressive, or controlling to the extreme; or who has other character flaws that are threatening or even dangerous. For many reasons it can be extremely difficult to be honest with yourself about these red flags. Maybe you've fallen head over heels in love, or he has many winning traits but also has a dark side, or you're looking to be saved or protected and someone seemingly strong offers such security. Serious threats may be present even in the most normal-seeming relationships, often with people who are successful and seem to have it together. Falling victim to these situations is nothing to be ashamed of. While these threats can take many shapes and forms, this section addresses some of the more common scenarios.

Sometimes it's difficult to differentiate between genuine threats and difficult, but manageable, problems. I call the latter *potential dysfunction*. This category includes issues such as acute anger, certain mental illnesses, addiction, and chronic moral or ethical problems. While these are not necessarily deal-breakers, they are going to make for a much tougher match. Sometimes experiences from our childhood make us latch on to difficult personalities.

When I told the illustrious professor,[11] relationship counselor, and bestselling author Dr. Pat Love (yes, that's her real name!) about my theory, she agreed. "Absolutely," she told me. "We're often attracted to people who remind us of our past. As a result, we can let the wrong people in and keep the right people out." These sorts of relationships are very challenging and are best managed in partnership with mental-health professionals. Meanwhile, if lying and stealing are not allowed, what about infidelity? I knew you'd ask. While certainly a red flag, infidelity is not necessarily an inherent deal-breaker. We'll get into why.

Finally, there is the other kind of red flag: *significant differences*. In this case, the relationship is threatened not by dysfunction, but by a very big tangible difference or challenge. The relationship is generally healthy and filled with passion, but one or more thorny issues exist that may cripple it over the long run. In other words, a relationship in which everything is great . . . except the sex. Or he doesn't want to have kids and you do. Or he's an Orthodox Jew and you're not. Or you're a Red Sox fan and he's a Yankees fan. Well, maybe not that last one, but the point is that for many people these differences would represent a potentially insurmountable hurdle.

Many other examples exist in which long-term compatibility issues come into play, but they do not necessarily mean a fulfilling relationship is impossible. Radical Acceptance requires you to be very clear and honest with your actual needs, not preconceived ones foisted on you by someone else or through perceived social norms. In effect, get ready to toss out that laundry list of traits you require of Mr. Perfect. At the same time, while Radical Acceptance requires you to manage many small (and even medium-sized) differences, do not shortchange yourself by coping with a major difference that you fundamentally cannot accept. My hope is that after reading through this chapter, you can better make that distinction if it applies to you.

Also, if your automatic reaction is to think, *Eh, none of this applies to me: next!* I encourage you not to skip forward too aggressively nor skim too lightly as there is quite a bit of useful, insightful data in here that could apply to you and helps pave the way for your Radical Acceptance journey.

SERIOUS THREATS

There are times when you just need to walk away from a relationship. There is no nuance here, no gray area. Attempting to manage any of the following scenarios will be detrimental to your well-being. If any of the following exist, do not be ashamed, do not be embarrassed. Walk away.

Physical abuse. This should go without saying, but do not stay with someone who physically abuses you. Full stop. There are no ifs or buts. This is especially true if you have kids. If you refuse to leave the relationship, you are enabling your abuser. To prolong the relationship is to prolong the abuse. Actions speak louder than words: by staying in the relationship, you are implicitly saying, "It is okay for you to abuse me." Here's the deal: if you truly love someone who is abusive, terminate the relationship and encourage him to get help. You can even help him find treatment. If he does and somehow manages to transform himself—this is a *tall* order, so don't hold your breath—maybe you can try again.

But you must not expect this miracle transformation to occur. Abusive people are typically products of abusive families. It is deeply ingrained within them, which makes it difficult to change. Moreover, do not use family history as an excuse to tolerate physical violence. Just because his father was abusive, for instance, does not make it acceptable for him to be as well. The statistics do not lie: in the United States, more women are killed by their boyfriends and husbands than by any other group. According to an Associated Press analysis, more than 80 percent of Americans who are shot and killed by spouses, ex-spouses, or dating partners are women. In other words, the vast majority of relationship violence is directed toward women.

Leaving an abusive relationship can be life-threatening. If you are in the least bit uncertain whether this is the case, you need to plan your extrication from the relationship very carefully. Let me say as vehemently as I can: you do not deserve to be imprisoned or enslaved or beholden to someone who is abusive. It may be scary or difficult to leave the relationship, but you must.

If this is you, please be very careful and ensure you enlist the help of law enforcement, at least two adults you trust, and ideally a reputable professional service or counselor who specializes in these matters.

Mental, verbal, or emotional abuse. This might sound as obvious as physical abuse, but mental, verbal, and emotional abuse can be extremely insidious. The National Coalition Against Domestic Violence estimates that one in four women will experience physical, emotional, or sexual abuse—and most cases are not reported to the police. This is a hugely alarming number—25 percent of women will suffer some form of abuse. It's crazy. If you suspect this may be happening to you, *do not doubt yourself*, and seek help immediately. When a relationship is characterized by frequent or regular nonphysical abuse, it is still abuse. The relationship must be terminated.

Emotional abusers often rely on a technique called gaslighting, in which information is twisted, spun, omitted, or fabricated in an attempt to make victims doubt their own memory and sanity. Emotionally abusive people may often belittle and put down their partners, only to deny this behavior when they work up the courage to bring it up. They may also try to persuade their partners that the abuse never happened, that they are crazy to be concerned. Emotionally abusive people may also trivialize huge issues by convincing their partners that their concerns aren't important. "You see everything in the most negative way," or "Where did you get a crazy idea like that?" are common phrases used by emotional abusers to make victims doubt their own perception.

Please, *please* do not doubt yourself. Never doubt your version of events. You are not crazy. A pattern of emotional abuse and put-downs can erode not just your spirit, but your ability to separate reality from fantasy. Most important, never blame yourself. Emotional and physical abuse is never warranted, no matter what. Cindy Southworth, vice president of the National Network to End Domestic Violence, tells victims: "You couldn't have seen this, and it's not your fault. You missed it because he's really smooth, and he knows how to make sure to back off the moment when your instincts start to tell you he's coming on too strong."

Are there gray areas? Can someone be kinda, sorta, maybe verbally abusive? No. What if it's a matter of two people who are normally civil and respectful to one another but who get in an insane, biblical fight; lose their tempers; and say some really crazy, mean shit to each other? It's cruel; it's out of control. It feels like Armageddon. There may be name-calling. It may even border on violent due to the shattered plate on the floor and the hurt or anger boiling over. Would this constitute verbal abuse? How do you know the difference?

Well, for one, if you regularly wonder whether you are being verbally, mentally, or emotionally abused, there's a better-than-decent chance you are. But if one or both of you totally lost control during one isolated fight, you're probably okay as long as this does not constitute a pattern. However, there are important issues that need to be addressed when both of you are calm. You will never forget the out-of-control fights, and you should never try to. This is where Radical Acceptance can really help. (We will discuss fighting and communication in part 2: The Five Steps for Happy, Lasting Love).

There also may be acute anger or other related issues, which I categorize below as potential dysfunction. These are red flags in that they merit some vigilance and perhaps additional counseling or other therapeutic measures.

I heard a great segment on WNYC in which John Hockenberry interviewed the famous radio host, author, and songwriter Delilah. (I *so* love this woman!) She described how her first husband was very abusive. Yet she kept going back to him! Ultimately she allowed this bad, unacceptable behavior to continue. She offered some wise advice about trust and how serious red flags translate into action: "If someone shows you that you can't trust them through their actions, believe them!"

If you're with someone who messes with you, treats you badly, acts in a way that erodes trust, or is abusive in any way, terminate the relationship. You can do better and you deserve better.

POTENTIAL DYSFUNCTION

Serious threats can form a continuum with potential dysfunction, and here is where things get can tricky. A problem might not be bad enough to constitute a serious threat, but it's nevertheless worrisome. Let's take a look at a few common examples, including anger issues, addiction, and infidelity. While these are clearly red flags, none of these situations inherently mean the relationship is doomed. However, in the extreme, they probably render the relationship untenable. Practicing Radical Acceptance alone will not likely be a sufficient means to manage these very challenging situations.

Anger problems. On the extreme-threat side, an acute anger problem is clearly a red flag, especially if it becomes violent or threatening.

Meanwhile, a modest anger issue might be dysfunctional at times, but it's fairly commonplace. Unless you personally cannot tolerate anger, it is not inherently a deal-breaker, nor does its presence imply you are settling. Periodic anger may simply be part of who another person is, and while ugly sometimes, it is likely manageable as long as that anger never translates into physical violence or verbal abuse.

But, at the same time, unchecked anger can lead to extremely dangerous or dysfunctional, unhealthy situations. It's up to you to decide if his anger crosses a line. As the Buddha said, "You will not be punished for your anger. You will be punished by your anger." That minor, nonviolent road rage can probably be cured with relaxation techniques or anger-management counseling—and you can learn to radically accept when he (occasionally) flips the bird at other drivers, but abusive behavior is never acceptable, and it's never forgivable. If he can control that anger, great. If that anger controls him, then get out. You can do better.

Addiction. This is another tricky one. Addiction is a disease; no one chooses to be addicted to drugs or alcohol, or the myriad other forms of debilitating addiction. You can absolutely stay with someone who is suffering from addiction, but Radical Acceptance is not going to help you. It fact, practicing it can be dangerously counterproductive. You can radically accept that he occasionally drinks that smelly scotch with his friends, but you cannot radically accept a serious alcohol addiction. I know couples who have fought one partner's addiction together and grown closer as a result, but your best bet is to enlist the help of an addiction treatment center such as the Hazelden Betty Ford Foundation, professionals who specialize in addiction treatment, and therapeutic groups such as AA (Alcoholics Anonymous) and Al-Anon.

As someone who has been close to multiple people befallen by alcoholism (and other forms of addictions), I know firsthand how completely brutal and damaging addiction is. I know what it is like for addiction to wreak complete devastation on individuals, couples, and families. It is tough to have a healthy relationship with someone who is an addict. It can sometimes be impossible, especially when the person you love is set on self-destruction. That said, I am fortunate to note that some of the people in my life who were most troubled by addiction did manage to escape its scourge and have gone on to live healthy, happy lives.

If the consequences of the addiction manifest themselves as physical violence or emotional abuse, please end the relationship. Chances are, the help he needs is not something you can provide.

Infidelity. As everyone knows, one of the hardest relationship obstacles to overcome is infidelity. Unfortunately, infidelity is quite common. While some 85 percent of Americans eventually marry, current studies of couples indicate that 20 to 40 percent of men and 20 to 25 percent of women will have an affair during their lifetime.

There's nothing worse than being hit with betrayal, that loss of trust—especially when you never saw it coming. To have a loving bond be thrown away so selfishly . . . can you ever recover? Yes, you can. Infidelity is not a deal-breaker in and of itself. Rather, it is often a symptom of a larger issue in the relationship. Harville Hendrix, the renowned relationship guru and cocreator of Imago Relationship Therapy, says that when it comes to cheating, both partners can inevitably be guilty. He may have had an affair with someone from the office, but it's possible that you were having an affair of sorts with your work, your friends, your family, or any number of other people or activities that prevent you from being tuned into him. Of course, this does not mean the affair is your fault, nor does it mean that cheating is okay. However, it's important to understand that the impulse to cheat is frequently a symptom of underlying problems in the relationship, and they often occur when two partners have become disconnected.

The tendency to stray is actually biologically engrained in us. Humans have three brain systems devoted to love: (1) The sex drive to attract potential mating partners, (2) Romantic thoughts to motivate us to focus on specific mating partners, and (3) Prolonged attachment to these partners to help raise and protect infants. In one of her brilliant

TED Talks,[12] biological anthropologist Dr. Helen Fisher notes: "These three brain systems: lust, romantic love and attachment, aren't always connected to each other. You can feel deep attachment to a long-term partner while you feel intense romantic love for somebody else, while you feel the sex drive for people unrelated to these other partners."

Infidelity blows up your relationship. However, this can be an opportunity. With the relationship in pieces, you can pick up each little slice and examine it. What worked? What didn't? From these ruins you can put together a new relationship that is more honest and more rewarding than the original. This is a beautiful chance to discover and embrace your partner's otherness. Slowly, carefully, you can rebuild what you had into something stronger. Couples who have worked through this painful process can emerge with healthier, more fulfilling, more transparent relationships than those who have not suffered from infidelity.

Infidelity does not have to spell the end of the relationship. You have to understand both its biological and situational context. Infidelity does not mean there is no more love in a relationship; rather, it usually means there is a diminished emotional connection. It is entirely possible to re-secure that bond, and there's a good chance that the relationship will emerge like a phoenix rising from the ashes if you are both committed to its repair.

SIGNIFICANT DIFFERENCES

Serious differences are hurdles that may or may not be surmountable. In this section I will help you determine whether a serious difference is truly a deal-breaker or if it's a manageable hurdle. In any case, the kinds of significant differences that I address will very likely weigh on you and your relationship, potentially quite heavily, for years to come.

One is a difference in cultural backgrounds. I love that Sanjay is an Indian who was raised with a strong Hindu upbringing. I love the blessings I've discovered from marrying into this culturally rich, family-focused part of the world. During our first several years of dating, I loved learning about his family's traditions and I enjoyed participating in them. Fast-forward seventeen years, add two young children, slather on endless stress from work, and I admit that at times I find certain of these activities and expectations burdensome. I must remind myself from time to time that while a certain family or religious activity may feel like an inconvenience or seem excessive, it's nevertheless important to him and offers me an opportunity to connect and engage with our extended family.

Moreover, I have enthusiastically embraced many aspects of his Indian upbringing. These efforts have endeared me to many of his friends and family and have been great for our kids. For example, I am the one that orchestrates the Diwali party that our family hosts each year at our kids' school. (Sanjay helps too of course, but I take the reins.) We go all out to make the party meaningful and enjoyable for the students and their teachers, and I take great pride because I know it means a lot to my family that I take this initiative. In another small example, I was moved to tears when we brought our eldest son home from the hospital where he was born and my mother-in-law lit a bunch of candles and prepared a small *puja* (or prayer) to welcome us home with our new baby. It was so beautiful and moving.

When you're in a significant-differences situation yet you're head over heels in love, biology is conspiring to keep you together—meaning hormones and neurotransmitters such as oxytocin and dopamine are flooding your system to assist with your physical and emotional bonding—it will be that much more important to listen carefully with both your head and your heart. And, *gasp!* Maybe even listen to your parents, family, or friends who are not under this addictive influence of romantic love. How you feel ten, twenty, thirty years from now may be very different compared with how you feel today, especially as the initial romance fades and the daily grind of life wears on. If you choose to embrace one or more of these significant differences and move forward as a couple, there's a good chance that you will have to redouble your resolve in the years to come.

Common categories of significant differences include racial and/or cultural, children, sexual compatibility, money, and religion.

Needless to say, there are many other significant differences that couples face, but in my experience the above are the most common and intractable. Other factors include differences in education, socioeconomic issues, and geographic differences. Even deep political disagreements can threaten the viability of a relationship.

Sometimes significant differences can be "fixed." Take sex, for example. Many couples have found ways to fix their seemingly incompatible sex lives. To better understand how this works,[13] I sat down in a crowded New York bistro with Ian Kerner, PhD, LMFT. Ian is a licensed psychotherapist who specializes in sex therapy and couples counseling. He is also the bestselling author of numerous books, including *She Comes First*, the most popular sex-advice guide of the last decade. Needless to say, Ian had a ton of fascinating insights to share! He makes a living by helping couples discover, or rediscover, intimate connections. From techniques such as "choreplay," routine hugging, and constant physical touch, couples can often solve intimacy problems through practice and hard work. Remember, trust is a crucial pretext. "You need to be in the kind of relationship that enables healthy sex," Ian agrees. "It's very important to try to be in as secure an attachment as possible."

Some sexual differences, of course, are much more complicated and can threaten even the strongest relationship. Ian told me about a married couple, let's call them Mike and Jane. Mike decided that he wanted to have a threesome with his wife and another woman. As he approached his fiftieth birthday, it was important for Mike to experience a higher degree of sexual adventurousness. To his dismay, Jane did not share this desire.

This caused strife in the relationship. Mike felt that Jane was rejecting him by belittling a genuine desire of his. Jane thought Mike was acting like a pig. Their sex life had completely disappeared. Through significant counseling, Ian helped form a dialogue between the two. Ian helped Mike explain what he was interested in experiencing sexually with Jane. With humility, Mike described his fantasy of seeing someone else pleasure his wife. His open, honest dialogue eradicated the ick factor and opened up the erotic potential between them. It turns out that Jane was not necessarily against the idea of a threesome. Rather, she had had a traumatic sexual experience in college involving a threesome, and her mind always returned to it when Mike brought up his desire to try it. This was a red flag for Jane; it was something she was not capable of giving him. When Mike finally understood this and Jane was able to listen openly to his desires, the relationship improved dramatically.

They started having sex again—really good sex, too. Moreover, Jane accepted that Mike had a legitimate sexual desire and no longer rejected him for it. When they'd go out to dinner, they would play a game in which they'd scan the room and identify whom they'd like to have a threesome with. "This led to sexual fluidity," Ian says. When they went dancing, they would make the night adventurous by playfully flirting with other men and women without ever actually bringing them home. In the end, Mike never truly needed the threesome to be fulfilled—he needed the ability to have a judgment-free space with Jane to explore fantasies.

In this case, Jane identified a true red flag; she just wasn't comfortable giving her husband what he desired, given her past. But with honest, open dialogue, the couple was able to transcend a potentially relationship-destroying problem and arrive in a highly fulfilling, happy new place together.

The caveat, of course, is that sometimes significant differences are just *too significant*. The following stories are about when significant differences proved too great to be sustained, as well as about when love conquered all and couples have succeeded despite their differences.

Here's a beautiful account about a couple I know who were madly in love with each other, but who faced a seemingly insurmountable obstacle. Anna and Ari are both brilliant and the best of friends, but Ari is an Orthodox Jew and Anna is a recovering Catholic. Anna put up with Ari's parents as best she could, but they insisted that she convert before she could marry their son. She initially agreed, but after more than a year of weekly meetings with the rabbi, Anna finally realized that she would be resentful in the long run if this were a condition Ari and his family imposed upon her. Anna determined that converting would be something Ari's *family* needed, not something her and Ari's *relationship* needed.

But Ari took his parents' side. While it very nearly broke her heart, Anna had to part ways with him, though they truly did love each other and they stayed in touch as friends. Finally, realizing that being with Anna was more important than being with someone who shared his faith, Ari confronted his parents and insisted that she be accepted into their family without having to convert. Mercifully, they agreed and did not force their son to choose between the woman he loves and the family he loves.

This was an invaluable gift to Anna and permitted them to reunite. As a newly married couple, they are closer and happier than ever. Understandably, Anna wanted to be accepted by Ari as she was. Ari took this to heart and eventually radically accepted Anna as she was. The two were honest with each other, and they made it work.

While I have seen relationships fail and succeed in the face of religious differences, I am encouraged by how many people manage to place love above religious beliefs. (w00t! Love wins!) I met a wonderful woman named Rachel when conducting research for this book. She told me a story about a guy, Ethan, she met on the dating site Hinge. After a magical first date, they texted each other all week. Rachel had never felt such a connection. But on Friday he suddenly stopped responding to her messages. Rachel was devastated. She thought she had been ghosted. Then, out of the blue, Ethan responded two days later and wanted to set up a second date. Rachel was still a bit doubtful, but she agreed. After he wouldn't share her scallops at dinner, Rachel realized that Ethan kept kosher. And then it hit her—he also kept Shabbat, which meant he completely unplugs during the Jewish Sabbath. He does not use his phone or any other electronics, lights, mechanical equipment of any sort, cars, and so on. As Rachel puts it: "I inadvertently started dating a modern Orthodox Jew!"

But their deep connection remained, even though the strict nature of his faith represented a significant difference for Rachel. After a long week of work, she wouldn't be able to curl up with Ethan on the couch watching Netflix, or even take the elevator up to their apartment. No weekend trips. No use of any mechanical or electrical devices during this time at all. But they had such a profound emotional connection, Rachel decided that Ethan's faith was not a red flag but something she would embrace. Rachel now observes Shabbat—not because she is converting to Orthodox Judaism, but because she wants to connect with Ethan, support him, and truly partner with him. In fact, she marvels at what it's like to spend "truly quality" time with him and his family starting at sundown on Fridays. No distractions from social media, emails, viral videos, or endless streams of texts. She has found it grounding, healing, and liberating—a wonderful way to focus on each other. In return, Ethan never pushes his beliefs onto her, and he has been amazingly open about discussing how he will balance his religion with a realistic, modern life when it comes to kids.

This brings us to one of the thorniest significant differences. Differences over whether to have children are among the biggest issues that spell "Splitsville." Naturally, there is no one way to deal with this. My friends Hope and Stan were a late twentysomething New York couple who loved each other dearly. But after being together for about two years, including more than one year of cohabitating, they broke up. Hope wanted kids and Stan did not. They tried to make it work, but

Hope really, really wanted kids. She could not imagine a life without them. Stan did his best to consider the possibility, but in the end he knew fatherhood was not in his cards. He cared about Hope deeply and realized that the most selfless, loving thing he could do was to let her go pursue motherhood with another person. Yes, it was heartbreaking for both of them, but it was the right thing to do. They have both moved on to new relationships and remain friendly.

Of course, deal-breakers aren't always what they seem. Sometimes we change our minds. Another couple I know, Raj and Emily, had been living together for about seven years. They were both in their late thirties, and Emily felt her clock was ticking very loudly. After many discussions that always led to his refusal to have kids, Emily finally walked out. She wanted kids so badly, and she knew she'd regret it if she did not take matters into her own hands. Emily reasoned that she would grow resentful of Raj and that the relationship would become too toxic. It had taken quite a while to prepare herself to walk away. Amazingly, once she did, Raj changed his mind. Now they have two wonderful children whom he adores. Raj is incredibly grateful that she gave him the ultimate ultimatum. (I know two other couples with a very similar story; one who compromised with having one child and another couple who ended up with not just one child, but three!)

Needless to say, this can backfire. Badly. Raj could have placated Emily and agreed to have kids only to find that he resented her for it. He deliberated about the relationship and realized that his reluctance stemmed somewhat from fear and uncertainty, as well as his desire to focus on his career and have the freedom to, in effect, play and do whatever he wished, not from an innate disdain for parenthood.

I understand that if you haven't had kids yet, this thought process can seem fairly theoretical. You don't know what you don't know. If you are on the fence about children, here's a little advice from a woman who didn't think about having kids until she was thirty-eight: it's cliché to say that having kids is the hardest yet most rewarding thing a person can do, but in my experience this is true.

Don't worry, this isn't one of *those* books. I'm not here to persuade you to have children. I would never try to persuade someone about such an important decision only to have them take my advice . . . and then regret it. I know quite a few happy childless couples that stand by their decision. But I also know some couples who probably did not make the right decision. My friends Ben and Liz did not have children even though Liz dearly wanted them. Ben was adamant about staying childless, and Liz determined that she'd rather be without kids than without Ben. While she has never explicitly disclosed regret, at times I can't help but see some sadness in her eyes. I wonder if deep down—or even not so deep down—Liz feels that she made a terrible mistake.

Having children is *the* biggest commitment you can make as a human. You must be honest with yourself and with your partner. And you must ask your partner to be honest with you about where he stands on children and take what he is saying at face value. And, yes, you may need to be prepared to lose the person you love to have babies.

. . .

Are you still with me? Good! This was a lot to take in, I know. The biggest takeaway right now is to be super honest with yourself about the potential red flags in your relationship.

We're going to move onto so-called deal-breakers and the oh-so common and challenging topic of settling. If you are single, there will be lots of great tips for breaking free of the endless cycle of dating that has become all too common these days. Finally, we'll cover concepts that offer self-empowerment and help pave the way to Radical Acceptance.

- Never use Radical Acceptance to justify red flags, especially behavior that is unacceptable, threatening, or even dangerous.

- If you're in a dysfunctional situation, be honest with yourself about its severity. Extreme mental health issues and character flaws are beyond the scope of Radical Acceptance and trying to apply it may be counterproductive in these scenarios.
- Where there are significant differences but a deep mutual desire to be together, Radical Acceptance can be very instrumental. Remember that the novelty of these differences may wear off and eventually prove to be extra challenging, so be prepared to redouble your Radical Acceptance efforts over time to achieve lasting love.

ARE YOU SETTLING? OR SABOTAGING YOURSELF? HOW TO TELL

NSTEAD OF THE bright red flags we explored in the previous chapter, we're now going to address the various shades of orange in your relationship that may be harder to discern. These could be deal-breakers, but they could also be manageable differences. We'll also be diving deeply into the question that plagues many women: Am I settling?

Radical Acceptance means appreciating all of your partner, not just picking and choosing the parts that are easy to love. Of course, all of the acceptance in the world isn't going to help a man who is actually still a child, who scorns responsibility and who would rather spend his weekends on the couch watching *South Park* than with you. Nor will it transform the man who makes you feel chronically insecure and anxious, the one who will never commit but who feeds you enough crumbs to prevent complete relationship starvation.

Okay, so what if you're not with a jerk or a man-child, but instead someone who's nice . . . but boring? What do you do when you're not necessarily head over heels in love, but you are with someone responsible and grounded, who is kind and generous? Or what if you're burned out from dating and can't bear to swipe right (or left for that matter!) again? These are common challenges that I will help guide you through.

In another common scenario, do you suffer from what I call the Beefcake Syndrome? This is when you have a preconceived ideal match in your head. Very often this person resembles the captain of your high school football team, or maybe these days he's a captain of industry. In any case, he is typically a two-dimensional character—your version of Prince Charming—to whom you have become attached and who is preventing you from being open to a wonderful three-dimensional, real-life person. I will help you figure out if you are sabotaging your chances for entering into a deeply fulfilling, long-lasting relationship before you even say hello.

Readers of this book, naturally, will find themselves in many different stages of relationships. In this section we are going to delve more deeply into two primary scenarios: In the first, you are perpetually single or dating a ton, but instead of finding lasting love you are bouncing from relationship to relationship. We're going to take a closer look at what might be preventing you from giving someone a chance, and then we're going to explore techniques for expanding your comfort zone.

In the second scenario, you are dating someone but experiencing uncertainty. Maybe he's getting on your nerves more and more often, or maybe he's just turned out to be . . . meh. He's not what you pictured. Perhaps there are differences you did not expect. Or maybe you are really into him, but you fight all the time. Or he has a ton of emotional baggage. (We're going to talk a lot more about this last category in step 4, but understand for now that while the presence of emotional baggage in a spouse or partner can be especially scary and confusing, it is manageable.) If any of these describe something you are grappling with, don't worry. Your relationship does not have to be at the mercy of these menacing gremlins.

There is a third scenario that I also provide a nod to: What about when you've been married or have been living together for a long time, and now you're at the end of your rope? I've included a brief section that speaks directly to readers suffering from this situation.

Many people suffer in relationships due to an expectations problem. I certainly did. We expect to be swept off our feet and epically romanced for the rest of our lives, and we're caught off guard when our beloved relationships ask so very much of us, when they present such conundrums.

No matter which scenario you fall under, there is one trait that unites them all: lovely, beautiful, remarkable *you*! We're now going to figure out how to change your narrative, to better enable you to achieve happy, lasting love.

IT ALL STARTS WITH YOU!

I'm going to ask you a handful of tough questions to help you explore those internal barriers that may be hindering your love life. Going through these questions is useful even if you are with someone you feel sure of. Almost all of us can benefit from changing our scripts (either a little or a lot). It's all about what you tell yourself and what you believe about yourself—both of which are subject to a dramatically empowering rewrite with a bit of courage and self-awareness. Try to write out your answers, ideally with pen and paper. I am always amazed by what the simple act of writing can reveal about what's bubbling below the surface. Endless research bears out this phenomenon. So often our psyches try to protect us, and this is a good exercise to try and get past those pesky defense mechanisms. Be as honest with yourself as possible.

This exercise may hurt a lot. But here's what I love about this kind of honest introspection: You are empowered to move forward with a new, more self-serving narrative. Once you have come face-to-face with these debilitating or even self-destructive parts of yourself, you can begin letting them go. You get to rewrite the script for your future self.

Inevitably, the patterns in our romantic relationships are inextricably linked to the patterns in our relationships with our parents and their relationship with one another (or to other adults they were romantically involved with). That's why it helps for you to be brutally honest with yourself and aware of what was going on when you were growing up, and how this all relates to your love life. Until you become clear and honest with your patterns and fears, most likely you're going to keep making the same mistakes, attracting the wrong kinds of people or floundering when you attract the right kind. If your parents had a bad relationship or you were abandoned or neglected, abused, or treated harshly as a kid, you are going to have a tougher time developing a healthy, lasting relationship. But you can do it by making an ardent effort. Radical Acceptance will help you. Depending on your specific circumstances, professional therapy may be warranted as well.

So, here we go.

When it comes to love: What are you afraid of?
- Really: WHAT ARE YOU AFRAID OF?
- Rejection? Getting too close to someone and being vulnerable? Not getting what you need? Being hurt or disappointed? Being ignored or neglected? Being abandoned? Being in conflict?

When you reflect on your love life, what kind of people have you been attracting? Think about your patterns.
- Are you forever pursuing someone "out of your reach"? Someone "beneath you"? Someone who is unable to commit? Do you always go after the proverbial bad boy? Or are you someone who always needs to be pursued?

- Are you afraid of what others will think about whom you are with?
- Have you often had to make excuses about your relationship?

And then there's your upbringing. What's at your core? What seems normal to you?

- What was your parents' relationship like?
- How much love and attention did you receive growing up?
- Do you feel you are worthy of a wonderful man's unconditional love? Or do you feel you only deserve crumbs?

If you are single, think more about your approach to dating:

- Is your list of deal-breakers nearly a mile long? Do you have a very specific picture of what Mr. Right looks, sounds, and behaves like in your head?
- What is the common cause of failure in your past relationships?
- If you've been single for a long time or go on date after date with different people, why do you think this is?
- What signals are you sending out to people you date? Do you unwittingly communicate that you have low self-esteem? That you are a little desperate? Or do you possibly telegraph the opposite—that you are fully self-sufficient (i.e. you don't need a man: you complete yourself!)?

• • •

I wish I could give you a hug and high five right now. Though you may feel emotional and worn-out from that exercise, I hope you're also feeling a sense of catharsis and clarity as you reflect on the challenges that have been brewing and bubbling within.

What are your two or three most significant takeaways? What are the biggest culprits that have been holding you back in your love life? Don't focus on too many right now. You can't boil the ocean. Focus on the biggest hurdles that are staring you in the face and be prepared to act on them.

I encourage you to pose the previous questions to a trusted friend. He or she can help you come to terms with your harder truths. We all have our blind spots and, occasionally, distorted self-perceptions. I am amazed how frequently even the most self-aware people can fall prey to this pattern. Consulting a trusted friend or family member about your vulnerabilities and patterns can be extremely helpful. Asking the right questions will give you invaluable insights into whether you are settling or otherwise sabotaging your chances for succeeding in love. Sometimes these truths are staring us right in the face, but we're afraid to confront them. It can take a truly honest, good friend to set us straight—or, alternatively, a *really* good therapist.

If you have abandonment issues, for example, and always find yourself in fight-or-flight mode, you are likely attracting people who are noncommittal or emotionally unavailable. I want you to commit to changing the parts of your narrative that hold you back. Tell yourself you are worthy of love and commitment *right now*. You are lovable, and you have lots of love to offer. Tell yourself this again and again. Sing it to yourself sweetly and confidently. Write it down.

Do your best to forgive whoever abandoned or neglected you. Try to extend compassion to these individuals. If that seems like a very tall ask, remember that harboring negativity is not good for you. Letting go of your hurt is less about giving people who let you down a pass, and more about taking steps to heal and liberate yourself. It may take years to fully come to grips with certain issues, but I believe that the vast majority of us can get there without years of therapy or endless introspection. At some point, trust yourself to say, "Enough. I'm moving on and leaving my abandonment issues behind."

Think about your fears. Everyone is afraid of rejection, but for some people this fear can be especially paralyzing, causing them to seek out incompatible partners who are not sufficiently energizing or stimulating—in effect causing them to aim "too low." For others, their greatest fear is to be alone. As a result, they'll accept being treated poorly or being incompatible, setting themselves up for an unhappy relationship.

An interesting set of studies[14] by researchers at the University of Toronto found that people who are fearful of being single—those who agreed with statements such as "I feel anxious when I think about being single forever," "I need to find a partner before I'm too old to have and raise children," "As I get older, it will get harder and harder to find someone," and "It scares me to think that there might not be anyone out there for me"—were much more likely to prioritize *being* in a relationship over being in a *quality* relationship. In other words, it's a tug-of-war between the fear of being single and the fear of being stuck in a relationship with the wrong person.

Do you have similar fears? Or are you the opposite? Do you fear that you can always be in a better relationship, and is this causing you to bounce from relationship to relationship without ever truly giving one of them a chance?

No matter what love stage you are in, listen carefully to your inner voice—the one that is wise, kind, and bold. Then tell all of those internal critics who are on an endless loop in your head to STFU.

And to remain quiet.

ADDRESSING YOUR DEAL-BREAKERS

Most people have deal-breakers. There's generally no getting around them. And some people have very specific deal-breakers. Don't be ashamed if your own come across as superficial or weird. You're not alone. Deal-breakers can be very helpful as a way to filter potential mates, but they can also be really limiting or even detrimental.

Based on responses to a survey YourTango conducted on deal-breakers, two-thirds of respondents reported that they have a definitive list of deal-breakers. Moreover, 40 percent said that having a list of deal-breakers helped them find someone who was compatible, and about 30 percent said that they are confident that their deal-breaker list would eventually lead to a successful long-term relationship.

How about people who decided to "overrule" one or more of their deal-breakers? What are the consequences of that? Forty-four percent said, "Yes, and it was a mistake," while 30 percent said, "Yes, and thank goodness—it led to a fantastic relationship!"

The three most popular categories of deal-breakers as determined by YourTango readers are:

- Insufficient personality traits (not funny or charismatic enough, etc.)—58 percent
- Insufficient sexual desires/satisfaction—54 percent
- Insufficient physical attractiveness (e.g., has to be the right height and weight, have good hair, etc.)—37 percent

Equally interesting are the responses we received on a battery of very specific deal-breakers. Can you guess what the number one biggest deal-breaker is?

Lack of hygiene!

Yes, 75 percent said lack of hygiene is their biggest turnoff! Meanwhile, 70 percent of people are turned off by someone who is frequently rude (to servers, customer service people, to you, etc.). Sixty-five percent don't want too much of a "player," and 63 percent can't stand someone hypercritical and judgmental. A three-way tie emerged for fifth place: 57 percent say control freaks (not a surprise), too lazy or not ambitious enough, and heavy drinkers. (Interestingly, 6 percent say "doesn't drink at all" is a deal-breaker.)

Below is a list of specific deal-breakers as reported by YourTango readers. It's incredibly interesting to see the various sorts of objections people claim to have. How do you relate to these?

48 percent said bad teeth

38 percent said being a cheapskate

35 percent said overly concerned with his/her looks

35 percent said too religious, while 8 percent said not religious enough!

30 percent said sloppiness

28 percent said differing values

28 percent said one of them wants kids and the other does not

28 percent said is too carefree/not stable enough

27 percent said always talks politics

27 percent said too short, while 4 percent said too tall

26 percent said not sufficiently educated

25 percent said dresses poorly

25 percent said shopaholic/spends too much money

23 percent said being too conservative, while only 8 percent said being too liberal was a deal-breaker

21 percent said too many tattoos

21 percent said bad taste/lacks sophistication

18 percent said conflict/disconnect among each other's friends/family

18 percent said works too much

16 percent said inappropriate sense of humor

15 percent said stubborn

14 percent said too thin, while 37 percent said too fat

12 percent said doesn't make enough money

10 percent said too pale, while 6 percent said too dark

8 percent said not enough hair

8 percent said dietary restrictions (e.g., you are vegetarian, he/she loves meat)

Here are a couple of examples of people who elaborated in their own words on their deal-breakers.

A YourTango reader from Johannesburg, South Africa, commented, "My biggest deal-breaker is respect when it comes to boundaries and communication. There was a man that totally disrespected both of those. I decided to walk away, he begged for a second chance, I gave it to him with set rules of conduct. Two years later we are now living together and planning a future together. We have had ups and downs but he knows where I stand." I love how this anecdote demonstrates the power of knowing what you need and successfully communicating it to someone.

A comment from a user in California makes a cogent case to not cling too tightly to a preconceived type: "I had always dated men who were six feet or taller. Dark hair and eyes. When I met my husband his looks weren't my type, but he was such a great guy and I felt so wonderful around him I kept dating him. Then his type became my type."

Hallelujah!

Having too many deal-breakers, or being overly attached to some of the more superficial ones, are common forms of self-sabotage. If you have an extremely specific picture of your life partner in mind, there is a good chance that you're missing many wonderful opportunities for love. But you don't have to continue to do so. The key is to understand your expectations, and then to push back on them as needed. You may very well determine that "settling" is a matter of perception, and that you have the opportunity to create a beautiful love with someone who completely surprises you, as experienced by the woman from California above.

Take some time and think of your own list of deal-breakers. Like many YourTango readers, you might have a picture in your mind of what your ideal mate looks like. Maybe he's six foot two, tall, dark, and handsome, a banker with an Ivy League education. Maybe he's the wounded, bearded musician with a trust fund.

Now I want you to reflect. Are you sabotaging yourself by having too narrow a picture of what this ideal mate looks like, talks like, and smells like? Are you being too superficial? To get real on your deal-breaker situation, let's consult the wise, hilarious, and oh-so-cool Dan Savage, the sex-advice columnist and all-around controversialist.

THE PRICE OF ADMISSION

A while back I was watching an interview with Dan online. He was at a speaking engagement when an audience member asked him: "I can't stay interested in a guy for longer than two months. What is wrong with me? I find a flaw and can't get over it. For example, if a guy chews with his mouth open, I could never see him again."

Dan proceeded to give some of the most succinct, right-on relationship advice I've heard, and it really cuts right to the heart of the Radical Acceptance framework:

> *You are the problem with you!*[15] *If you have a list of deal-breakers that has more than five things on it, you do need to wait around to get a sex robot you can program to be perfect in every possible way. There is no settling down without some settling for . . . We call this in my house "paying the price of admission."*
>
> *. . . You can't have a long-term relationship with someone unless you're willing to identify the things, you know, the prices of admission you're willing to pay, and the ones you're not. But the ones you're not, the list of things you're not willing to put up with, you really have to be able to count it on one hand. And it can't be superficial bullshit like chews with the mouth open.*
>
> *People, when they're young, have this idea . . . "There's someone out there who's perfect for me" . . . "The one" does not fucking exist.*

Every person is going to have his or her price of admission—those flaws and rough edges that you are never going to be able to change. If you can't accept them, the problem is with you, not with them. Your decision is to either pay or not pay the price of admission, not whether you can negotiate the price down or sneak your way through without paying anything at all.

The price of admission can mean unpleasant characteristics—he chews with his mouth open—but it can also mean bigger-ticket items. These might be religious observances, children from a prior relationship, or a certain degree of conflict, due to the combustible nature of your personalities. The price of admission isn't inherently bad, and quite often, can present an opportunity for enhanced intimacy and growing closer.

There's a story I like to tell about a woman named Caitlin who, though just twenty-six years old, had already experienced a lifetime of heartbreak. She grew up in a small town in upstate New York. She began dating Jeffrey in high school and they stayed together through college. They got engaged their senior year and were married at twenty-three. She and Jeffrey never fought. They never bickered. They never had serious conversations about their relationship. When she tried bringing up difficult topics, he would slip into his shell until she backed down.

Then, all at once, it was over. Just a year after their wedding, Jeffrey asked for a divorce. It came as a complete shock to Caitlin. "I can't do this," he said. "I don't want to try anymore." Caitlin sees now that the warning signs were present long before that final traumatizing conversation. Eventually something broke inside Jeffrey and he was unwilling to do the work to improve their relationship.

The next year was very difficult for Caitlin. She had to balance the fallout of her divorce with her job at a major media company, but she stuck it out. Eventually she decided to dip back into the dating world. She was living in New York, after all, and she was still so young despite all she had endured. She joined OkCupid and put herself out there. Not long after, she met a smart and good-looking guy named Brian. They had wonderful chemistry and hit it off immediately. A year later they moved in together.

What is new about Caitlin's current relationship is that her and Brian's prices of admission are both out in the open. Caitlin must accept that Brian is stubborn and defensive. Brian must accept that Caitlin can be inside her own head, and because of her past relationship can interpret unhappiness as a sign of imminent danger. With Brian, she will express an opinion with which he may vocally disagree. In the early phase of their relationship, this would escalate into an argument. She was initially caught off guard when he would say: "I disagree with you, and here is why." Caitlin would perceive this as an attack, rather than him simply expressing himself. Nowadays, she recognizes that conflict isn't inherently bad, and that it can represent an opportunity to strengthen the relationship. Initially the fights were difficult and new for her, but there was something liberating about them. For the first time she could freely express herself, and she knew that Brian was freely expressing himself.

They have their problems, of course. Caitlin admits she can get defensive, and Brian isn't afraid to tell her when he thinks she's wrong, not unlike Sanjay and me. But over time they learned to radically accept their differences. Brian understands that Caitlin is hypersensitive to small resentments that can build up and eventually crush a relationship—that's what happened to her marriage. He knows that when she is asking him about his feelings, she isn't accusing him of being unhappy. She just wants to be sure everything is okay between them. Meanwhile, Caitlin understands that unlike Jeffrey, Brian won't back away from conflict, and she is learning to see that as a positive, and as a way to deepen their connection. They still have their fights, but they are constructive. While a higher degree of conflict was never something Caitlin was seeking in her next romantic relationship, it has been a completely worthwhile and growth-inducing price of admission. Through really accepting one another, including their differences and challenges, both she and Brian understand that they are not enemies when they fight; they are two players on the same team practicing how to be better toward, and with, each other.

EXPECTATIONS AND THE CONCEPT OF SETTLING

Can you count your deal-breakers, as Dan says, on one hand? If you can't, then you might be sabotaging yourself by having too specific or narrow a picture of your ideal mate. Sure, everyone wants to be with an ultrasuccessful, brilliant, perfect man who looks like Ryan Gosling. But as an alternative, let's say you find someone who is reasonably success- ful, smart, but super corny and a little pudgy with a modest bald patch. Can you still experience tremendous love even though he doesn't meet your preconceived criteria at face value? Can you still experience deep, lasting love with someone who takes up one or two hands worth of deal- breakers? *YES!* But only if you decide to open your heart (and mind) and cultivate love.

Now, let's get real. Clearly this person must possess a boatload of redeeming traits. There should be aspects intrinsic in his personality, or about your interactions together and how he makes you feel, that you eventually find alluring and endearing, things that you can build upon. Maybe it's his wicked sense of humor, or that he's endlessly knowledge- able, or super generous? Maybe he adores you and makes you feel like a queen. If you have a list of very specific deal-breakers, or if you don't keep your mind open to the possibility of a second date, you may never discover these beautifully innate qualities that can take some time and nurturing to surface.

I have a college friend, Tanya, who developed her idea of Mr. Per- fect in high school and never changed it. This is the Beefcake Syndrome, again. It begins as your typical all-American story: Tanya was a cheer- leader and she always dated the handsome quarterback. How perfect, right? This was all well and good for Tanya during high school and col- lege, but the problem is that throughout her twenties and thirties, Tanya maintained the exact same image in her mind. He was tall, dark, and handsome, and he would sweep her off her feet.

Tanya fell into a thoroughly destructive pattern in which she would never give any potential suitor a chance unless he fit a particular physi-cal mold. Unsurprisingly, she never found a successful, lasting match. And yet, she *still* is holding out for John T. Quarterback to magically materialize. Maybe he will, but in the meantime Tanya has sacrificed more than twenty years that she could have spent building a lasting re-lationship, not to mention the possibility of having her own biological children, which was very important for her.

You can't talk about settling without addressing the topic of chem-istry. Of course, chemistry is amazing when you can get it, but it is far from the be-all, end-all. Moreover, for most people, the chemistry that was so electrifying in the beginning eventually ebbs and fades. This is not necessarily a bad thing. This is where the fleeting electricity of ro-mance and chemistry give way to deep, long-lasting attachment.

I advise people who are desperately seeking deep, long-lasting love and attachment to be as open as possible and to not demand instant chemistry on day one—or for it to linger beyond year one. Instead of surface-deep deal-breakers, broaden your requirements to allow the widest range of possibility. How about: He must be kind, smart, and honest; he must care deeply about you (eventually!); and you two must be able to have fun together. Chemistry may, in fact, develop over time. There is a wonderful story at the end of this chapter that demonstrates the stealthy, innocuous ways that chemistry can develop!

Take a moment to reflect on the past few months of your life. How often have you said no? How often have you said no to that concert or no to that dinner party or no to that after-work drinks or even no to that dorky-looking guy at the bar who tried buying you a drink? If you're in a relationship, how many times have you said no to your significant other, even casually? Maybe it was saying no to eating at that hole-in-the-wall restaurant or no to watching that weird independent film on Netflix or no to planning an adventure vacation. They tend to add up fast.

In the previous section I introduced you to my friend Rachel, who began dating an Orthodox Jew named Ethan, and managed to fall in love with him despite his very restrictive lifestyle. If Rachel had known that Ethan kept strict Shabbat—that he couldn't go out or even use his phone, elevator, or stove on weekends—she likely would not have agreed to the date in the first place. While she is comfortable and accepting of their differences now, Rachel would not have consciously left her comfort zone by such a large degree had she known about his strict adherence to his faith.

Before she met Ethan, Rachel had been in a long-term relationship with a man named Dev. Rachel and Dev were one of the few college relationships that stuck. They met during their freshmen year and stayed together through all four years. They moved to the same city together, ready to start their lives. Dev was brilliant and passionate and an incredibly hard worker. They were perfect for each other . . . except when they weren't. Rachel felt Dev was highly critical of her and her life goals. Trying to find a consensus about simple problems was like scaling a mountain. Rachel was uncomfortable talking about their problems with him, so she talked about them with her friends instead, and that only made Dev angrier when he found out. Meanwhile, Dev felt strongly about his Hinduism and Rachel wasn't ready to abandon Judaism. When it came to kids, they couldn't agree about how they should be raised. They broke up and got back together again several times, but it simply wasn't working. Eventually Dev received a job offer across the country. Rachel told him he should take the job, but that she wouldn't follow him.

They broke up for good, and Rachel struggled to regain her independence. She was totally heartbroken. As fortune would have it, though, she had started working at a start-up that granted her very flexible hours. Deciding she needed to leave her comfort zone, she began a "year of yes." People and activities she would normally say no to, Rachel began saying yes to. Yes to strange concerts and art shows and activities. And most important—yes to people. All sorts of people. Yes to that boy on the subway who asked her out, yes to that nervous guy at the bar. Saying yes allowed Rachel to break through her angst and to be okay with her breakup and with her life.

Rachel began dating and dating and dating. Not because she was hoping to find a lasting relationship right away, but because she enjoyed meeting people and having an adventure. Embracing the year of yes was fun and stimulating! She went out with many interesting people and many people who were, well, odd. She once had a breakfast date with a guy who wore a three-piece suit—she struggled not to laugh the entire time. Sometimes Rachel dated three, four guys at a time. It was one of the most liberating experiences of her life.

Rachel still had her deal-breakers, of course, and many of the guys she dated would never pass muster for an actual relationship, but she was having fun. She experimented with pushing her comfort zone, and she learned that what she thought were deal-breakers maybe weren't deal-breakers, and vice versa. It took a year of opening her heart to prepare Rachel for Ethan. She probably would have never said yes to him if she hadn't said yes to many other possibilities before him. Now she is with her soul mate and her life is transformed, beautifully and brilliantly, in ways she could have never imagined.

This is a wonderful example of building your foundation for Radical Acceptance. Liberate yourself from preconceived ideas that may be holding you back. Say no to the self-sabotage of being too narrow and judgmental. Have the confidence in yourself to open your heart and say yes! Note, for those of you who normally cling to control, I realize this can feel really scary and maybe even impossible. But if you're willing to cede control, to not obsess over the outcome, to tell yourself that it is okay to have experiences that may not end up being perfect, you are likely to be rewarded.

The caveat, of course, is to always be aware of when your comfort zone is merely pushed and when it is invaded. Have the confidence to say no when you need to.

BODY LANGUAGE

When it comes to making decisions about your relationship, it helps to be calm and confident. No matter if you're dating or if you're in a relationship, this begins with body language. In 2012, the Harvard University social scientist Amy Cuddy[16] gave a wonderful TED Talk about the degree to which our body language affects confidence levels and impacts mental and emotional states, creating a powerful physiological feedback loop. By being aware of your posture, you can reduce anxiety and stress levels, boost your confidence, and send positive signals to those around you. Cuddy and her team classified various body positions as "high power" and "low power."

High-power poses are open and relaxed. When standing, that means legs shoulder width, elbows out, chin up, and hands on your hips. When sitting, it means your legs spread out or one leg propped on the other. One arm can be sprawled out on a nearby chair, or spread out on the table. Maybe they are flexed behind your back. But most importantly, you are open and relaxed. You are calm, confident, and ready for anything.

Low-power poses are the opposite. When standing, both your legs and arms are crossed, your knees bent. Your chin is down and your eyes are looking toward the floor. When sitting, your knees are together and your feet crossed. Your hands are locked together, you're rubbing them together or along your arms and legs. Your shoulders are hunched. This body language represents being closed and guarded.

Your body language doesn't just influence other people's perception of you; it actually determines your biochemistry. Dr. Cuddy and her team demonstrated that high-power poses increase testosterone levels by 20 percent and decrease cortisol levels by 25 percent. In other words, your body position directly affects your mood and confidence. Having run a media company for many years, I know that positive body language is a must when working with others, spending time with your partner, and especially dating. Crossing your arms, for example, presents a defensive, unengaged posture—and studies have even shown that closed body language actually causes us to absorb less information. Likewise, slouching in your chair suggests boredom. Even though you might not be consciously feeling these emotions, your body language is communicating them in a big way.

When I walk down the street, I am mindful that I feel energized as I look up and hold my head high, keep my back straight, and look around me. Often I make eye contact and smile at strangers. Quite a boost!

Before you leave the house (or when you're in a public bathroom, or wherever), try one of my all-time-favorite mood boosters: the Wonder Woman pose. Stand up tall, puff out your chest, stick your chin up, and place your hands on your hips. Think Beyoncé at the Super Bowl. Look straight ahead and hold this pose for two minutes while breathing deeply. You'll feel more relaxed and more confident. This is a great routine to start off your day.

Trying to catch someone's eye on Tinder? A University of California, Berkeley study[17] of three thousand participants found that users were 27 percent more likely to get a yes with an expanded posture—meaning arms or torso outstretched— compared with contracted, slouched poses.

No matter if you're on a first date or at dinner with your partner of ten years, be sure to keep your body language open. Point yourself in his direction and make steady eye contact. Be sure to smile and try to nod when he is speaking—it shows you are engaged, attentive, and interested. The key is that you are forging a strong connection, no matter your relationship status. Your body language is a crucial asset here.

As women get older and the pool of potential candidates narrows, we sabotage ourselves by holding out for a preconceived perfect match. This stark pragmatism burst onto the scene in 2008, when a writer named Lori Gottlieb published her seminal essay, "Marry Him! The Case for Settling for Mr. Good Enough" in *The Atlantic*, sending seismic shockwaves virtually everywhere:

> *My advice is this: Settle!*[18] *That's right. Don't worry about passion or intense connection. Don't nix a guy based on his annoying habit of yelling "Bravo!" in movie theaters. Overlook his halitosis or abysmal sense of aesthetics. Because if you want to have the infrastructure in place to have a family, settling is the way to go. Based on my observations, in fact, settling will probably make you happier in the long run, since many of those who marry with great expectations become more disillusioned with each passing year.*
>
> *. . . As your priorities change from romance to family, the so-called "deal-breakers" change. Some guys aren't worldly, but they'd make great dads. Or you walk into a room and start talking to this person who is 5'4" and has an unfortunate nose, but he "gets" you.*
>
> *. . . My long-married friend Renée offered this dating advice to me in an e-mail: "I would say even if he's not the love of your life, make sure he's someone you respect intellectually, makes you laugh, appreciates you . . . I bet there are plenty of these men in the older, overweight, and bald category (which they all eventually become anyway)."*

It was a controversial but brilliant article, and it led to an equally controversial and bestselling book. In one sense it's a cautionary tale: For years, Lori dated and broke up, dated and broke up, all in pursuit of that one, objectively perfect mate. She never found him, and all of a sudden she found herself forty years old and at the terminus of her childbearing years. With the help of a sperm donor she became a mother, and the article delineates the extraordinary hurdles single mothers face when dating. In essence, Lori argues: strike when the marital iron is hot, ladies, because it won't last forever. "I'm the ghost of what could happen to you if you don't broaden your idea of Mr. Right," she cautions.

As brusque as Lori is, she is mostly right. (There is good news, don't worry—I'll tell you in a moment where I think she got it wrong.) As women age, our priorities change from romance to family—not for everyone, of course, but for many. As a result, our deal-breakers need to change as well. For example, right out of college maybe you would never think of dating a balding, potbellied short guy with a hammertoe. But when you hit thirty-five, he now has a steady income, is the epitome of generosity, loves to cook, and would make a fantastic dad. And who knows? Maybe he gives a mean massage—and has an impeccable fashion sense.

So, here's where Lori gets it wrong. Creating lasting love isn't like finding a roommate. Simply finding a warm body to rely on, procreate with, and share the bills with will absolutely feel like settling. You have to *want* to be with this person, after all. That warm body you find might have a stable income and a kind spirit, but what if he can't make you laugh? What if the sex is bad? What if the sex is *really* bad?

Lori would probably say something along the lines of, "Get over it." Instead, I argue that you both deserve to be in a relationship that makes you happy, where you can truly be into each other. But here's the caveat: *You have to work for it.* That initial infatuation (if there ever was one) isn't going to sustain the relationship for decades. It almost never does. Hence the sky-high divorce rate! The love that sustains the relationship isn't the love-at-first-sight variety; it's the love that is cultivated at year two, year five, year ten, and beyond. It's the love that you create on your own, and it never comes easy. Feelings of deep attachment take time to develop, but they endure for the long haul.

So what is the middle ground between Lori's cold, harsh practicality and holding out for the One? This question reminded me of a friend of

mine who joked that "in about five to ten years we're going to get a tip-
ping point. People are going to start having arranged marriages because
the choices are just too paralyzing."

That got me thinking. Sanjay is actually the product of an arranged
marriage. Interestingly enough, unless both spouses are thoroughly repellant to each other, arranged marriages can actually grow to become
more successful than marriages born from passion.

A Harvard professor[19] named Dr. Robert Epstein looked at numerous cultures in which arranged marriages are commonplace, including
Pakistan, India, and heavily Orthodox regions of Israel. He interviewed
more than one hundred such couples and compared the data with more
than thirty years of research into Western marriages, which have seen
sky-high divorce rates. What Dr. Epstein concluded is fascinating: "In
the West marriages are easy to get out of. But in arranged marriages,
the commitment is very strong. They get married knowing they won't
leave, so when times are harder—if they face injury or trauma—they
don't run away. It brings them closer." Indeed, while the divorce rate in
the United States hovers around 44 percent, only about 1 percent of
couples in India, where most marriages are prearranged, end up divorcing. (Though, to be fair, divorce is much less accepted in India than it is
in America.)

Many Western marriages are the end result of a short period of lust
and intense physical attraction. Initial feelings of romantic love are extraordinarily high. Unfortunately, these feelings diminish over time—in
fact, Dr. Epstein's work suggests that feelings of romantic love can fade
by as much as half within eighteen months. Romantic love is often referred to as an addiction because your brain is so hopped up on neu-
rochemicals. When the reality of the marriage is unable to live up to
the early bliss of the relationship, divorce or discord often loom. Many
couples feel frustrated with each other and are unlikely to try and battle
through rough patches when they fear they cannot rekindle that initial

spark. Moreover, they feel like they shouldn't have to battle—that if they were *really* meant to be with this person, it wouldn't be so difficult.

Conversely, significant thought and consideration go into arranged marriages. Issues that often pose significant problems for Western couples—such as income, family compatibility, and life goals—are all weighed and calculated before an arrangement is decided upon, and therefore are less likely to represent pressure points during the marriage. While the love in arranged marriages might begin at zero, it grows over the years to the point where, Dr. Epstein found, it can surpass the love in unarranged marriages within five years. Within ten years, the love can be twice as great, often because the initial commitment of the arranged marriage forces them to work together through rough patches.

So what can this tell us? Lasting love is earned. *You can learn to love someone.* The catch is, you will likely only learn to love him if you go all in. I'm not saying enter an arranged marriage in this day and age in the Western world. But, whether or not he's your preconceived version of Mr. Right, you have to commit yourself entirely to the relationship. If he is kind to you, if he is smart and sweet, and you feel safe and happy around him, then no, you are not settling. There is so much more to discover about him. Chances are you haven't even begun to scratch the surface.

I'll share one of my favorite Aziz Ansari quotes that sums up this situation quite helpfully:

When you hear a Flo Rida song[20] at first you're like, "What is this, Flo Rida? It's the same thing you've always done. I'm not listening to this song." And then you keep hearing it and you're like, "Oh my God, Flo Rida. You've done it again! This is a hit, baby!" And that's what people are like. People are like a Flo Rida song. You need to hear them a couple of times before you really get what they're about.

You see, there is likability—and discovery—through repetition. And sometimes, like with Flo Rida, you have to give a new potential relationship time to grow on you.

YOUR SITUATION: YOU ARE SINGLE AND HAVE BEEN FOR A LONG TIME (OR AT LEAST IT FEELS LIKE IT)

The Radical Acceptance program includes a modified framework for dating. I call it Radical *Assistance*. (Although arguably it also offers many helpful insights to people in longer-term relationships, too. Taking steps to "date" your husband helps keep your marriage fresh. Virtually all that follows will also be useful to you if you're in a long relationship.) While the first step of Radical Acceptance is, "Just love him or just dump him," this choice is obviously not realistic during the early stages of dating. Instead of "Just love him," let's stick with "Just like him." That's all. *Easier said than done*, you're probably thinking. *Why should I try to like him when there are hundreds of other potential matches just clicks and swipes away?*

And therein lies the paradox: With so much choice, why should you ever settle for less? But with so much choice, how do you ever know when you've found the right person? In theory, more choice is better. But often times, as the psychology professor Barry Schwartz famously points out[21] in his book *The Paradox of Choice*, our obsession with choice encourages us to seek that which makes us feel worse. When it comes to relationships, an infinite supply of potential partners has made us *less* likely to settle on a potential mate, not more likely. In short, we get easily overwhelmed.

In his book *Modern Love*, the hilarious Aziz Ansari recounts[22] a focus group that he ran in New York City. Aziz and his team observed as Derek, an average-looking, perfectly ho-hum guy, scanned through OkCupid. "The first woman he clicked on was very beautiful, with a witty profile page, a good job and lots of shared interests, including a love of sports. After looking the page over for a minute or so, Derek said, 'Well, she looks O.K. I'm just gonna keep looking for a while.' "

When Aziz asked him why he was turned off, Derek said: "She likes the Red Sox."

And it's true: With online dating apps, we can have deal-breakers as ludicrous as sports allegiances. A potential mate can check almost every single box yet still not be good enough. I have a friend, Cara, whose struggles with dating really exemplify this growing problem of too much choice, coupled with the tyranny of being attached to a pre-conceived "type." Double Jeopardy! She had been in a relationship for five years before it finally ended. When Cara began dating again, she had a very specific image in her mind: She wanted to be with a banker or a high-powered lawyer. The tall-and-dark, strong-and-powerful, master-of-the-universe type. You get the idea. This was Cara's Mr. Right, and she was determined to find him.

But Cara eventually became disillusioned. Living in New York City, there isn't exactly a shortage of Wall Street–type guys who fit the bill. And so she began dating. And dating. And dating. She tried OkCupid. She tried Hinge. She tried Tinder. She tried Bumble. Some apps worked better than others. The typical date was after-work drinks, occasionally coffee. She'd often have several dates per week. It was trouble making a connection with anyone. On the surface these guys fit the bill—they worked in finance or law and were rising fast. She dated older guys and she dated younger guys. And while many of her dates passed muster on paper, Cara would find some issue wrong with them. Maybe something about their personality or that there wasn't sufficient chemistry. It was always . . . meh. Of the fifty dates she went on in one year, maybe seven or eight turned into second dates. Far fewer became third or fourth dates. Some guys were witty and charming over text, but for the life of them, they could not make conversation in person. Others she liked, but they would abruptly stop corresponding with her.

Over time, Cara learned that her requirements—being uber-successful, having a prestigious title, having a wardrobe of black power-suits—were not working for her. There were an endless number of guys who met this criteria! Cara's experience is a classic case where the paradox of choice is in full force, preventing her from making it from drinks on date one to toasting their first anniversary.

Breaking this endless cycle of dating is where Radical Assistance comes in. It begins with changing your expectations. Instead of waiting for a guy to sweep you off your feet on the first date, just try to find a way to like him. Think of your mission as getting to a second date (and then the third!).

"Just think of reasons to say yes.[23] The problem with the first date is that you know so little about that human being that you focus too much on what you know. As you get to know him more you're going to see past his bad table manners and you'll see his great sense of humor, that he's enormously kind, that he likes dogs, that he's dying to have babies. All the data show that the more you get to know someone, the more you like them. And the more you think they are like you. You just have to get through the first date and to the second date."

—HELEN FISHER

Try not to think about his breath or his haircut (or lack thereof) or his unfortunate color coordination. Unless the stars align, Mr. Right isn't going to burst into the bar on a gleaming white horse and sweep you to his Upper East Side duplex. In reality he lives with two other guys in Queens, and they may or may not have had a bedbug infestation a few weeks prior. Just focus on the positives: Does he make you laugh? Does he seem honest? Unless he is repellant to you, for now, see what you can find that is positive and redeeming.

HOW FLIRTING CAN HELP YOU DATE MORE EFFECTIVELY

Note: Actively flirting with your husband or significant other is a big YES!

As Amanda Chatel reported on YourTango.com, "After conducting research regarding flirting in places where people go looking for love, psychologist Dr. Monica Moore found that 'it's not the most physically appealing people who get approached, but the ones who signal their availability and confidence through basic flirting techniques like eye contact and smiles.' "

I love this data because it places so much power in your hands, even if you weren't born looking like Halle Berry. As we talk about again and again in this book, when you feel sexy, attractive, and desirable, this confidence is transmitted directly to your date. It's all about how you speak and comport yourself.

Amanda offers up several interesting facts about flirting. Here are my faves:

"Women who touch while flirting get more dates." While men need to play it cool when it comes to this one, women who lay it on thick reel in the dates. There are three levels of touching: friendly (shoulder push or tap); plausible deniability (touching around the shoulder, waist, or forearm); and nuclear, which is the face touch. When you can, without being creepy,

go nuclear. (I go into the enormous power of touch at great length in part 3.)

Is everyone taking notes?

"Angling your head can also determine how you come across." Scientists at the University of Newcastle in Australia have found that you're most alluring when you angle your head forward, so you're forced to look ever-so-slightly upward. This creates a more feminine look, and we know how guys dig that. (Helen Fisher calls this the "copulatory gaze," and notes how common this is in cultures across the globe.)

"It has amazing health benefits." Weird, right? But those who get their flirt on and do so regularly are walking around with higher white-blood-cell counts, which means they're really, really healthy.

If you find yourself turned off by him, or filled with doubt because you're not instantly turned on, ask yourself why. Is he genuinely a jerk? Does he not meet your list of qualifications? Is the problem with him, or is it really with you? Be aware of these questions throughout the date, but stay in the moment. Make the guy you're on a date with your priority. Find a way to say yes! to date number two. Let the paradox of choice stop with you.

The first date is just a look-see. It's window shopping. If, like my friend Cara, you find yourself in an endless cycle of first dates, stop after five, or max, ten. Reflect on the guys you've met and pick one to spend more time with. You can't possibly have been able to really get to know them. Unless all of these guys are total slimeballs, give at least one a chance. If you find that everyone you meet is a no, there is a good chance that it is not about them but about you!

It may be helpful to remember this quote from Louis C.K., "Self-love is a good thing, but self-awareness is more important. You need to once in a while go, 'Uh, I'm kind of an asshole.'"

Okay, I am (mostly) kidding. I realize that for many people, dating can feel like a bruising, depressing experience, one where wearing a protective mantle feels as necessary as lipstick. I have heard from many women about how especially bad dating is in a place like New York City, where the sense of entitlement is rampant and people often behave very badly toward each other. I can see why a vicious cycle that breeds negativity and asshole-like behavior could easily emerge as a means of self-preservation.

But, seriously: If you're going on first date after first date, try to introspect and see (1) if your preconceived ideas are so high or specific that you're basically ruling guys out in the first thirty seconds and if (2) as a result, you're sending him negative signals and killing any chance of connection that could possibly occur? And/or (3) you are not doing a good job screening prospects.

Remember, it helps a *lot* if your inner narrative is "Yes!" You want to make it as easy as possible for him to be interesting and comfortable.

There is a very insightful quote that, if taken to heart by all people who dated, would make dating a transformative experience. Maya Angelou once said, "I've learned that people will forget what you said, people will forget what you did, but people will never forget how you made them feel." How can you make your date feel good about your encounter? And no, I don't mean by plying him with faux compliments or being overly nicey-nice; I mean by being kind, nonjudgmental, and openhearted to him, even if you know there's not a match.

I hear this all of the time: "Dating is a numbers game." In other words, that you have to keep on dating and dating until you find the perfect match.

Well, I have news for those who think that's true.

Dating is not simply a numbers game. This fallacy alone is likely the reason so many of us embark on endless cycles of fruitless dates. This is why I urge you to go 150 percent of the way without being cloying or fake. Be real. Be kind. Be interested. Get to know him. Don't interrogate him, but have a short list of questions ready to ask.

Say yes to that second drink. (But no more! As Cara told me, "You can love anyone after two whiskeys!") Extend him tenderness—even a tiny little sliver of it. And no, I don't mean that you should feel sorry for him; rather, do what you can to suspend judgment while you get to know him. Even if you're pretty sure that the relationship won't go anywhere, go for a second date anyway. And who knows? Maybe you'll discover some new, impressive side to him!

When you open your heart, he will feel it. And most important, you will feel it.

RADICAL ASSISTANCE HIGHLIGHTS. GREAT FOR DATING!

Just like him or just dump him. Think of it as networking or making a new friend. If you can't like him, move on!

Get to know him! Make it as easy as possible for him to be interesting—and for you to see a more real, slightly more intimate side of him—without getting too nosey, of course. Getting him to share some personal anecdotes is wonderful. Don't ask questions that can easily be answered with one- or two-word answers. Inspire him to reflect a little bit and give you something to work with. Here are some easy suggestions: What is your idea of a perfect Saturday? Who in your family are you closest to? (And what is this person like?) What is one of your favorite childhood memories? Who was your favorite teacher and why? Of course, you don't want to turn your date into an interview, so be willing to share your own answers to these questions, too. Before you know it, you're likely to be engaged in conversation that actually feels natural . . . and hopefully, fun!

Your job is to get a second date. If you're not getting a second date more frequently, you're either not screening well or you're not doing your job on the date. It may sound a little harsh, but as someone who wants you to succeed in love, I'll say it: the problem is probably with you, not him!

Stop, reflect, introspect. If you're not feeling a connection, think deeply about what is turning you off. Is the problem really about his personality, or is he stirring up ancient feelings or insecurities within you?

Radical communication. If you want to know why you aren't connecting after going on dates with lots of different people, ask for feedback. Really! If a date clearly didn't lead anywhere but you felt that he was a decent guy, try texting or calling him later for some honest feedback. Be genuine. If a few people give you the same feedback, you are empowered to make a positive change. I know this may seem scary or downright crazy, but it's an excellent exercise for leaving your comfort zone and learning about your blind spots. Asking for feedback is not about putting yourself on trial! Make it casual and earnest. Perhaps ask if he'd like you to return the favor.

Accept him here and now. Let your inner narrative say YES! Have an open heart.

Make him your priority. Neither of you is a commodity. Don't let the paradox of choice win! Go 150 percent of the way without being cloying or fake. Be real. But be kind, be interested, and suspend your judgment.

YOUR SITUATION: YOU ARE WITH SOMEONE . . . BUT YOU'RE NOT SURE

Okay—so you're dating someone. Maybe you've been together for a little while; maybe you've been together for a long while. It's going fine . . . but you're not sure if he's the one. What if there's someone better out there and you're making a mistake choosing this guy? What if he's great . . . except for when he's not. Maybe you're into him, but you fight all the time. Or his work is more important than you are. Or maybe he has some serious emotional baggage that you're not sure you can deal with.

Here's the good news: It's okay not to be sure. Perhaps you need to get to know one another better. Go on a long road trip, try to remodel your kitchen, or some other demanding project that will test how you do together in adverse situations. There may be many wonderful sides to him that you haven't even experienced yet—and you won't be able to find them unless you *try*. But eventually, you will need to commit. As I discuss in the next chapter, you'll have to decide whether to just love him—or just dump him. When you commit yourself to him 110 percent, it will become clear whether or not the relationship is worth pursuing. Either the relationship blossoms or you walk away with confidence knowing that you went all in.

There are a variety of unlovable traits that can be very tricky to tolerate, but which can ultimately be manageable differences. We will come back to this topic again later in part 2 of the book. Does he have an overactive ego? A bad temper? Low self-worth? Is he overly critical? Taken to the extreme, any of these will be deal-killers, as noted in part 1. But these kinds of traits do not have to be deal-killers at more modest or "normal" levels. This section also offers many insights to people who are in a long-term relationship and is a nice ramp to the next chapter, Just Love Him.

My friend Olivia found herself in a stage of indifference that so many women find themselves in while dating. She had recently gone through a pretty devastating breakup and was having a tough time getting over her ex. Then she met Curt at a restaurant while out with friends. Olivia shot him down numerous times before her friends persuaded her to give him a chance. She finally agreed to have dinner with him, and they went out a handful of times after that. But she wasn't enthralled. *There's no way I'm going to end up with this guy*, she told herself. Olivia wanted to be swept off her feet, and she couldn't get past her initial ambivalence toward Curt. He was cute and sweet, but there wasn't a connection.

Eventually Olivia broke it off altogether. But several months later she ran into Curt on the beach, and this time she allowed herself to be more open. She decided to put the work in. He wasn't her ideal match, but he was kind, had a good job, and he was extremely supportive of her. Olivia decided to open her heart and commit fully to the relationship. Sure enough, she was absolutely astounded by how much she had missed about him the first time around. Once she decided to put aside that nagging apprehension and just say, "I am going to really give him all I have," everything came easier. While he has his flaws—he has serious anxiety issues, for example—she still describes him as everything she ever wanted, and the love of her life.

"The first time someone says or does something that bothers you," Olivia later told me, "instead of being encouraged to work it out and see where the relationship goes, we often just don't want to invest the time. Why bother when you can go on Bumble or Tinder? This leads to very shallow relationships." Olivia ended up questioning her initial apathy toward Curt and realized it had nothing to do with him. The problem had been with her. She was still recovering from her earlier heartbreak and simply wasn't open. Within six months they were engaged, and they are now happily married.

While her story has a happy outcome, it is not particularly unique. Passionate love can materialize with people where there was an initial lack of chemistry. There may not be an initial spark. Love takes time to develop, and it takes a ton of work. There is no getting around it.

IF YOU ARE IN A LONG-TERM RELATIONSHIP AND ARE READY TO CALL IT QUITS

I can hear many of your shouts (or whispers) of protest. For those of you who are at the end of your rope, whose marriages or relationships are on life support, I can see your faces filled with doubt, your eyes puddled with hurt. I have been there, too. I understand your anger, fear, and sadness. You have been suffering for a long time. Maybe a very long time. If you have kids, chances are you feel your options are limited. I understand you're tired of struggling, tired of feeling lonely, tired of feeling angry and neglected. You're tired of feeling heartbroken and disillusioned. You're tired of feeling tired, for God's sake. Sister, I understand your angst.

At this stage, you have nothing to lose by putting your whole heart into Radical Acceptance. Give yourself a decent amount of time for Radical Acceptance to take root. Everything will not be magically fixed in one month. Maybe not for several months. You must search for meaningful signs of progress that indicate hope. These signs are your ramp to true reconciliation in your relationship. Pick a realistic time frame in which you want to see improvements and then GO. TO. THE. MAT. Practice Radical Acceptance with your whole heart and mind every day, starting with your commitment to just love him. Take the lead and do all that you can to fortify your relationship and rebuild it on a foundation of love, tenderness, and non-judgment.

At some point, tell him that you're committed to him and to your relationship and that you're willing to go to the ends of the earth for him. Then tell him that you need him to come along, too. I always say that actions speak louder than words, but sometimes you really do need the words to be filled with emotion, conviction, and hope.

A friend of mine who harbored a lot of doubt and overcame big challenges in her relationship shared this: "Andrea's advice has always been to take the high road. Radical Acceptance is exactly that. Radical Acceptance asks me to recognize my pettiness for what it is and to step beyond it in my relationship with my boyfriend. It also asks me to recognize his shortcomings and not take them personally."

Think about this for now: No matter if you've barely been dating or if you've been together for years, what if you were to cut him some slack? To be more caring? To give him the benefit of the doubt? Rather than wringing your hands and harboring doubts, what if you were to *GO ALL IN* for him and your relationship? In the following section we're going to discuss this in depth.

- Reflect on your inner narrative and the relationships you have had, including the kinds of people you tend to attract. If you keep letting the wrong people in and the right ones out, identify what message you're telling yourself and projecting to others. You are worthy of tremendous love and attention; those endlessly critical, doubt-filled voices in your head can STFU.

- Dating is not a numbers game. Keep your heart and mind open as much as you possibly can.

- If you have too many deal-breakers or refuse to pay a price of admission, you're likely sabotaging your chances for lasting love. You *can* develop a deep, love-filled relationship even if he doesn't sweep you off your feet out of the gate. Don't settle! But do remember that regardless of whether or not there are fireworks in the beginning, you'll still have to go all in and work to make love last.

- Are you at the end of your rope and ready to call your long-term relationship quits? Commit to practicing Radical Acceptance long enough to see positive changes emerge. Then GO. TO. THE. MAT. to restore your relationship.

PART 2

THE FIVE STEPS
FOR HAPPY,
LASTING LOVE

RADICAL ACCEPTANCE: STEP 1

JUST LOVE HIM
(OR JUST DUMP HIM)

OKAY—SO, YOU'VE FOUND someone. He's fun, he's attractive, he's an accomplished cook, he has a stable job, he loves kids. He's great . . . well most of the time, anyway. Sometimes you can't believe how hypersensitive he is. Or how judgmental he is. Or how controlling. Or how uncommunicative. Or how crazily obsessed with the Lakers. Or how wishy-washy. Or how forgetful. Or that he spends half his time in the gym. Or on the couch. There are aspects about him that you may find hurtful, aspects you may even hate or resent. Now what?

Earlier in the book we explored different kinds of deal-breakers. We looked at when you may be settling, or when you might be sabotaging your chances of enjoying a mature, fulfilling relationship. We've progressed now to a scenario where you've been with someone for long enough to really get to know him and you've sorted through the annoyances and the manageable challenges. In other words, you care about him and he has very high potential as your significant other, but there are issues.

Are you wringing your hands about him and constantly worrying about your future together? Do you actively harbor doubts about your compatibility? The question is: Are you ready to just love him?

This simple question is the first exciting, foundational step toward Radical Acceptance. And it's also the most terrifying. If you're not ready to just love him and his annoyances, the answer is clear: just dump him.

Say what?

I know it sounds harsh. But there is an enormous power in this bold, binary beginning to Radical Acceptance. That is because there is enormous power in true commitment and you are making a decision to commit. Being committed fundamentally changes your energy; it changes your consciousness and aligns how you think and behave accordingly. Commitment enables you to more easily take the long-term view in your relationship—versus being captive to a reactionary short-term one. *True* commitment enables you to create a strong, stable foundation for your relationship with great clarity.

If you're not normally a decisive person, engaging yourself with such a stark choice can fundamentally realign how you approach life—no matter which decision you make. You will be a stronger person.

Before we get too much further, note that deciding to just love him does not mean committing to marriage nor to being together forever in any other manner. It means committing now and for the foreseeable future. It means you're giving unconditional love a fighting chance. You're saying, "I choose you. And I intend to keep choosing you." Aspects of the relationship or some of his flaws may still be painful, but you will no longer perceive them as removable warts—they're just who he is, and you're ready to make peace with them. You are simply deciding: *Can I love this person right now, as he is?* If you can't, then get out.

But doesn't having to accept his warts just reignite the quest for a perfect partner? No. It does the opposite. It forces you to look at a person you care about, acknowledge all of his shortcomings and flaws, and then say, "Okay. I can live with that stuff." It's a lot harder than it sounds. It is an active decision, one that you may be tested on day after day (we'll get deep into how to do this in the following chapters). Here, we're going to address whether deciding to just love him will make you a doormat (it won't!), as well as whether you should talk with him about the flaws or shortcomings you see in him or the relationship (generally, yes).

Now, there is a very big difference between what might have been passing as commitment in your relationship and what "true" commitment actually entails.

If someone had asked me prior to my development of Radical Acceptance whether I was committed to Sanjay, I would have said "Yes, of course! I love him! We live together and have been together for years!" And all of that was true. But if this questioner continued to probe, I would have disclosed that I nevertheless harbored doubts about him and about us, and that I managed to keep the specter of an escape route alive somewhere in the shadows of my heart and mind. I didn't actively nurture this doubt or that specter, mind you—except when I felt hurt and lonely. But rather than understanding how I needed to make peace with our challenges, or realizing doing so was even possible, I found myself frequently resisting or battling the possibility of accepting him, which was emotionally exhausting.

Sanjay and I were physically and psychologically together. But there was a piece of me that I was holding back. I realized how much damage and dysfunction that piece of me inadvertently wrought, not to mention how it prevented the kind of unconditional love we both deeply desired. When I finally figured this out, everything changed. Dramatically.

There were a few obstacles that prevented me from having done this previously. One, I lacked the wisdom (and perhaps maturity) to understand the power of Radical Acceptance and how powerful the decision to "just love him" truly was. Two, Sanjay's oversized personality was sometimes difficult for me to navigate. He is brilliant and charming and generous and handsome, and though he's mellowed considerably, he can be very set in his views. Over time, I have realized how much of our drama was as much about me as it was about him.

The bottom line is that I was finally able to look at him and at our relationship and say, "Yes, I know about your shortcomings and our challenges together as a couple but I am now all in—I am fully committed in my heart and in my mind to you and to our relationship. I choose you and intend to keep choosing you." During difficult times I have found this to be a very powerful anchor.

To just love him means you're 150 percent invested in the relationship, that you are committing to going the extra mile for him, and not expecting him to meet you halfway, out of the gate, every step of the way. There is a very good chance you will be leading the way in this fundamental aspect of our relationship. It can feel one-sided and a little bit scary, especially in the beginning, but assuming you're with a good guy, taking this lead will hugely pay off for you both.

The decision as to whether you should love him or dump him will reveal some degree of clarity to you. Ideally, perhaps, you will decide to just love him. But do not worry if you realize you can't. This can be a blessing, as it enables you to move away from a relationship you cannot commit to, and devote your energy to finding one that you can.

But what if you still don't know? What if it's still not obvious that you are ready to commit 150 percent to your relationship? You may think, *I care for him a lot . . . but I am not sure I am ready to just love all of him.* How long should it take to figure this out? How certain do you have to be? I have three guidelines.

First, *there is no standard length of time you must be together after which you must decide to love him or dump him.* You should know this person well and have ideally gone through some ups and downs together. If you've been dating a handful of months and aren't sure, by all means, keep dating, have fun and don't feel pressured to make this decision prematurely. However, if you have been together for years (whether married or dating) and you feel uncertain whether you can make this level of commitment and really mean it, I urge you to really be honest with yourself and with him. Either decide to just love him and make peace with the annoyances or terminate the relationship.

This leads me to my second point. *Making this decision comes down to trust.* You must trust yourself, and you must trust him. I have written this book to help you understand yourself and your relationship better, and to more confidently make crucial decisions about your life. By reading others' stories and taking these insights to heart, you'll have a strong framework for objectively assessing your relationship. The rest is up to you. No one can or should make the decision for you.

And, finally point number three: the decision to make a definitive yes should energize you. If you feel fatigued or disappointed, then you probably should say no. Say it decisively. Being in limbo is no-man's-land. It's a dangerous place to be in a relationship.

When you do decide to just love him, hallelujah! That's epic. You can move forward with confidence. You can align your thoughts and actions and pave the way for a successful future together. This choice that you are making *to love* should primarily feel powerful and affirming. I cannot emphasize this strongly enough. It may feel a little scary, too, and that's okay (and even healthy), but if you continue to feel a nagging sense of doubt, it may mean that you need to revisit your decision to just love him.

I am not saying that by this stage everything will be perfect in your relationship: that he will no longer have flaws, that you will no longer fight, and that everything will be 24/7 roses. You will likely have to reaffirm the decision to just love him at different points in your relationship. That's also okay. It's normal. And it's even possible that you may later come to realize that you can no longer just love him.

Remember, trust yourself to look these gremlins in the face and say: "I am not afraid of you—buzz off." Or, "You are too much. We cannot coexist. You win. Adios." Trust is fundamental when choosing to just love him. If you're not sure you can trust him, give it some time. If you're like, "I don't know what to do!" trust yourself that you're merely journeying through a necessary exploratory phase. Be vigilant; be proactive. Give him the benefit of the doubt where it makes sense, but do not get lulled into a false sense of security. If you don't eventually feel like you can trust him, your relationship is not a good candidate for Radical Acceptance.

I know that this may feel like the most endlessly elusive decision you can make, but you should not feel tortured by saying yes to loving him! After you distinguish between character flaws and deal-breakers, no one can tell you how to make this decision. You may want some trusted family members or friends to weigh in with their observations—or, better yet, to ask you good questions to help you to come to the right conclusion—but the key is for you to eventually have real faith in the relationship, in him, and in yourself. Remember, you are not necessarily committing to love him forever at this stage. Rather, you are committing to choosing him, right now, and to keep choosing him. It ultimately comes down to trust.

Trust may be instantaneous or it may take weeks or months to find to a definitive answer. Tell yourself that is okay. Don't feel rushed. If you feel anxious, close your eyes. Relax the muscles in your face and breathe in several deep breaths. Be mindful to exhale nice and long. Try to be still; drink in your stillness and savor the quiet. There's deep wisdom here. Listen to it. Know that doubt and "on-the-other-hand" scenarios may also bubble up. A lot. This is okay. This is normal. Eventually, come back to your stillness, your quiet, your wisdom. Come back to that place within you where you can confidently say YES to what is right for you. And then keep saying yes to yourself, cultivating ever more of that deep wisdom that resides within you. That's the seat of grace.

. . .

Here is a sample list of flaws or challenges that are manageable for some people. It doesn't mean each one is manageable for you. I list these in part to destigmatize, and hopefully to neuter, challenges that are quite common.

He's a little bit boring. He tends to micromanage you. He boasts a lot around your friends. He is overly negative or critical. He lacks career drive. He is hyperambitious. He always interrupts you. He is a mama's boy. He is a slob. He is a hypochondriac. He has a bad temper. He is a little wimpy. He has poor hygiene. He is egocentric. He is a bit of a redneck. He is pretentious. He shirks responsibility. He has an obsession with sports or music or any other very loud pastime. He is a know-it-all. He is overweight. He is underweight. He has no hair. He has too much hair. He is six inches shorter than you. He is into kink (and you're not, or vice versa). He is very needy. He never follows through. He manages to press every button you never even knew you had. And so on, forever.

Try making your own list. Don't worry—it doesn't make you a bad person, even when you acknowledge the annoyances that he has no control over (He's too short! He's too tall! He's allergic to everything, and so on). By identifying challenging traits, you'll be empowered to more constructively manage and make peace with them. (We delve into how in subsequent chapters, I promise!)

Almost any of the above examples in the extreme would likely be deal-killers. Of course, any instance in which someone with a true character flaw—say he's a frequent, pathological liar; philanderer; or someone who habitually manipulates you—all bets are off. Just dump him.

My goal here is to simply say, if you're with a person who has a whole host of very redeeming traits and who loves you, but also exhibits some of these more challenging ones, he probably deserves a chance. None of these are inherently fatal flaws in and of themselves.

Let me tell you about my friends Sheila and Shay. They had been dating for about four years. Shay was very successful in his career and financially well off, though he had difficulty expressing his emotions through talk—he preferred demonstrating his love for Sheila with thoughtful gifts, dinners, and trips. Sheila, on the other hand, was much more of a free spirit. She had little interest in material things or conventional definitions of success. She had a troubled past and a string of dysfunctional relationships, and more than anything she wanted to bond with someone in a deep, healing way. Shay, too, had a difficult past—he endured a devastating divorce that he did not see coming. Sheila and Shay loved each other a lot. Nevertheless, she wanted something that Shay still could not give.

I remember speaking to her when she was assessing the relationship. "Sheila," I told her, "Shay adores you. Deep emotional discussions were never his strength. You've known that since day one. He finds other ways to express his love." She paused to think for a while, then replied that she had been deliberating whether to stay with Shay for a long time. She had so much doubt. She loved Shay's loyalty, his generosity, his kindness, and their shared passions for music, art, wine, and travel. Yet she felt lonely. Emotions for her represented such profound highs and lows, so much energy. She wanted her partner to share in her euphoria and her melancholy—not merely hold her hand through it all. Maybe she should wait a little bit longer to see if Shay changes.

"Sheila," I said, "Just love him. Sure, if you could wave a magic wand, it might be to summon a shaman with whom you could go and live in the desert. But if that's what you really wanted, you would have done that long ago. You picked Shay, and for very good reasons. He has some real challenges expressing himself emotionally, but don't compare him against a fantasy in your head. He loves you, and he really tries. Look at the man in front of you and decide whether or not you can love him. He's not going to start practicing Reiki or talking about his chakras. But I really believe he will always try his best to make you happy."

For the longest time, Sheila couldn't decide whether or not it was time to commit, whether it was time to accept his occasional aloofness. If she couldn't, the relationship was doomed. In this case, she needed an ultimatum. I asked her directly: "Sheila, can you love this man without expecting him to change? The way he is, right now. Yes or no."

She sat quietly for a while. There was something inside her she seemed to be fighting. Then, suddenly, she cried, "Yes!" And then again. "*Yes!*" She knew Shay very well, and she knew it was time to go for it. Had her and Shay's path been rocky? Of course. But with that simple answer, the tenor of the relationship changed. The relationship became more solid, offering fertile ground for them to grow closer. And they did. Sheila became more appreciative of Shay and learned to accept that while he may not demonstrate it as outwardly as she did, Shay too was emotionally sensitive. They soon married, and they've been together for five years strong.

You likely won't have some overbearing person like me on the phone to force you into an ultimatum, so you'll need to be the judge of when you're ready to decide and know you can trust your judgment.

Always remember: there is deep wisdom within you!

. . .

Now, if you *still* harbor doubts and are having a tough time being able to make the commitment to just love him, the following possibilities will likely help shed some light as to why. We'll talk about a variety of scenarios that may be preventing you from being able to just love him. *The key is to ask yourself the obvious but often scary-to-face questions: Why can't you say yes? Or no for that matter? Why are you willing to be in limbo?* I've listed many of these common situations below. Then we'll briefly discuss each one.

- You are afraid to be alone.
- You are waiting for someone better to come along.
- You are afraid of what might happen to him if you break up.
- You have children in the picture whose well-being you must consider.

- You depend on him for something other than the relationship itself, such as money, shelter, status, visa, or you want to be married, have kids, etc.
- You are afraid to completely commit yourself to him (or maybe to anyone).
- You love him but there are aspects of him that are very troubling.
- You love him, but you fight a lot—there's tremendous conflict in the relationship.

Before I delve more deeply into each of these, I ask you to be really, *really* honest with yourself here. Whether you instantly reacted to any of the items noted above or, as you keep reading, one or more really resonates with you, do yourself and your partner a huge favor by facing the truth of your situation and responding accordingly. Once you get real with what is happening, I urge you to take the high road—for your sake and for his. In most of these situations, you may have been with him for the wrong reason up until this point, but you can choose to build an honest, lasting, loving relationship with him now. You can decide to just love him and give your relationship a shot at unconditional love. Here we go.

You Are Afraid to Be Alone

There's not much I can say about this, but you're with someone for the wrong reason. At some level you probably know that. You could get lucky and find someone who helps you avoid being alone and who is also very lovable. In that case: congratulations! But, in all likelihood, your best bet is to really look within, perhaps even see a therapist, and figure out what's causing so much fear and anxiety. If you can get over this fear of being alone, there is a much better chance that you'll have the fortitude and good judgment to build a lasting (and loving) relationship.

You Are Waiting for Someone Better to Come Along

This is a big one. Are you the type of person who keeps scanning through the radio even when a perfectly good song comes on, simply because there might be *an even better* song playing on another station? Do you get buyer's remorse after every big purchase? You can't treat a potential life partner like buying a new car. No matter if Prince Charming himself sweeps you onto his sparkling white horse, you'll still wonder if Prince Florian would've come along on his even *faster, more sparkling white* horse if only you'd waited longer. After all, Florian has cooler friends.

But it doesn't work this way. Prince Florian may not have back hair, but he probably has an ingrown toenail or two and a host of emotional insecurities. The grass-is-always-greener maxim applies to relationships too, and it often boils down to a lack of trust in yourself, or fear of making a mistake.

There are many reasons not to get involved in a relationship, but the fear that you're missing out on someone better should not be one of them. No matter whom you're with, that fear is going to stew in the back of your mind. If you're hesitant to commit to a relationship, take a moment and truly ask yourself why.

Take a look at your deal-breakers list and see if they apply here. Are you hesitant to commit because of who he is, or because of who he is not? Do you love the man in front of you, but wish there was more? Here's the honest truth: no matter whom you're with, that feeling is always going to be present until you decide to love him for who he is—not some future version. If there are no bona fide deal-breakers keeping you from committing to him, then the fear of settling can be clouding your judgment of the relationship.

You Are Afraid of What Might Happen to Him if You Break Up

It is generous of you to stay with someone because you're afraid of what might happen to him if you break up, but you're definitely in this relationship for the wrong reason. This type of codependent relationship is not sustainable. You will not be happy, and he will not be happy in the long run. In extreme cases he may need therapy or possibly even medical attention if he truly falls apart after breaking up. I realize this can be extreme and that you could be dealing with someone suicidal or dangerous, either to you or to others. In any of these cases, I urge you to seek professional help, enlist your friends and family, and possibly even notify the police. No one should be trapped in a relationship due to fear of what may happen should they terminate it.

You Have Children in the Picture Whose Well-being You Must Consider

We have all read articles on how messed up kids often become whose parents should have gotten divorced much earlier. There's a lot of research about how not only is it okay for kids to survive their parents' divorce or breakup, but they do much better as a result of it. In other words, kids do better with an amicable, early divorce as opposed to being forced to live with two parents who fight relentlessly and who are perpetually angry or depressed. Do not stay together for the kids. Stay together for the relationship—and then only do so if you're willing to go the distance to make it truly loving and fulfilling.

You Are Afraid to Completely Commit Yourself to Him (and Maybe to Anyone)

Ah. The fear of commitment. This is especially common for children of parents who had a deeply unhappy marriage or experienced other dysfunction growing up, including not receiving secure attachment in their formative years. It's probably going to take some real soul-searching and possibly therapy to conquer your fear of commitment. You may even discuss this with a close friend or family member whom you trust and who will keep it real with you. Chances are if you have a history of being unable to commit, someone who knows you well and cares about you can help you talk through what's really going on. Again, I urge you to be honest with yourself. If you're unable to commit to a really good guy due to harboring a fear of commitment, that sentiment is likely not going to change until you come to terms with it. It's you—not him—and in all likelihood, whether its Prince Florian or Prince Charming at your behest, you'll still have issues.

You Depend on Him for Something Other than the Relationship Itself

You depend on him for something such as money, shelter, status, a visa, or anything along those lines. Perhaps you feel the need to marry and have kids at any cost.

While these scenarios seem to be dramatically different, the conclusion is the same for each. No matter why you've been together, you now have the option to just love him and commit to building a truly sustainable relationship. If you're really in it for the money or the visa and aren't sure about the guy, I hope for both of your sakes that this book helps you cross the Rubicon and that you become committed to building a strong, healthy, fulfilling relationship—or that you get out. If you are with him because you have an agenda to be married or have children, again, you can choose now to truly love him—for everybody's sake.

If you cannot, I urge you to be transparent with yourself and with him. It's impossible to imagine a truly happy marriage in the long run in which there is no transparency about why you're together.

You Love Him but There Are Aspects of Him That Are Very Troubling to You

We touched on this various times above. You have a pretty good idea of what his flaws and shortcomings are, but you also know how wonderful, kind, smart, funny, generous, and awesome he can be. It's time, proverbially, to fish or cut bait. Can you love him—really and truly, as he is, without always harboring an agenda to change him? If not, then the answer is pretty clear. I know how excruciating this decision can be. You may be deeply attached to someone who is deeply flawed or possibly whose flaws are not that deep but they are like kryptonite to you. It doesn't matter either way, as unless you are ready to truly just love him, you'll likely always have a relationship that leaves you feeling bruised, tired, and unfulfilled.

You Love Him but There's Tremendous Conflict in the Relationship

This is similar to the previous point. He may not have fatal flaws, but something continues to create a ton of friction for you.

I would like to underscore this important point: some relationships come at too great a cost, and not for some obvious fatal flaw or glaring difference like we've seen above. You and your partner may ostensibly have all of the right ingredients for a successful relationship. Maybe you've tried to just love him and the relationship remains too rife with conflict for you to pursue it. Maybe you love him but don't feel enough love from him—though it's possible he doesn't have enough love for himself to begin with. In other words, you are ready to just love him, but he isn't. He has proven unworthy or incapable of accepting your love. You may know this in your gut already and simply need to come to terms with it.

Frankly, for whatever reason, whether it's him or you, the combustion you create is somewhat immaterial. If the relationship comes at too great a cost, then you must terminate it and find someone with whom you can build a lasting, loving relationship. The following story underscores this point.

My friends Stephanie and Mark had been dating for two years when they got engaged. They planned an extravagant destination wedding in the Caribbean. They were both in their thirties, had good jobs and lots of mutual friends, they loved traveling and the outdoors—the time was right. However, though they loved each other, they fought. A lot. They fought day and night, and it put serious stress on the relationship. Finally, after a particularly brutal fight, Mark couldn't take it anymore and he called off the wedding.

"Andrea," he later confided to me, "I felt like it was a constant battle. Stephanie was always on my case. I felt like it shouldn't be that hard and painful. I was willing to work at our relationship. I really did try to please her." When they first met, Mark had already established a routine with his friends involving your typical heavy-duty-dude-bonding activities: hunting, exotic fishing trips, late-night poker games replete with cigars and plenty of Macallan. When Stephanie objected, Mark agreed to dial these activities back considerably, but he didn't want to give them up altogether. After all, he enjoyed them. Mark even invited her to tag along, but Stephanie wasn't interested.

"I was willing to compromise, but she wasn't," Mark told me. "I figured it would only get harder after we got married, so better to call it off before we walked down the aisle. I knew I couldn't give her what she needed, and I realized that I didn't want to forsake so many other things I like to do."

To that I say: Hallelujah! Forget about who is in the right or the wrong. Maybe Mark truly was spending too much time with his friends and not enough with Stephanie. Or, perhaps Stephanie really was suffocating Mark with her demands. It doesn't matter—everyone's needs are different, and rarely is anyone ever fully right or wrong in a relationship. It's how you connect and love and support each other; i.e., it's the relationship that is right or wrong. The point here is that Mark tried adjusting his behaviors, but in the end he realized that he simply could not accept the demands Stephanie placed on him and the friction in the relationship.

Mark had identified that this relationship just came at too great a cost, and he moved on.

. . .

I referenced a handful of additional points above that I'm eager to flesh out now to help you succeed in this first crucial step toward Radical Acceptance.

DON'T MAKE HIM A FIXER-UPPER

There's a cliché about how women go into a relationship with the expectation to change a guy, and how guys go into a relationship expecting the women won't change. Perhaps you see him as a project and daydream about how you will upgrade him (or that marriage or kids or the right job will make him right for you)? I will address how common and damaging this cliché is, and how it can be replaced by a much more evolved, empowering approach that serves you both. Remember: changing someone else is an act of aggression. Changing yourself is an act of love.

Harboring an expectation of change from your partner is one of the most dangerous ways to treat the relationship. By committing to love a future version of him, you are rejecting the current version.

Another common mistake is projecting your own ideals onto him, and then expecting him to meet them. Here's a story that illustrates this point.

Liang and Yin had been friends for a long time before they began dating. Yin had always thought Liang was cute and funny, but not exactly her type. She was typically drawn to the king-of-the-boardroom alpha male. Liang had no such ambitions. In his late twenties, Liang was working hard at a consulting firm and advancing quickly, but he didn't like conflating his identity with his career. He was an artist at heart and one day imagined himself moving to Europe with his guitar. He was successful and good at his job, but he didn't need to run his company to be fulfilled. When they married, however, Yin was determined to change that.

Yin was beautiful and very charming—seductive, even—and she had a successful career. She confided in her friends that she wanted to "work on" Liang to step up his game. She wanted him to become a partner at his firm, and he needed to start playing the part. Yin tried updating his wardrobe, dragged him to the hottest restaurants in Houston, and insisted that Liang trade in his seven-year-old Honda Accord for something fancier.

I asked her why she was so intent on changing Liang. "He's so kind, funny, and sweet—oh God! And *so* smart!" I said. "Why do you want to change him when he offers so much to you?" I realized that to an extent Yin was projecting her own values onto her husband. She loved Liang dearly and wanted him to succeed. But she also wanted him to *look* like he was succeeding, and this troubled me. "Yin," I asked her directly, "is this really about Liang? Or is this about you?"

After a defensive exchange, she finally got honest with me (and herself). She had always cared a lot about what other people thought about her, and part of her desired a "trophy husband" she could show off to her friends and family. But Yin eventually realized how lethal these expectations could be to her relationship, and she backed off. She accepted that Liang did not need to flaunt his success to feel successful. Sensing her attempts to accept his values and acknowledging he was allowed to enjoy the fruits of his success, Liang eventually bought a BMW, and he's enjoying it a lot more than he thought he would.

People do change, but it's rarely at anyone's behest. Up above I suggested that you make a list of his traits you'd like him to improve on. Maybe they're small things like his wardrobe or his love of fried food. Maybe they're bigger things like his career ambitions, or maybe how he micromanages you. Now imagine that he can't significantly change them. Can you still love him? Can you possibly find compassion for the unattractive traits, traits that may even cause him pain? Are you in love with the man beside you now, or the man you wish he would one day be? Be honest with yourself, and don't think you're a bad person for saying no.

NO ESCAPE ROUTES!

I noted at the beginning of this chapter that I used to keep an escape route of sorts open somewhere in my mind when things were difficult in my relationship. And while this escape route took the form of being less than fully committed, as I would think how I could escape the hurt, anger, and pain I felt in our relationship, there are other kinds of escape routes that I urge you to recognize and avoid in your relationship. These include things like having endless access to an unlimited pool of potential suitors thanks to online dating to escaping into work or other forms of avoiding your partner.

Online dating offers greater selection while also promoting greater impatience and less tolerance. Dates have become commoditized and people are now easily disposable.

The ADD nature of modern dating has its benefits, but don't let the allure of a bottomless well of single men represent an escape route for your current relationship. After a particularly bad fight, it's easy to think about the thousands of new people that are on Tinder right now. *He's not working out*, you're thinking, *but surely there's someone else out there who will!*

We will touch on this further in "Apply the Platinum Rule and Make

Him Your Priority," but it's worth touching on briefly now. Escape routes can also take the form of avoiding your partner—either actively when you're not getting along or because something else feels like more of a priority for you. For many successful women, it's their work. Even when we weren't fighting, I realize, I had an escape route: my company. There were always more revenue goals to achieve, more capital to raise, endless emails to reply to. I could lose myself in my work. If I couldn't improve my relationship, I could improve my business.

The problem is that escape routes are never secret. Losing myself in work sent signals to Sanjay that I preferred my business over him. Late hours at the office were late hours I was choosing not to spend at home, which only fueled our arguments. Committing to a relationship means committing time and being truly tuned in to your partner. Whether you know it or not, nurturing your escape route is courting relationship failure.

What escape routes are open in your relationship? From disabling your Match.com profile, to removing your Bumble app, to curbing your workaholic tendencies, to seeking out quality time with him instead of your best pals, to simply not allowing doubts about your relationship to loom large—setting aside a known escape route will do wonders for your relationship and allow you to focus on just him.

BUT . . . DON'T BE A DOORMAT

Radical acceptance means accepting characteristics you don't like about someone you love—there's no way to get around that. You need to make peace with the manageable problems for the good of your relationship— and we'll get much further into how you do this in the chapters that follow. He's being a know-it-all with your friends at dinner; he's being especially crabby; he's digging his finger in his ear and elsewhere; he's being hypocritical. And yet I ask you to love all of him anyway!?

Doesn't this sound an awful lot like taking the path of least resistance? Isn't this just letting him do whatever he wants with impunity? Won't he take advantage of your passivity and become even worse? Are you just being a doormat?

No, no, no, and no.

Loving someone fully and without judgment is the opposite of being a weak pushover. For many women, this is the hardest aspect of Radical Acceptance to accept. Being able to accept him for who he is requires tremendous strength, fortitude, emotional maturity, and self-awareness. You are not abandoning generations of feminist struggles to acquiesce to his every desire, or giving him license to be a jerk. Quite to the contrary, accepting his flaws and annoyances is a way to extend tremendous compassion and empathy to him—to give him permission to be who he is without judging or shaming him is the essence of unconditional love. More than anything, it takes grace. You want and deserve the same from him, after all!

That all said, it can be difficult to shake the misconception that Radical Acceptance makes you a doormat (again, decisively, *NO*, it does not). You are *not* going to grin and bear all. To the contrary, you are going to voice to him exactly what makes you uncomfortable in the relationship. We will address this in much more detail in step 3: Radical Communication, but generally, I urge people to communicate what's working and what's not working in their relationship to their partners. Not to nag, needle, or castigate, but to communicate.

I am often asked about tools to avoid becoming a doormat. I go into significant detail in part 3 about being your beautiful, awesome best self, which is the best way to guard against being a doormat. If you love yourself and you know that other people would love to be with you—in other words, you have other options—you will readily operate from a place of abundance. The key is to have a strong sense of self-worth and a healthy sense of what you want from the relationship. Being a doormat is fundamentally about operating from a place of scarcity and doubting your worth. You may wonder from time to time if you're putting up with too much. That's okay. It can be a natural part of this process. When that happens, remember:

- You can trust yourself.
- Radical Acceptance will inevitably cause you to be reflective and introspective. You should give yourself plenty of latitude to figure things out, especially as you recalibrate how you can lovingly extend more compassion and latitude to him.
- *You* are choosing to be with this person.

If after attempting Radical Acceptance for a meaningful period of time you continue to reevaluate your decision, and you genuinely feel he is taking advantage of you, or that he is not stepping up to the plate, he is probably not a good fit for you. You may also have some work to do to develop your sense of worth and your understanding of what a healthy, loving, mutually respectful relationship looks and feels like.

I always encourage people to share their feelings or concerns with their partners in open, loving, nonthreatening, nonjudgmental ways. This can be tricky—especially when emotions are running high—but it goes a very long way to being able to be detached from a certain outcome.

If you can't stand something he does, talking about it can get it off your chest, which can be very cathartic for you, and provide a useful insight to him. At the same time, this may stir up conflict with him—especially if you communicate it in a way that is aggressive or judgmental. The next few sections will be super helpful for doing this successfully.

I urge you to reflect on those traits that bother you before bringing them up. As I have noted numerous times and go into more detail in Step 2: Stop, Reflect, Introspect, something may be going on inside you to make you react so strongly to whatever he does that bothers you so much. That said, nearly all people find it annoying to be criticized or micromanaged. If you can become a little more detached from this reaction and try not to take what he's doing as personally (I know that may sound like asking a fish to ride a bicycle but I promise it gets easier!), you'll be able to have a more calm and rational discussion about it, which is likely to cause him to feel less threatened and reduce the likelihood that this devolves into another fight. The key is that you're initiating this conversation to get your concerns off your chest and to establish boundaries. Sure, you'd love for him to no longer do these things, but the message needs to be: they make me crazy, but I love you anyway and I'm really trying to make peace with them. If you cannot accept something, let him know as calmly and clearly as possible, but be prepared to move on if he can't step it up.

Exciting and empowering, right?!

- At a certain point you must decide: can you love the man you're with, here and now? If not, then just dump him. Do not make him a fixer upper. Remember: Changing yourself is an act of love. Trying to change someone else is an act of aggression.
- Deciding to just love him should be mostly energizing and affirming. If it's a decision you're constantly revisiting or it leaves you filled with doubt, it's probably not the right decision.
- Be honest about any escape routes that may be open in your relationship. They will prevent you from being truly committed.

RADICAL ACCEPTANCE: STEP 2

STOP, REFLECT, INTROSPECT: GET OUTSIDE OF YOUR OWN EMOTIONAL REACTIONS

YOU'VE DECIDED TO love him! Amazing! Cue the confetti falling from the ceiling! Well . . . Maybe not quite yet.

Even if you have committed to loving him, inevitably you will want to reject something, maybe several things, about him. *That extremely annoying thing he does* is creating murdering thoughts. Who hasn't experienced thinking, "Oh my God, I'm going to kill him!" In any case, there's a very good chance that something he's done will elicit a strong emotional reaction from you that will only make matters worse.

Before you do that, pause. What's *really* going on here? As we touched on earlier, the behaviors or traits your partner exhibits that make you angry, hurt, or disappointed generally don't happen in a vacuum. Your history, expectations, vulnerabilities, and your various defense and protective mechanisms are all likely kicking in. In other words, your emotional baggage may be causing you to react or overreact in ways that exacerbate bad cycles and strain your relationship.

This chapter is about how not to react in these situations. You're not going to be suppressing these urges; rather you will channel them into more productive ends. Your emotional reactions don't come out of the blue. They tell you a lot about yourself, and they represent an opportunity to glean better insights using a technique I have developed called "Stop, Reflect, Introspect."

We'll talk about how defense mechanisms such as control and the need to be right can often sabotage relationships. We'll delve into the value of vulnerability in a relationship and how protective measures, such as blame (bad!), and beneficial elements, such as empathy (good!), are connected to healthy relationships.

Here is a short "Stop, Reflect, Introspect" primer before we delve in deeper. If you begin feeling you are losing control of a situation, if an argument gets out of hand, or if negative, nagging thoughts are taking over your brain and you are at risk of reacting in any number of destructive ways, from lashing out to shutting down to silently stewing for hours:

Stop. Take a deep breath, or even better, two or three. Do not allow your emotions to hijack the situation. No matter how infuriating or wrong he is, stop yourself from reacting *in that moment*. Buying yourself even a few seconds can be crucial.

Reflect. What caused his behavior? Did you see it coming or was it spontaneous? What is making you upset? What is making him upset? Did he have a bad day? Did you have a bad day? Are either of you hungry or tired? Is his behavior linked to his deeper vulnerabilities? Try to pretend you are a neutral observer with a bag of popcorn watching from the sidelines. What would her impartial opinion be? Are you being entirely fair to him?

Introspect. Now turn inward. Do you feel vulnerable right now? Is it possible his behavior is inadvertently triggering one or more of your deep-seated insecurities? Is a painful pattern repeating itself? Can you summon a tiny bit of compassion for him and yourself?

Stop, Reflect, Introspect offers you a powerful means to get *outside* of your emotional reactions, enabling you to quit reacting and to respond more thoughtfully and constructively to the triggers that would otherwise trip you up. It helps you terminate, or at least attenuate, the vicious cycle in which so many couples find themselves: hurt and resentment breeding yet more hurt and resentment. The goal is to replace this with a *virtuous* cycle, which Radical Acceptance helps you to do.

In the face of these unlovable traits and challenging behaviors, the very ones that push your buttons and cause you to be defensive, and sometimes downright aggressive, I will first help you learn how not to react impulsively. Awareness is your BFF in a big way here, and it is half the battle. Next, I will encourage you to take a few moments to understand what is *really* going on around you as well as inside you (e.g., "Why do I feel so freaked out right now?" "Why is what he is doing or what he just said so threatening to me?" "Why is he behaving so aggressively?"). You'll learn to give yourself a quick time-out to cool your jets—especially if you have a propensity to cast blame, seek control, or be defensive.

The Stop, Reflect, Introspect formula is one that I am going to reinforce and urge you to practice, like everything else in Radical Acceptance! This process flows beautifully and naturally into step 3: Radical Communication. After you Stop, Reflect, Introspect, a common next step will be for you to communicate your feelings or perceptions in a way that facilitates a better understanding between the two of you, including positive body language. Building and maintaining a very strong sense of safety and trust is key to both of these steps, as I detail below.

You will eventually realize that unless your partner is really a jerk—in which case refer back to step 1 and just dump him!—he's probably not deliberately trying to push (nor skewer, impale, or smash) your buttons. As we explore your sensitivities and what's going on with you, it is also a wonderful opportunity for me to remind you how to extend lots of tenderness and compassion to yourself. As you learn to radically accept yourself, you will be increasingly well equipped to radically accept your partner.

BREAKING DOWN OUR EMOTIONAL REACTIONS

If you're anything like me, there's a good chance that when he does something you don't like or exhibits a trait you disapprove of, blame, defensiveness, and/or a need for control are fighting to rear their ugly heads. Let's break them down.

Blame. We can't begin to radically accept without addressing the topic of blame. I know I am guilty of having blame-filled thoughts when something goes wrong, but often I find we share in the blame, and those thoughts are in fact unfair and misplaced. I really try to call myself out when this is happening and I urge you to, also, given how insidious and destructive blame is.

There clearly are times when a screw-up occurs and blame is "legitimately placed." Someone was at fault. Then there are times when blame directed onto another person is misplaced because there was a failure in communication, both partners dropped the ball, and the blame actually deserves to be shared. In truth, the conversation should never center on who is to blame. No matter if it's totally, obviously, 100 percent *his* fault, or if both of you share responsibility (which is the case the vast majority of the time), blame in any form is toxic and counterproductive.

This truth is illuminated by the incredible research conducted by Brené Brown, a research professor at the University of Houston Graduate College of Social Work. Brené has spent many years studying human emotions, particularly vulnerability, courage, worthiness, and shame. She is the author of three wonderful books, *The Gifts of Imperfection*, *Daring Greatly*, and *Rising Strong*. In a lecture for the Royal Society for the Arts,[24] she said something that really resonated with me: "Blame is a way to discharge pain and discomfort. It has an inverse relationship with accountability."

This was a huge "aha!" moment for me.

As a coping mechanism, blame is a cathartic, reflexive way to deal with unpleasant feelings. Unfortunately, by definition, blame creates opposition. It's no longer about *us*, but *me* versus *you*. In effect, you are saying: "I am right, you are wrong. I am good, you are bad." Blame is an emotional, impulsive reaction that obscures what is *really* going on in the relationship.

The reflex to blame others can be rooted in a theory called "psychological projection," and is a defense mechanism people deploy as a means to cope with difficult feelings and emotions. In short, we blame others for doing or thinking the same things we are. It's also usually subconscious—we don't even realize we're doing it. The theory was developed by Sigmund Freud, who noticed in his sessions that many patients accused others of the same feelings they themselves harbored. The classic example is the husband who cheats on his wife but at the same time angrily accuses her of doing the same thing. We are ashamed of our own behavior, but instead of coming to terms with it we project our negative emotions onto another person in the form of blame. When I am unfairly blamed for something, I am usually able to take it less personally now because I understand that it's a coping mechanism for that person. I am also that much more mindful of what's going on within myself when I am predisposed to blame Sanjay (or anyone, for that matter).

To illustrate the point, Brené tells a great story of being in her kitchen with a full cup of coffee. She drops the mug, it breaks into a million pieces, coffee spills everywhere. Whom does she immediately blame? Her husband! He was supposed to be home earlier. If he were, she'd be in bed with him instead of drinking coffee alone in the kitchen. This is meant to be a humorous story, of course, but with it Brené reveals a lot about our own personal vulnerabilities and propensity to rationalize misplaced blame.

Blame is also often rooted in a phenomenon social scientists call "fundamental attribution error," which is the tendency for us to attribute other people's behavior to their intrinsic (flawed) personality rather than situational causes. For example, say that some bozo cuts in line at airport security. Most of us are going to assume he's a narcissistic jerk who doesn't care about anyone else. And maybe he is. But it's also possible that he's a total sweetheart who *normally* would never do such a thing, but in this case he's about to miss a flight home to see his dying grandmother. Of course, many of us would rarely give someone like him the benefit of the doubt. Indeed, the research suggests that the vast majority of us never do.

When it comes to our love lives, we also tend not to give our partners the benefit of the doubt. Instead we judge and blame. In the past when Sanjay was critical of me, my impulse was to think: *There he goes again! He doesn't respect me. He doesn't trust my judgment.* I wouldn't really think about the reason he was critical, or evaluate whether it was valid.

Be honest with yourself now: When something goes wrong, do you immediately point fingers? Do you quickly look for the cause of the problem outside of yourself?

I urge you to be truthful and ask yourself why you do this. Do you feel absolved of responsibility when you do? A good technique is to think how *you* could have helped the situation. Sanjay and I have a running joke about an old saying, "Whenever you point one of your fingers at me, there are three fingers pointing back at you." It's a bit cheesy, but it helps defuse the situation and allows us to replace blame with a little bit of levity and humor.

I want you to think about how many times in the past week you've blamed someone. And I mean for *anything*. It can be your boyfriend who forgot to pay the cable bill and so your Internet was cut off for three days, or that coworker who didn't return your email so your project was late. I don't care how right you were and how *wrong, wrong, wrong* they were. Then think about your state of mind. Did you feel vulnerable? Could you have done something differently to facilitate a better outcome?

Now comes the fun part: force yourself to give them the benefit of the doubt. Instead of invoking a character flaw—He's lazy! She's a jerk— think of a situational factor that might have caused these people to behave the way they did. Maybe your partner forgot to pay the cable bill because he has been going full tilt to complete a big assignment. Maybe that coworker is overworked and just didn't see your email. Your job here is not to justify objectionable behavior, but to train yourself to empathize with those at fault and to explore where you could possibly have stepped up to the plate a bit more.

I don't want you to become an apologist for bad behavior— sometimes people are bona fide jerks and deserve all the blame you can throw at them. Rather, I want you to become more self-aware. *Why* are you blaming this person, and could your blame really be more of a harbinger for some kind of vulnerability? Do you feel a sense of self-righteousness that is perhaps misplaced? Is there an "I'm right, he's wrong" duality at play here that feels perversely satisfying?

Let's talk a little about vulnerability, which is often closely connected to blame. As you discharge pain and discomfort through blame, you are trying to avoid being vulnerable. You are hurt, angry, injured, and so on. And when you assume responsibility for being at fault, you are thrusting your vulnerability front and center for everyone to see. This can be extremely scary. As we all know, it is not easy to say, "I screwed up." Moreover, when blame is cast, there is judgment and a clear absence of compassion or understanding, which threatens safety and instantly erects defensive barriers.

Brené Brown is an advocate for the awesome power of being open about your vulnerabilities. Over her many years as a researcher, doctoral student, and professor she has conducted thousands of interviews and focus groups, amassing a treasure trove of stories in the process.

She began dissecting her data and teasing out the differences between people who enjoy a strong sense of love and people who struggle for it.

One variable she found was courage:[25] People who were successful in love tended to have, as Brené says, "the courage to be imperfect. They had the compassion to be kind to themselves first and then to others, because, as it turns out, we can't practice compassion with other people if we can't treat ourselves kindly." Stemming from this, she also found that they have "fully embraced vulnerability. They believed that what made them vulnerable made them beautiful. They didn't talk about vulnerability being comfortable, nor did they really talk about it being excruciating."

It's a bit of a paradox. We all want to be seen for who we are, but we are afraid to show ourselves. Yet we also want to be fully accepted. These two desires are not mutually exclusive, but it takes tremendous courage for us to put our full selves out there, warts and all, and still expect acceptance. As Brené said in her TED Talk,

> I ran into this unnamed thing[26] that absolutely unraveled connection in a way that I didn't understand or had never seen. And so I pulled back out of the research and thought, I need to figure out what this is. And it turned out to be shame. And shame is really easily understood as the fear of disconnection: Is there something about me that, if other people know it or see it, that I won't be worthy of connection?
>
> . . . What underpinned this shame, this "I'm not good enough," which, we all know that feeling: "I'm not blank enough. I'm not thin enough, rich enough, beautiful enough, smart enough, promoted enough." The thing that underpinned this was excruciating vulnerability. In order for connection to happen, we have to allow ourselves to be seen, really seen.

Blame and shame appear to be inextricably linked. We blame others because we're ashamed of ourselves—our insecurities, our shortcomings, our mistakes. Instead of addressing these things and taking responsibility for them (or debunking them!), we project them onto others. The next time you are blaming your partner—or if he is blaming you—take a moment and think about the deeper significance of that blame. What is it concealing? Is there shame involved? Are there one or more defense mechanisms involved? If you still feel a need to blame, try casting it on human psychology rather than him.

The desire for control. Why do so many of us seek control? A lot of it pertains to stress and to trust issues. Think of the mother in line at the grocery store with two unruly kids amped up on sugar. They're running around, knocking things over, annoying other shoppers . . . that poor mom just wants to make them calm down. The more control you have of a situation, the less stressful it is. Think about your recent fights. Wouldn't it be amazing if you could just *make him understand*?

There is a strong case to be made that millennials, as a generation, are especially wired for control. A young, superbright student at Columbia Business School named Michelle remarked to me how everyone her age is "ultraprogrammed to have control." She told me that "We have to be in control. We have to control everything. We are expected to be in control and we expect it of others, too."

The digital revolution is having so many unexpected and unintended effects on us socially and emotionally. Millennials especially have grown up in the age of instant gratification thanks to digital media and technology. So many things they want have always been available on demand. We all seem to suffer from these expectations now to some degree. We all have the control to choose how to interact with someone. *I won't answer this call; instead I'll text when it's convenient for me.* As we talked about earlier in the book, even potential relationships are just a swipe away. In this digital age, so many of us are finding it incredibly difficult to be patient with one another, to cede control and not have our relationships "on demand."

In my observations, aside from millennials, those who are

particularly susceptible to control issues include type A personalities, entrepreneurs, children of addicts, ambitious overachievers, and highly creative types. I'm sure other subgroups will identify with this propensity but the common denominator is: We want things how we want them. We have a lot to do, damn it, and we'd sincerely appreciate everyone's cooperation! We want to conduct our lives and work on our own terms, and we can get very cranky when others interfere or question our judgment. When it comes to relationships, we get uneasy when there's a threat to our agenda, even if that agenda has not been overtly shared or mutually agreed to.

If any of this resonates with you, well, you know what you need to do. No, the answer is not at the bottom of an extra-strong vodka tonic, as good as it might sound right now. Admit that you have control issues and that you are accountable for what you do and say. When you get snippy with your partner because he didn't do what you wanted him to do, hit the pause button and call yourself out as needed. Remember that you can (and must) trust your partner.

Take yourself to task when your control issues, or that incessant need to be right, are causing you to act like a spoiled child. Holding yourself accountable and acknowledging when you fail will be one of the greatest ways to not only keep your control issues in check, but also to create a greater sense of harmony in your relationship.

I find control issues still sometimes create silly spikes of frustration in my marriage. He wants to get to the airport two hours before a flight; I prefer to cut it closer. He wants to stop to browse; I want to get home. Now, we are much better about not letting dumb little things spoil the moment . . . and then escalate into something more menacing.

This might sound a bit out of left field, but it works: I occasionally do minimeditations focusing on the word *surrender.* It's a great technique that helps bring me out of the constant drive for dominion. Fairly frequently I'll counsel people who suffer from control issues—whether in their relationship or in other areas of their life—to just surrender. "Control is an illusion, after all," is a common refrain of mine—a reminder as much for myself as it is for others.

This often elicits a skeptical reply. "Really? Surrender? Just give in?" I then explain that to mindfully surrender means yielding and accepting. It does not mean capitulating or tossing in the towel. *By temporarily ceding control, you are in fact mastering the highest form of it*—the ability to pick your own battles and to put the relationship ahead of petty squabbles. Deciding to surrender means handing yourself an opportunity to be liberated.

Defensiveness. If there is anything tougher than a controlling nature, it's defensiveness. We've all been there. Your partner accuses you of something, and no matter how right or wrong he is, we reflexively fight back.

I want you to reflect for a moment. When was the last time a loved one—your partner, a parent, a close friend—remarked that you had hurt his or her feelings? In the movies we always envision a tearful apology followed by a big bouquet of flowers to make amends. But this is hardly ever the reaction, is it? Instead of immediately apologizing for hurting someone, our first reaction is to be angry or defensive. It's like Newton's third law of motion: every action has an equal and opposite reaction. The same is true for relationships.

Blame and defensiveness often come together to perform a pretty ugly tango. I remember being in line at the grocery store watching a couple melt down right in front of me.

"STOP interrupting me," the woman snapped at her husband. "You *always* interrupt me and I can't get my point across. We need to get—"

"*Excuse me?*" her husband countered. "*I* always interrupt *you*? That's hilarious, because just last week, *you* interrupted *me* when I—"

"*There you go again!* You just interrupted me *AGAIN*. Every single time—"

"No, *you* just interrupted *me!*"

The conversation just spiraled down from there. I wanted to hand them both a Xanax. One interrupting the other in order to accuse the other of interrupting. It's a ridiculous example, but it demonstrates how our first reaction to an accusation is often not with regret or compassion, but with another accusation. These arguments turn into a zero-sum situation: Whatever is gained by one side is lost by the other. If you acknowledge his pain, that means *you* are at fault, that *you* must lose something by apologizing. Your very survival is at stake. It's a fight for existence.

Love is not war. Both your experience and your partner's experience can coexist. It's not one or the other. You can be angry that he didn't take out the trash while he can be justified in believing that it could wait another day or two. When we learn another person is angry, our first reaction is to often fight for ourselves. Rather than trying to understand his anger (which is underpinned by hurt), we try to conquer it. But we're missing the bigger point: that hurt exists. Acknowledging someone else's pain—and yes, even apologizing for your role in it—is not a threat to your survival.

The next time you feel defensive, try to cool your jets for a moment. Don't think about whether his accusation is justified. Instead, accept that he is hurt (or frustrated, or not heard, or whatever), and do your best to understand it. In many cases, his hurt is due to his own vulnerabilities and not exclusively to your actions. Try to listen without judgment to what he is saying, and, especially, what he *isn't* saying. Hurt often hides in criticism.

TIME TO STOP, REFLECT, INTROSPECT!

I don't expect you to be able to conquer all of your emotional demons, but simply being aware of their existence and how they affect your relationship is a huge step forward. Now we're going to discuss the Stop, Reflect, Introspect technique for managing emotional upheavals before they wreak havoc. But first I'll begin with a story.

Sanjay and I were with our kids on a summer vacation in Beaver Creek, Colorado. I was really looking forward to this trip; we had been working so hard for so long that we had barely seen each other. I was feeling really disconnected from him. This was our chance to spend some quality time together and with the kids in the beautiful Rocky Mountains. There was only one catch: Sanjay's extended family was coming, too.

Now, for the record, I love Sanjay's family and enjoy spending time with them. They are generous, loving, and wonderful. We all get along very well and have a lot of fun together. (Cue the epic at-home dance parties fueled with Bhangra music and the Bee Gees.) Sanjay is extremely close to his family, and I was prepared for us to be spending a lot of time together that week. (As a *big* aside, the incredible emphasis he places on family and the very high expectations he has of me in our relationship have been hugely influential in my Radical Acceptance journey. Sanjay's focus on family and relationships has opened my eyes and heart to how much more connected spouses—and families—can be. I am lucky to be with someone so devoted to his own nuclear family as well as to his family of origin.)

Our vacation also happened to coincide with the World Cup. I could care less, but Sanjay and his family are huge soccer fans, so he was pretty much checked out from the start of the trip. Instead of hiking outdoors and enjoying the rivers and mountains, Sanjay was cooped up inside watching soccer with the group.

Under these particular circumstances I felt angry and hurt that he had tuned out from me. I wanted to be around my husband and our kids, spending quality time together. I wanted to hike and climb and breathe the fresh air—all things that we can't do in Manhattan. Moreover, I wanted him to make me his priority. And, of course, I wanted him to *know* this, without me voicing it. (Isn't it obvious? Why can't he read my mind!? I know it's an irrational expectation, but I still sometimes get lulled into it. Sound familiar?) I didn't want to tell him. I didn't want to ask him. I just wanted him to give me a lot of attention and TLC. After all, asking for attention can seem incredibly perilous. You risk feeling exposed and being rejected, feeling naggy or needy. You want him to know you well enough and to care about you enough to anticipate what you want—without your having to spell it out (never mind the fact that asking for what you want and expressing your expectations is healthy). But even more damning than my desire for Sanjay to read my mind was that I wanted him to *share* my mind: I wanted him *to want to spend this time with me.*

You know where this is going. He had something else planned.

Since we had invited everyone on vacation with us, Sanjay was eager to play cruise director with his family—including entertaining them as they watched soccer. It was Germany vs. the United States, the Netherlands vs. Argentina, Brazil vs. Colombia . . . *argh, who cares*?! I spend 98 percent of my life in New York City staring at a computer screen, sitting in an office. And yet I worship the outdoors. Spending quality time together outside was what my mind, body, and soul craved. But instead of fresh air and birdsong it was bags of Cheetos and the drone of idiot play-by-play announcers.

The following moments are forever frozen in my mind: We were about halfway into our vacation. I was reading a book and relaxing by myself in our unit. There was the sound of a key in the door and Sanjay entered the room. *Finally,* I thought. *He's here to spend time with me.*

Hah! Or not.

It turns out he just wanted to pick up beer or Doritos or God knows what from the pantry for his family who were watching—*ding ding ding!*—even more World Cup soccer! As he was leaving, I remember opening my mouth to really let him have it. I was so incredibly, righteously pissed off. It was reactive and irrational and fraught with ancient feelings of rejection, but I could care less. And then . . . and then . . .

I stopped.

It's not about him, I realized. *It's about me.* I thought about the pressure he felt to be ultra-attentive to his family—as well as the joy this gave to him. I thought about how much he loves soccer. And then I thought about my own insecurities and why I was so affronted by his behavior. Instead of yelling at him, I walked over and gave him a hug.

"I love you," I told him. "I wish we could spend more time together, but I know you have a lot on your plate with your family. And the soccer matches."

"Why don't you come downstairs and join us?" he responded.

Of course, I wish he had said: "Honey, may I whisk you into the woods and stare into your eyes and savor your essence, you beautiful goddess?" But okay. I knew that his mind-set was completely rational. I knew he was doing the best he could.

This experience became the basis for Stop, Reflect, Introspect. I always think back to that moment, about that nanosecond during which I made the decision not to react, but to consider the situation more delicately. I'm going to walk you through my thought process in that moment and explain how this story can teach us about the beauty of gaining control of almost any situation, starting with gaining control of our own reactions.

Stop. I can still feel my tongue jammed up against my teeth in that moment, desperately trying to break through and launch a tirade against Sanjay. "This was supposed to be our vacation!" I wanted to yell. "And you're ruining it." But I stopped myself. I stopped myself even before I reflected on what he was going through, even before I introspected on how my own insecurities were influencing my emotions.

Remember: *He is not the opponent. It is your emotional reaction that is the opponent.* You are on the same team. In this section we are going to practice the first and most important step of Stop, Reflect, Introspect. It's the most important because nothing else can happen until you do it! Are you ready for it?

Stop!!!

Hit the brakes! If you're in an emotional fight, if you're losing control, thinking corrosive, toxic thoughts, nothing good is going to happen. At this stage, huge red lights are flashing in both your brain and his brain. *Survive! Defend! Attack!* Yes, you are both in full-blown survival mode. Millions of years of human evolution are taking over and your biological predispositions are now at the wheel. If you sense this happening, there is only one thing you can do: stop.

Practice is the operative word here, especially if you are stressed, tired, hangry—I am the *worst* hangry person in the world—or, shall we say, *passionate* when you get angry. The key is to be ready to stop before the next flare-up occurs. As you're reading this book and (hopefully) feeling calm, close your eyes and visualize yourself not reacting or flipping out when he does something that you find completely boneheaded or hurtful. *Visualizing* yourself doing this successfully again and again is almost as effective as actually practicing it in real life.

Even if you don't react verbally, your facial expressions can give you away. There are seven universal recognized facial expressions: anger, disgust, contempt/hatred, sadness, fear, happiness, and surprise. Studies show that humans can recognize these expressions within one-fifteenth of a second. Even if you stop yourself from yelling when he says he forgot to make dinner reservations, he might still pick up on your momentary eye roll or pursed lips. Going forward, try to be aware of your emotional "tells." These "microexpressions," as they are called, signal to your partner how you really feel. However, even if you grimaced initially, you can move forward by using positive body language, a neutral voice, and as much empathy as you can muster.

Imagine yourself taking a deep breath or two or eight or as many as needed to *keep your cool.* Feel how good it feels to exercise that tiny but enormously powerful kernel of emotional control. Try reciting one or more mantras. Maybe even smile and think about how you can extend some tenderness toward this person whom you love dearly—rather than treating him as the opponent.

Depending on how volatile your relationship is and how reactive you are, you may need to do this again and again, maybe dozens of times, before it starts to become more reflexive. But if you genuinely practice and visualize stopping, it *will* get easier. While you might still feel pissed off and may still fight, your fights will become less scary and counterproductive. Meanwhile, your hurt feelings will likely become less frequent, less intense, and less damaging.

Try developing mantras. I have found it very effective to ask myself: *Am I radically accepting Sanjay now?* Or, *Am I taking the high road here?* I remind myself that we are on the same team and that we are creating a harmonious relationship. These small phrases have become so engrained that I rarely have knee-jerk reactions—minimal eye rolling, regrettable outbursts, smart-ass comments, or incessant ruminations. These mantras help blunt those tingly feelings of anger and frustration that rise into my arms, back, chest, and neck.

You don't necessarily need to have a lot of volatility in your relationship for this technique to be helpful. After all, not all of us routinely flare up emotionally. Maybe you're the passive-aggressive type who rolls your eyes or makes a sarcastic comment when triggered. Or maybe you're the purely passive type who retreats, withdraws, and stews on partial boil. There are many ways we react when our partner says or does something we can't stand. The point is to stop yourself before your negativity turns into a fire hose of charged thoughts and feelings. The goal is to buy yourself some control and take power of your emotions before they overpower you.

I know sometimes it feels good to be reactive. It feels good to yell or fire back, to give your anger and frustration a much-needed megaphone. And, yes, sometimes it's perfectly appropriate. After all, we're human; we have emotions for a reason. It's natural to get angry or hurt. I'm not asking you to become a robot or to suppress your feelings. Rein yourself in before an emotional outburst or negativity escalates the situation. Of course, if he calls you a cow, then by all means let him have it (and then you should probably dump him). But if he's, say, offhand-edly critical of you, or if he forgot the avocados—*again!!!*—then try to use the Stop technique before you capitulate to a cascade of negative words, thoughts, or facial expressions. Remember, negativity is incredibly contagious.

A powerful biofeedback loop exists among our mind, body, and emotions. For example, when you hear bad news or even imagine something horrific, you feel a pit in your stomach or a shiver down your spine. While you may not notice it, your heart rate and breathing patterns are typically the quickest to change. This sort of mental-physical feedback is occurring all day, whether or not you're aware of it. The good news is that you have a degree of control over this loop. You can change what's going on with your thoughts and emotions by altering your posture and physical movement. Likewise, you can change what's going on in your physical body by altering your thoughts and emotions—and vice versa.

"The moment you change your perception is the moment you rewrite the chemistry of your body."

—AMERICAN DEVELOPMENTAL BIOLOGIST DR. BRUCE LIPTON

When you feel worked up and need to *STOP*, there are two very effective things you can do:

First, tell yourself, "This is no big deal. I'm the queen of cool and I've got this." This is where enlightened leadership really matters—when it's hard and takes a ton of emotional resilience. Think about those superstar leaders who exude grace and calm when everyone else is freaking out. That's you, sister! Positively and proactively managing your perception enables your nervous system to follow suit.

This is a *huge* gift to give to yourself.

Second, breathe—deeply and consciously. Really. There is ample scientific evidence about how this is one of the most effective ways to calm your autonomic nervous system. Ancient Indians figured this out when they devised *pranayama*, known as controlled breathing. (You yogis out there know what I mean.)

In fact, research has shown that the way you breathe can affect your perception of others. Dr. Stephen Porges, research professor in the Department of Psychiatry at the University of North Carolina at Chapel Hill and Distinguished University Scientist at the Kinsey Institute, explained to me that in his workshops he has proven that couples in conversation who take long inhalations and short exhalations appear to be judgmental and evaluative to each other. But those who inhale quickly and exhale gradually are the complete opposite. These couples are calmer, more engaged, and less defensive.

The simplest method is to breathe in several breaths deeply and exhale S-L-O-W-L-Y through your nose, pulling in your stomach as you exhale and pushing it out as you inhale. Try to slow down to a pace where you take five breaths in a minute. This rate has proven to be very calming for the autonomic nervous system. Many people take shallow breaths up into their chest, especially as they get anxious, angry, or afraid. Avoid doing this, as it's very similar to holding your breath. This only increases anxiety. To learn more about the transformative power of breathing, check out *The Healing Power of Breath* by Richard Brown and Patricia Gerbarg.

Performing a few easy yoga stretches along with deep breathing is also a helpful way to restore your cool. You don't need a swanky Lululemon outfit or a special mat. Try moving through a few sun salutations, or holding the tree pose for a count of ten, and when you've finished, give yourself a silent, almighty *namaste*. This is a beautiful chance to honor the light in yourself. Whatever crap may be dogging you, know that you are good and that you deserve to both give and receive love. You got this.

When I am stressed or upset, I also sing a calming song or put on very upbeat music. Breathing experts also corroborate the efficacy of singing to calm the autonomic nervous system. Even if I am righteously pissed off, taking a few deep breaths and singing along to "My Sharona" always transports me to a more sanguine place.

Taking a calming walk can also do wonders—especially in the woods, a park, or anywhere with trees. Recently, *Time* magazine ran a fascinating article,[27] "The Healing Power of Nature," trumpeting the power of trees to make you feel better. Japanese researchers from Nippon Medical School in Tokyo determined that "Trees and plants emit aromatic compounds called phytoncides that, when inhaled, can spur healthy biological changes in a manner similar to aromatherapy."

It turns out that time spent in nature can help lower blood pressure and cortisol, the stress hormone; increase white-blood-cell count, which helps strengthen the immune system; and can help reduce symptoms of depression and anxiety. Also, in part thanks to the moments of awe that nature can offer, it can lower inflammation and cause people to be more kind and generous to one another. Research shows that the benefit of being in nature will stay with you well after you have returned to the great indoors. In other words, if you want to feel more relaxed, improve your health or simply need to cool out, try to find ways to regularly spend time in nature.

Learning techniques to stay calm and relaxed, including learning to *STOP*—and being able to easily access them, should you tend to be reactive—is essential to ensuring safety in your relationship and has the huge added benefit of promoting your health and well-being.

STRESS

While learning these techniques, also look seriously at your stress levels. Stress is toxic and insidious. Sometimes we cannot pinpoint where it comes from, but it can lead to projecting our anger and tension onto other people. I know that when stressed I am more likely to be impatient, judgmental, and reactive with not just my husband, but also my kids, parents, friends, and employees. How many times have you said to your partner, or to anyone, something along the lines of: "I'm sorry I snapped earlier. I'm just really stressed out at work. It's nothing to do with you."

Stress is your responsibility. You are not allowed to blame stress for your actions toward others. As a mature adult, it's a cop-out. It's lame and irresponsible. (And, yes, I am totally guilty of it. That's why I bring it up!) It's important you apologize when it happens, as it may from time to time, but better yet, take to heart how stress influences your emotional reactions (not to mention your overall health) and commit to reducing your stress levels. Stress has so many unintended effects on the people around us—physically, emotionally, and mentally—and we notice so few of them.

There are a million books out there on how to reduce stress, and YourTango.com is full of great tips for managing stress more productively. A pillar of Radical Acceptance framework is stress management, so don't let this slide! I sometimes go to a coffee shop after work to write in my journal to relieve some stress before going home. I don't want to bring any of that tension into the living room. This buffer enables me to return home with grace and a sense of humor.

One thing I urge you to do is meditate regularly. Maybe for two minutes a day or for twenty—whatever you can manage. Do it a few times a day if you can, especially if you can only squeeze in a few minutes at a time. Use visualizations and affirmations. When things were tough with Sanjay, I would take a few deep breaths and tune out the incessant barrage of thoughts and *to-do lists that normally occupy my brain. I'd tell myself "There is great harmony and love between Sanjay and me," and then I'd visualize Sanjay and myself in tune, connected, and in the zone. I'd use some of the mantras we talked about earlier in this chapter.*

Don't worry if meditating doesn't work for you at first. Find a technique that you are comfortable using and just get used to making it a part of your routine. The positive impact on your body and on your brain is irrefutable. Heck, you and your partner can even try meditating together. Believe it or not, this is a proven technique for couples therapy.

Reflect. Okay, you have a taste for what it's like not to react. Right on! So now that you've chilled out, what next? Glad you asked. You may still be stewing over his behavior. Believe it or not, the hard part is over.

Now, reflect. Think about the situation as dispassionately and objectively as you can. What's going on with each of you? What factors influenced the behavior you objected to? Has he been stressed out about something? Have you? Is your blood sugar low? Has he just had a bad day, or are the problems deeper? Is there unresolved conflict lurking below the surface that seems to be sparking a similar pattern for many of your fights? Be curious and inquisitive. And remember, there's a good chance that whatever you're having trouble accepting might be about you, too.

Let's return to my vacation-in-the-mountains story. After I stopped myself from freaking out in our condo, I tried to remove myself from the moment. I imagined a neutral observer watching all of this unfold. Obviously I understood my side of the story, but then I thought about Sanjay. I reflected on how he is the eldest son in an Indian family—this meant he felt a great responsibility for everyone in the house. I reflected on how I loved this side of him. Sanjay is determined to spend time with his family and look after them, and at the moment, that meant watching soccer. I would have preferred if he had sought me out for some special time together; he would have preferred if I were with them watching Argentina go down in flames.

Reflecting is a great time to be both compassionate and dispassionate—that is, to see things from his perspective. Try to move past your instinct to blame, control, or be defensive. Don't think about right and wrong. Just do your best to understand what was going through his head and the overarching dynamic between the two of you. Try to give him the benefit of the doubt. Your relationship deserves it.

Introspect. You've stopped, and you've reflected. Now it's time to turn inward. As we've talked about, there is a good chance that your emotional reactions to what he says or does (or does not say or do) are intrinsically linked to your past or inherent sensitivities. Maybe not—it's possible he's just being a complete idiot. But now is the time to consider your own vulnerabilities and how they might be influencing your emotions.

Think about these for now:

- Why is his behavior so painful? So threatening? So annoying?
- Did he manage to push a very delicate button that has "nuclear" or "seminuclear" written on it?
- Do you feel vulnerable? And if so, why?

In that condo in Colorado, after I stopped, after I reflected, I thought about my own vulnerabilities. The emotional, vulnerable part of me was acting like a needy child who felt rejected and unimportant. It's a part of me that I have spent much of my life trying to outrun and outgrow.

While I wanted Sanjay to focus on me, I was able to accept that he had another agenda at the moment—it didn't mean he didn't love me. I realized, eventually, that this was a turning point in my life and in our relationship. This is probably obvious to readers more evolved than I was, or to those who have done a ton of therapy! But I finally understood that when Sanjay's actions (or in this case, inactions) made me feel hurt, and angry, I had the choice to examine those feelings and to quit accepting them at face value.

Had I not taken that nanosecond to exercise restraint, the outcome would have been much more predictable. I would have said something negative and hurtful. Then he would have become angry. A fight would have ensued. I would have felt even more angry and hurt, and I would have eventually withdrawn, my body charged and shaky. Those icky, tingly stress hormones would create a deeply unpleasant sensation throughout my body and perhaps that's how I would have spent day four of my summer vacation. Instead, I learned a triumphant lesson.

Introspecting can be tricky to master because it involves being exceptionally honest with yourself. It's not just looking inward. Sometimes, introspecting means acknowledging your darkest, scariest, most broken parts or irrational fears. We try to suppress or ignore them, but they're lurking there. You can start small. Think about your most common arguments and try to understand what triggers them. Were there any early experiences that make you particularly susceptible to certain situations? Does your partner know about them?

Here's a quick story to illustrate what I mean regarding triggers, starring my friends Sebastian and Frida, who were dating at the time. Frida tells the story as follows:

I was out for a while and had returned home in the middle of a warm, summer day. I walked into the apartment and found Sebastian there with a friend—a man I had never met. Our place was drenched in gorgeous sunlight . . . and cigarette smoke. The two of them were each smoking a cigarette. IN THE MIDDLE OF OUR EFFING LIVING ROOM.

Internally, I totally freaked out. I CANNOT STAND cigarettes.

I ignored the friend and looked at Sebastian with horror and venom. I dashed into our bedroom, changed into running clothes, and made a beeline for the trail behind our place. I literally ran away from something as offensive to me as my boyfriend and some random dude smoking in my apartment. I was seething.

As my feet hit the dirt, my anger eventually gave way to introspection. I knew my reaction was irrational. Why did I just freak out? I am a grown woman—what the hell! *I must have looked like a crazy person. This wasn't about Sebastian, I knew. This was entirely about me. I'm no princess (just ask any of my friends from high school or college), but I have never smoked a cigarette. Not one puff. Not even any I-didn't-inhale bullshit for me. Nada. That said, I have lots of friends and family members who used to smoke. Some still do. My grandma Julieta, whom I adored, was a veteran smoker. I don't recall ever having an emotional reaction to any of these people smoking.*

But . . . my parents are lifelong smokers. I grew up with a lot of smoke. I can only surmise that my freaky, irrational reaction was because of how much as a kid I hated my parents smoking and then even into adulthood. I love them dearly (plus my kids worship them!) and I don't want to lose them prematurely from something so preventable.

Eventually I returned home. The friend was nowhere to be seen. Sebastian watched me enter and blinked. He was like, "WTF?!" I explained to him my behavior as best I could, and he mostly understood. Sebastian radically accepted that this reprehension was part of me. While his smoking bothered me to no end, it became less of an emotional trigger for me. Eventually, he quit altogether (thank God!).

Of course, your dude will sometimes say or do something that has nothing to do with your deep-seated anxieties, but it will still be annoying or frustrating. Even then, learning not to flip out will serve you well. When it truly is about him and not you, Stop, Reflect, Introspect is a chance to exercise restraint and learn what else might be going on with him. Maybe he had a tough day at work, and this is your opportunity to communicate and extend him empathy.

No matter what, your ability to not be reactive and to replace judgment with compassion and empathy will serve both of you extremely well. Taking this one crucial step further, by you keeping your cool, you will be much better able to help him calm down through using one or more of the following: a non-threatening tone of voice; positive body language; positive, sincere words; reassuring physical touch—a hug, holding his hand, touching his arm or knee. Rather than escalating the situation, you can trigger a phenomenon called co-regulation. Oh man! It is SUPER powerful. We'll talk more about why and how it works up ahead!

GETTING REAL ABOUT YOUR VULNERABILITIES

The moral of the story above is to explore your vulnerabilities. Be curious about them. Seek out a therapist if you need to. When you are ready, please share your insecurities with your partner. If he knows what makes you react irrationally, hopefully he will try to be protective and extend compassion your way.

As you become more conscious of vulnerabilities, you can also embrace them. Dr. Pat Love likes to take that one step further.[28] In her fantastic book *You're Tearing Us Apart: Twenty Ways We Wreck Our Relationships and Strategies to Repair Them*, Pat explains that we need to differentiate between current pain and archaic pain. This goes hand in hand with Introspect. Think about your most recent fight with your partner. What was the moment you felt the most angry? The most vulnerable? Now think back and try to identify the earliest times you felt that same sensation. For instance, if you're angry that he doesn't spend enough time with you, when was the first time in your life that you felt neglected? The more you practice this exercise, the more you will understand the vulnerabilities that long predate your relationship. Instead of suppressing them, do what Pat does: Put a heart around them! Don't just accept your vulnerabilities, *love* them by drawing mental hearts around them. This is a powerful opportunity to foster compassion for yourself and for others in your life.

In my case, I know I have been hugely to blame for Sanjay getting angry with me for my inattentiveness. It took me a long time to truly understand this. It was tough for me because our expectations for the relationship were quite different. We literally come from different sides of the planet, and we had to work through truly enormous cultural differences. What adds further complication is that a number of people I am close to have suffered from alcoholism, eating disorders, depression, and other such challenges.

I put this out there because I know that alcoholism, drug addiction, depression, anxiety, eating disorders, and other such maladies cause so many of us to seek escape from those incredibly painful parts of ourselves. There is so much shame and so much suffering silently bubbling beneath the surface. Growing up in these circumstances causes so many people to feel we're out here alone, that we're simply "not enough." It's messed up because it's just not true. Making matters worse, these problems make it difficult and sometimes even impossible to connect truly, openly, and honestly with others, creating further hurt and dysfunction.

These issues are ubiquitous in our society. Upper class, middle class, lower class—we're all in it together. If you can relate to those circumstances, I hope that what I am sharing resonates with you. You are not alone in what you're experiencing, and I hope you know that these issues may be a major culprit in your relationship—whether in finding love or making it last. I know how painful it is to feel emotionally isolated, to feel broken, to feel a deep void, to feel like you have to keep parts of yourself hidden or constantly try to wrestle them to the ground.

Mercifully, I have seen and experienced firsthand how profoundly healing it is to give voice to these deeply personal challenges, and to actively extend compassion and understanding to others who are battling similar demons. Being able to talk with friends, colleagues, and family members about these kinds of battles with an open, loving heart is a powerful opportunity to help and heal one another. It's never too late to do this for yourself or someone else.

I am a workaholic, and this has been the hardest trait I have asked Sanjay to accept. I barely drink, I don't do drugs, but my addiction to work and achievement certainly have a dark, encompassing shadow side. While it's different than having a raving crack addiction, being addicted to work and feeling the need to prove myself have real consequences. It's a form of escapism. It creates distance. It forms a protective shell and squelches the feeling of togetherness. My sense is that it has been very difficult for Sanjay to understand and accept how my selfworth and identity are inextricably linked to my work.

When it comes to Radical Acceptance, I often feel it is a lot less about my accepting him than his accepting me. I realize that at times I am no picnic. And while Radical Acceptance continues to be a journey for us, we both have come a million miles. Yes, I still work a lot. Yes, Sanjay occasionally feels neglected. But a major internal shift has occurred within me, thanks to our relationship. My intense work habits aren't quite so much about survival anymore, my sense of belonging has increased dramatically thanks to our Radical Acceptance practice. My ability to forge a deep, loving, ultrahonest dynamic with Sanjay has been fundamental to my becoming more of what Brené Brown calls "wholehearted"—that is, to feel a strong sense of worth and belonging.

I share this because I know so many people struggle with a sense of belonging and with feeling a strong intrinsic sense of worthiness. If you are like, "Oh my God, she just described me!" then welcome to the club! You're beautiful, you're worthy and you're *NOT ALONE*. I hope that Radical Acceptance helps you, too, become wholehearted.

. . .

Hello? Are you still with me? I want to say "Hallelujah!" if you have been able to take all of the above to heart, and if you understand how you can be carrying and expressing yourself more wisely, more productively, and with more compassion—for his sake and yours. In moments of stress or conflict, I have tried to impart you with a mandate to pause, to better understand what's going on, and to take measures so that you *DO. NOT. REACT*!

Remember: Stop, Reflect, Introspect. If he does that thing you can't stand, *Stop* yourself from reacting impulsively. *Reflect* on the situation and try to understand what is going on (and that this, too, shall pass). Then *Introspect* by exploring your vulnerabilities and how your own issues might be coloring your reactions to his behavior.

When you can get a hold on your own emotional reactions, you will be amazed how everything else seems to flow naturally. At the same time, please be patient with yourself! This will be easier for some people than others. (Sorry, to the Aries out there—I feel your pain. Tauruses, I'm looking at you!) Brain chemistry, neuroscience, epigenetics, and other factors will impact the degree of emotional control you are able to wrangle, but it is possible to be aware of your reactions and rein them in before they wreak havoc. This will require a sincere, honest commitment and a lot of practice—but I promise it's worth every ounce of effort you invest!

- Avoid blaming your partner and be mindful when this instinct arises for you, as there's a perverse logic to it. Remember: "Blame is a way to discharge pain and discomfort. It has an inverse relationship with accountability."

- Stress is your responsibility. There are a ton of ways to manage stress and adopt techniques that help you become less reactive, including controlled breathing.
- Get real about your vulnerabilities and what makes you feel reactive. You may very well be responding to hurts or sensitivities that are as much or more about you as they are about what he's doing or saying.
- He is not the opponent. Your emotional reaction is the opponent. You are on the same team.

RADICAL ACCEPTANCE: STEP 3

RADICAL COMMUNICATION: CREATING A SAFE SPACE TO BE HEARD AND *REALLY* SEEN

NOW THAT YOU have decided to just love him in step 1 and started to take charge of your emotional reactions in step 2, you are ready to radically improve the communication between you and your partner.

Let's start with masks. We all wear them. We all have something to hide. We all have aspects of ourselves that we are afraid to reveal—our experiences, our feelings, our fears, our vulnerabilities. We keep them quiet and hidden because we are afraid of being perceived as weak, of being criticized. And we're all afraid of that greatest existential threat of all: rejection. Radical Communication is a powerful technique for casting off your masks, enhancing safety and trust in your relationship, and replacing the fear of rejection with the joy of being seen. If you have safety, you and your partner are much more likely to take off your masks, to be who you really are, to be vulnerable, which is where emotional intimacy flourishes and honest feelings emerge. (Yes, even the really scary ones. In fact, *especially* the really scary ones.)

In this chapter, we'll build upon the foundation started in step 2 for creating safety within your relationship so that you can open up and really be seen by one another. You'll also learn what sabotages communication, from deflecting blame onto him to using words like *always* and *never*, to constantly needing the last word in your arguments. I will share key, actionable highlights of Imago Relationship Therapy, the masterful communication framework designed by Harville Hendrix and Helen LaKelly Hunt more than thirty years ago.

You'll see how taking the high road directs you to a place of strength and abundance, even when you might feel like being petty and hurtful. A crucial starting note is that everyone sees the world differently, even though we like to imagine that everyone else thinks like we do! As Harville Hendrix told me, "Most people live in a symbiotic consciousness,[29] which means they assume that others see the world much the same that they do. It's so simple to say, but that's the root of all conflict on the planet." The techniques in this chapter won't help you "win" arguments; rather they will help you develop the tools to better understand and learn to be okay with opposing points of view, even if you do not agree with them.

Every couple experiences conflict, but each responds to it differently. No matter the form it takes, conflict emerges when one or both partners feel they are fighting for scraps. They are not getting what they want. They are not being seen or heard. They are in a place of emotional scarcity. In my case, I would feel that I had to fight tooth and nail to win praise from Sanjay, while he felt he had to move mountains to get me to prioritize him over work. Often instead of addressing conflict in a productive manner, couples pick and nag and retreat and lash out, among countless other ways of revealing their thoughts and emotions nonverbally. If you are one of those who tends to withdraw, bury your feelings, or feel afraid to honestly express yourself, you will be able to take meaningful steps toward opening up. These suggestions will help you express what is going on inside of you before you explode (or implode). This can all be developed with practice.

Radical communication will help you feel brave and confident in ways that you and your relationship have never known before.

CREATING SAFETY IN YOUR RELATIONSHIP

"Safety is nonnegotiable.[30] **If you want a good relationship, it's got to be safe—predictably safe and reliably safe. Both predictability and reliability are essential."**

—HARVILLE HENDRIX

Safety must be established for any sane person to risk being vulnerable and to willingly expose her- or himself. After all, if you think someone is going to laugh at, deride, judge, or reject you, why would you ever open yourself up? You wouldn't, and neither would your partner.

Let's start with how your brain perceives threats and how you can counteract this propensity. A region of the brain called the amygdala is partly responsible for memory, decision making, and regulating emotions. The amygdala also governs the flight-or-fight response that typically occurs when conflict starts to brew. Either we seek to escape the conflict, or we dig our trenches and prepare for war.

When Sanjay says or does something I perceive as hurtful or maddening, a physiological response occurs. Sensing a threat, my amygdala releases hormones that either prepare me for battle or provide the extra energy to flee. No matter which happens, my heart rate surges, my muscles tense, my blood pressure rises—and then, too often, these impulses translate into fighting words that fall right out of my mouth. Oops.

There is so much fascinating information and research out there about the biofeedback loop connecting the brain and body.

POLYVAGAL THEORY

I am going to offer a relatively simplified explanation of the Polyvagal Theory (PVT), which we briefly touched on in part 1. The theory was developed by the illustrious Dr. Stephen Porges. I am excited to share these highlights because PVT will help you understand yourself better, and help you interact much more productively and lovingly with those you care about.

PVT describes how neural circuits have evolved from reptiles to mammals, to regulate humans' autonomic nervous systems. The most recent circuit has evolved as a "social engagement system" that features connectivity between the brain stem and the heart, along with muscles of the face, neck, and head, through the ventral vagal nerve, aka the vagus. While this is a great simplification, the "social" vagus effectively uses oxytocin and vasopressin to communicate safety and trust between the brain and the nervous system.

When you feel safe, your autonomic (subconscious) nervous system enables you to engage socially and be physiologically relaxed—that is, with a normal heart rate and easy breathing. If you perceive danger or the presence of social cues that indicate emotional threats, the PVT describes how you react physiologically: your heart rate increases, breathing becomes shallow, and an increase of cortisol may trigger a fight-or-flight response.

Dr. Porges explains that we can calm this stress response and establish effective connections with others by using our facial muscles, making eye contact, modulating our voice, and simply listening.

In an interview, Dr. Porges explained[31] that "Using gestures of engagement, and more playfulness, helps to regulate each other's physiological state. The notion of connectedness is a biological imperative. The goal as mammals—and as good spouses—is to interact in a way that regulates each other's physiology. It is a responsibility for individuals to interact to make each other feel safe. It is not just healing, and enjoyable, but it has great impact on our mental and physical health because it supports the circuits of health, growth, and restoration!"

Dr. Porges notes there's a "hierarchy of calming," and it starts with your ears during interactions, aka "co-regulation" with another person. When you hear warm and melodic intonations, the muscles in your ears relax, followed by the muscles in your eyes and face. Your breath deepens, your heart calms, and your autonomic nervous system relaxes. Understanding this process is crucial when you are in an argument with your partner. Nothing good can come from heated, over-the-top arguments because both you and your partner are in fight-or-flight mode. You can only resolve conflict when you return to a calm state. "It's totally predictable," Dr. Porges says.

Once triggered, it can take some people a while to shift physiologically back into a safe, calm mode. So please be patient with yourself and your partner.

Neil Sattin, who interviewed Dr. Porges[32] and has written extensively about PVT, adds, "A basic understanding of *our autonomic nervous system provides insight into why we react the way we do in conflict and crisis, while also laying the framework for what we can do to help bring ourselves back into a physiological state in which we are available for connection, love, and intimacy."*

Neil adds that Neuroception is the term that Dr. Porges created to describe how our body can sense something and react to it without it necessarily penetrating our conscious awareness. Our nervous system makes decisions and changes our biobehavior without our realizing why. For example, if we detect risk or danger in the environment, we might have a "sympathetic" excitation (sweat, jumping out of our skin, etc.). Our bodies literally know things that our minds haven't yet discovered.

Neil also warns, "Escalation is not co-regulation! In most relationship conflicts, both individuals feel like victims—so in order to de-escalate a situation and move in the direction of play and connection, one person must step up and take charge of noticing the pattern, and changing the way of engagement. This means meeting your partner on their level—often through touch, gentleness, and a "prosodic" (i.e., soothing) voice. Hug your partner—not in an effort to fix, but rather in an effort to connect and bring back safety."

Another thing you can do to calm your—and his—autonomic nervous system and foster safety includes offering a loving touch to your partner (place your hand on his hand, arm, or leg). Safe touching triggers the release of oxytocin, which helps people experience bonding. If you take steps to feel calm and safe, you can more readily listen without judgment and offer compassion to your partner, helping him to return to a place of calm and safety—physiologically and emotionally.

The Polyvagal Theory is helpful because by understand-

ing the very basics, you'll understand how to facilitate trust and safety in your relationship(s). You will understand that your body and brain (including your mental and emotional states), are inextricably linked and that by keeping your body (and your partner's body) calm, you can minimize the tyranny of fear, anxiety, anger, stress, and other undesirable emotions that wreak havoc on relationships.

. . .

You owe it to each other to ensure that you don't piss off your amygdalae—or your autonomic nervous system! As we saw in step 2, being able to take hold of your emotional reactions strengthens your relationship, prevents your amygdala from going rogue, and keeps your nervous system calm. The same goes for him. If he believes that you will flip out anytime he says something you don't like or find upsetting, he'll probably avoid difficult conversations. He'll refrain from sharing those parts of himself that could help you gain a better understanding of him, that could help you love him more deeply. He needs to know he is safe to do so. And vice versa.

As always, be aware of your body language, as it can undermine safety instantaneously. You might be a master of words (or holding your tongue!), but your body language, facial expressions, tone, and even your "vibe" will give away your true intentions. It's all about what I like to call *alignment*. Keeping your intentions, thoughts, feelings, and actions in sync—that is, aligned—means that you rarely have to calibrate how to express yourself in a particular situation. Alignment also enables you to be honest and transparent, offering you a much better chance of either finding someone who will love the real, authentic you, or solidifying your current relationship on a firm foundation of honesty and openness.

By extension, the next crucial ingredient in creating safety in your relationship is communicating in a loving and supportive fashion. Once again, neurobiology and that oh-so-powerful body-brain feedback loop is going to take center stage here! (I truly love this stuff.)

A fascinating series of studies was performed by a group of researchers who were curious about the skyrocketing divorce rates of the 1970s and 1980s. Dr. John Gottman, who led the studies, set up a "love lab" at the University of Washington to gain a better understanding of what was happening with divorced couples on a neurobiological level. In the process, Gottman and his colleagues determined some compelling results that help explain why some couples succeed and others fail.

The experiments were popularized[33] again by a 2014 article by Emily Esfahani Smith in *The Atlantic*. The researchers' equipment measured couples' blood flow, heart rates, and other vitals as each partner talked about their relationship. These included positive conversations, such as how they met, and negative conversations, such as major conflicts they were facing. After obtaining their data, the researchers followed up with the couples six years later to see how things had gone.

Based on his data, Gottman divided the couples into the "masters"—couples who had stayed together happily—and the "disasters"—couples who had either broken up or remained married but were terribly unhappy. It turned out that six years earlier, the disasters were the most excitable during conversations. The simple act of talking to each other caused these couples to enter fight-or-flight mode, constantly bracing for an attack. With some, seemingly benign questions like "How was your day?" caused hearts to race. Even during pleasant conversations, these couples' bodies were ready to pounce at any suggestion of criticism. Many of the "disasters" appeared calm during their interviews, but their heart rate, blood pressure, and sweat glands told a far different story.

Meanwhile, the "masters" were genuinely calm throughout their interactions. They were serene and in tune with each other, even when they were fighting. Their heart rates remained low, they breathed easy. Most importantly, they trusted each other. Even during difficult conversations, *they knew they had each other's back*. They could take on any difficult situation that might arise because they knew they could do it together. Psychological calm turned into physical calm.

"There's a habit of mind that the masters have," Gottman explained to *The Atlantic*. "They are scanning the social environment for things they can appreciate and say thank you for. They are building this culture of respect and appreciation very purposefully." Meanwhile, "Disasters are scanning the social environment for partners' mistakes." By observing how various couples interact, Gottman is able to predict with as much as a 94 percent certainty whether couples will stay together or break up.

And what's the number-one factor that determines whether a couple will stay together? Contempt. The researchers found that individuals who focus on putting down their partners miss 50 percent of the positive aspects their partners bring to the relationship. In short, it's scrutinizing the partner for anything in which they can possibly find fault. Even if it's nothing big, put-downs can make your partner feel small or invisible, that nothing they do will ever please you.

The takeaway is that safety matters. There is a ton more that can be said on that topic, but following the five steps of Radical Acceptance can transform your relationship into a bastion of safety. We will explore a handful of additional practical means to enhance safety in this chapter. Conversely, routine sarcasm and contempt will place your relationship on a dark road. No matter what you are talking about, try to keep in mind how he is reacting to your tone. Are you implicitly criticizing him? Are you putting him down? Even if you don't mean to, does he think you are? These small moments add up over the course of days and months and years.

VULNERABILITY AND BEING SEEN

With an abundance of safety present, we have set the stage to allow both of you to be vulnerable and to be truly seen. Beautiful. I love it.

Vulnerability establishes a virtuous cycle in which he can reveal his true feelings, weaknesses, and insecurities, and you can meet them with tenderness. The more compassion you extend, the more willing he will be to show himself, and the more likely he'll be to relax those defensive, protective mechanisms he engineers to control the situation and protect himself. He knows you will not judge him. I have certainly seen this work in my marriage—and its ugly opposite. When I reject parts of Sanjay, I bring out the worst of him. This makes me want to withdraw more—cue the downward spiral. Thankfully, we have also managed to achieve a virtuous cycle: As we extend compassion and tenderness to each other, we bring out the best in each other.

Shame shuts down connectedness by preventing people from really showing themselves and from being seen. As Brené Brown says, "Shame is the most powerful, master emotion. It's the fear that we're not good enough. Jungian analysts call shame the swampland of the soul." Sure, it's a risk to show yourself, but the upside is enormous. Imagine if you could share all of the negative, frail, ugly, confused, weak parts of yourself and know you will still be loved? Being seen not only offers you liberation from fear and the need to continue to hide something, it also enables you to connect in a deeper way. Through this process, I have decreased my weaknesses, and even transformed some of them into strengths.

There is enormous power in being the one-and-only, wonderful, authentic you. There's a great scene in the film *The Big Short* in which a financial genius with Asperger's syndrome reflects on his first Match.com profile. He stated he had "only one eye, an awkward social manner, and $145,000 in student loans." The woman he eventually married contacted him and said she was looking for someone real and honest—and he fit the bill to a T. I urge you to be the best, most honest version of yourself out of the gate—even if the thought makes you wince a little. Don't try to put on a different mask for every person in your life, especially for your significant other. Your vulnerabilities make you real and can give you strength if you really own 'em. And if you resist, deny, or seek to escape them, vulnerabilities can be toxic.

"Be yourself. The world worships the original."

—INGRID BERGMAN

SABOTAGING COMMUNICATION

What sabotages communication? What is sure to result in ugly, horrific, explosive fights? Well, a lot of things, of course. But generally, when safety and trust are absent, frustration and negativity flourish. We have touched on a few of these, but I want to underscore the most common saboteurs, those which breed fear and prevent successful communication.

Here are the big ones: withdrawal, rejection/the silent treatment, anger/yelling, name-calling/abusive language, sarcasm, blame, "always/never," defensiveness, eye-rolling, and needing to have the last word.

Do you fall victim to any of these traps when you communicate with your partner? Does your partner fall for them when communicating with you? How do these behaviors make you feel when you inflict them on your partner, or when he does the same to you? We'll talk about each of these in depth, but I want to say unequivocally right now that feeling angry is okay. Being hurt or frustrated is okay. This all will happen. What matters is how you manage this negativity and discomfort. Our goal here and now is to identify habits that sabotage communication, and to prevent that small fight from snowballing into a bloodbath.

Learning to fight right, to fight well, and to fight constructively can strengthen your relationship. That said, after lots of research and after reflecting on my own life, I am convinced that couples should work toward not fighting. This doesn't mean that they won't disagree. Rather, it's finding positive ways to manage disagreements. I'll address this in greater depth in part 3. But for now, baby steps, guys! First let's learn to fight more calmly and more constructively.

Lao Tzu, the ancient Chinese philosopher and founder of Taoism, once said, "When I let go of what I am, I become what I might be."

Oh, our menacing egos.

I know how easy it is to cling tightly to your almighty ego. Most of us fall into this trap, though we do it subconsciously as a means of self-preservation. Unfortunately, this is often a mirage. It's when we can let go of our egos and not feel afraid of being perceived as wrong or weak or imperfect that we are actually stronger. Our body chemistry rewards us accordingly and we are more equipped to connect with others. Conversely, when we feel stressed, when we feel the need to defend ourselves, that is when the ego starts to rear its frail, ugly head—and things start to go sideways. Or maybe even downhill, fast. Loosening your grip on your ego typically means letting go of fear and letting go of your need to control things. When you do this, you can be truly open—to others and to a better, future version of yourself. It also helps a ton to let go of the outcome. Whatever is challenging you, try to detach yourself from the outcome. This is such a powerful skill, and it allows you to listen to your partner on a fundamental level.

We have all heard the trope, "Would you rather be right or would you rather be happy?" Be willing to let go of your need to be right—in other words, be willing to let go of your ego—and you will be happier. Guaranteed.

I promise this can be learned! For some people it feels excruciatingly difficult, and I feel their pain! Having the moral high ground or a sense of self-righteousness is a truly potent feeling. But needing to be right can be very self-defeating. The you-won-the-battle-but-lost-the-war scenario is almost guaranteed when this dynamic arises. How many perfectly pleasant moments have been squandered by ridiculous I-am-going-to-prove-I-am-right arguments? I see it all the time, even with couples in strong, healthy relationships. When it comes to relatively trivial matters that are subject to debate, I try to "ego-check" myself by asking, "What's going on here? Why do I feel the need to prove that I am right?" It's amazing how much more easily I am able to let go thanks to that bit of practice. And how much more readily Sanjay responds in kind!

Much of what follows should be common sense, but, let's face it: we all are self-destructive from time to time, especially when we feel hurt, angry, or threatened. My goal is to burrow a bit into your consciousness so you can call yourself out as needed. If none of the following situations apply to you, great! You're a big step ahead of most everyone else. Like the rest of us, though, you probably fall into at least one of the following traps once in a while.

Here we go, let's address each topic one by one:

Anger/yelling. You are going to get angry when you try to radically accept him. You'll get angry when you try to shoulder some of the blame for his screwup and he doesn't immediately reciprocate. Yup, this will happen. This is where you need to practice emotional control, not yelling and not letting your anger boil over. If you're feeling really angry or out of control, I urge you to retire temporarily to a safe space. Here you can collect yourself so you don't precipitate more hurt by saying something you will later regret. When you are deep into a fight, both your and your partner's brains are in full-blown survival mode. Neither of you can listen coherently. Dr. John Gray, author of the mega-bestseller[34] *Men Are from Mars, Women Are from Venus,* agrees with this assessment. "Once the argument is heated and someone is getting defensive, the argument has to stop. You can't try to fix it. You can't go into active listening from there. It just doesn't work. When people fight, blood flows to the middle part of the brain. This causes us to be reactive. We repeat the same arguments and the same fights. We just hurt each other more and more and shut down."

The next time you are in this situation, suspend the argument by taking a deep breath and telling your partner: "I love you very much, but I need to take a break. I don't want to say something to you that I will regret. Let's resume this discussion after we have had the chance to cool off." Eventually, you do need to reengage your partner in conversation. You can let disagreements simmer for a while, but never let them fester. Closure is important. Once you are both calm, try to revisit the argument—it's amazing how a little time-out can encourage resolution.

If you're still having trouble reaching resolution, try to reconcile without words. Touch him, hold his hand, give him a hug or a kiss. As John concurred, "When talking doesn't work, just do things that say 'I love you.'" You may have to agree or disagree. That's okay and perfectly normal.

Withdrawal from conflict. This one can be tricky. As noted above, temporary withdrawal is a great technique if you or your partner feel emotionally out of control, exhausted, or generally feel a constructive conversation is not possible in the moment. However, there is a difference between temporarily withdrawing from an argument to cool down and reflexively withdrawing anytime there is conflict. The former is healthy and positive while the latter, a form of rejection, breeds resentment and destroys safety.

If you or your partner tend to withdraw from conversations that are uncomfortable or unpleasant, constructive communication can be extremely difficult. However, as we'll talk about shortly, Imago Relationship Therapy can help create a safe environment, precluding the need for constant withdrawal.

Rejection/the silent treatment. Whether you threaten rejection ("That's it! I'm getting a divorce!") or actually leave (with the exception of cooling off, as we discussed above), constructive communication is next to impossible. Rejection is about as big of a threat as you can proffer, and the silent treatment falls under this. It's damaging, it's psychologically destructive, it hurts—it just sucks all around. If you are angry with him, talk it out when you feel calm. The silent treatment, or passive-aggressively claiming everything is "fine," is a form of gaslighting. It is not healthy, it's abusive, and it has no place in your relationship.

Name-calling/abusive language. This needs no explanation. Name-calling and abusive language are very destructive. Even if you are justified in your anger, one insult, one regrettable word can instantly make the fight go nuclear. These are the fights that stay in the back of your mind, and they're the ones that end relationships. No name-calling. No abusive language. Set those ground rules if needed and stick to them!

Sarcasm. Sarcasm can be very insidious. Unless done with cheer or humor, it will likely undermine your communication and alienate your partner. "But I'm always sarcastic," you might be saying. "That's how I communicate. It's part of my charm. He understands that." Okay, maybe. I will never ask you to change a fundamental part of your personality, but everything is different during fights. This is when sarcasm goes from endearing to incendiary.

If you are in a disagreement, sarcasm is like pouring on jet fuel. After all, it's derived from the Greek word *sarkasmos*, meaning "to tear flesh, bite the lips in rage, sneer." Even if you are hurt, even if he has been rude, *just stop*. Sarcasm during an argument is mutually assured destruction. Believe me, I know: I used to be guilty of being sarcastic around Sanjay, especially when he lost his temper. The result is a self-feeding downward spiral that can only end in a more hurt and prolonged conflict. Instead, I try hard to take the high road, especially when I'm feeling hurt and want to hit back.

Blame. We talked about blame extensively in step 2. Blame is common, but wholly destructive. When you're inclined to blame, it's a signal that a dose of introspection is warranted. When he blames, don't get defensive. Extend tenderness and try to understand what's causing the blame to emerge. As times goes on, ideally you'll find that blame evaporates from your relationship.

Defensiveness. This goes hand in hand with blame. Defensiveness is another common bad habit that can erode a sense of unity and partnership. When your partner is acting overly critical or accusatory, try to listen and reflect rather than reflexively defend yourself. It's perfectly fine, of course, to help your partner understand your perspective. The truth is, there's a fine line between being defensive and offering clarification. Failing to toe this line effectively can create a destructive cycle. But if you learn not to take the bait, and work to change the narrative of your fighting, your disagreements can be more constructive and less painful. I should know!

Always/never. Never say "never" again when arguing with your partner! Be ultracareful not to make sweeping generalizations; they will almost certainly derail the conversation. "Always" and "never" are loaded, accusatory terms. Remember, you will never get the outcome you desire (unless, of course, your desire is mutually assured destruction), and your partner will feel put down.

When your partner uses "always" or "never"—as in, "You *never* pick me up on time," or "You *always* interrupt me"—remember to not take these phrases literally. Seriously. I have spent a lot of time in the always/never rabbit hole. During disagreements with Sanjay I would play detective, trying to unearth contradictions or finding ways to disprove that I always or never did whatever he was accusing me of doing or not doing. Rather than trying to understand what he was actually trying to say, as unpleasant as his tone was, I chose to find contra-examples. Argh! So dumb. If your partner says "always" or "never," listen to the message and interpret those words in your brain as "oftentimes" or "rarely." If you make the effort to scrub these words from your vocabulary, he will notice, and (hopefully) he will reciprocate over time.

Eye-rolling and other nonverbal cues. Employing nonverbal tactics like eye-rolling alienates other people. When you make faces or roll your eyes, you might as well say, "Hey, idiot! What the hell is the matter with you?!" because that's how these nonverbal cues are interpreted—

especially during fights. Think about what your body language, tone, and facial expressions are saying to your boyfriend or spouse. Did you ever watch that TV show *Lie to Me*? The series followed a group of psychology professionals who are hired by law-enforcement agencies to scrutinize suspects' facial expressions and determine who is lying and who is not. There is so much truth hidden in our faces!

A great way to minimize negative body language is to minimize negative, judgmental thoughts. If you're thinking something negative or are feeling reactive or resentful, make the effort to control how you express yourself. Rolling your eyes or muttering during an argument will never, ever, in a million years endear your partner to you. Even if he says something especially odious, try not to react! Yes, even when you feel like he is being a completely self-righteous pain in the butt. During your next fight, try nodding understandingly instead of rolling your eyes or pursing your lips. You'll be amazed how a little bit of earnest listening and positive body language can defuse even the most protracted conflicts.

Needing to have the last word. If you need to have the last word, here is what it should be: "I love you." Then, feel free to add: "Let's have sex," or "Let's go grab a beer," or "Let's watch a movie." Unless you're a prosecutor during a criminal trial, having the last word is never useful. It only serves to drive a wedge between you and your partner. This gets back to the topic of control and the unhealthy tendency to sacrifice the happiness and the health of your relationship to prove that you are right. Take the long-term view about nurturing a happy, lasting love life. Even when you feel justified, or that you just *need* the final word for validation, let it be a loving, endearing word or even a concession. I sometimes tease Sanjay and say, "Oh my goodness. For the third time in all of history, I was wrong. I'm sorry. Let's go make out!" Or better yet: "Let's go to Shake Shack!" (Lucky us: there's one down the street from our apartment!) We are able to move on from the ugliness with humor and grace.

· · ·

The above examples are a few of the common ways couples undermine communication and their relationship. From being sanctimonious and smug to being passive-aggressive to using negative body language, there are no shortage of ways to put your partner down. Whatever your own form of communication sabotage is, commit to no longer practicing it. This behavior is bad for you, it's bad for him, and it's bad for the relationship.

I know what you're thinking: *Don't I deserve some quid pro quo? Shouldn't he play by the same rules as I do?* Yes you do, and yes he should. After all, you aren't the only one who occasionally rolls her eyes or drops in a sarcastic comment. But reciprocation takes time, and it may require you to take the lead. If your partner consistently yells or employs the silent treatment or any of the other techniques we talked about, I urge you to address this behavior calmly but directly. These next sections will help you do so constructively.

Please remember that while I do encourage you to address this kind of problematic behavior, he may have a really tough time changing this part of himself. Alternatively, you can tell him how painful his behavior is in a constructive, loving way. If he proves incapable of changing it, you may have to chalk this behavior off as one of those unlovable parts to which you will attempt to extend tenderness. Maybe he was verbally abused growing up and he has a really tough time talking through conflict in a way that is rational. This doesn't mean it's game over; it means that you have to be very clear about how you relate to and communicate with this part of him. If it's crippling your partnership and you can't take it any longer, you may have to reassess the viability of your relationship.

LEARNING TO *REALLY* LISTEN

One of my favorite quotes is by Paul Tillich, the Christian existentialist philosopher: "The first duty of love is to listen." *YES!* Right on! Of course, we can all easily agree to this . . . but how often do we really do this? How often do we actively listen to our partners?

Do me a big favor: The next time your partner is speaking to you, no matter what it is, just listen. And when I say just listen, I also mean with your eyes; i.e., look at your partner's face and body. Drop your need to interrupt, or to think about something else, or to steer the conversation in another direction. AHEM: DROP YOUR NEED TO LOOK AT YOUR PHONE! ALL CAPS FOR A REASON, PEOPLE! Just focus on what he is saying, even if you don't agree with him. *Especially* if you don't agree with him.

Consciously focus on his body language and tone. Remember, the vast majority of communication is nonverbal. So often we multitask and merely hear a bunch of words when we should be looking at our partners and seeing what their faces and bodies are telling us. Reflect after you try this. Do you notice a difference when you focus solely on listening to him? Do you feel a greater connection when you shift your eyes from the TV or iPhone to his eyes? Try to do this again and again. See what happens. I bet your communication will dramatically improve by this small but profound change in your behavior.

Don't believe me? Well, Dr. John Gottman, whose research we looked at in the previous section, has some compelling data that corroborates my claims. He was fascinated by the tiny, seemingly forgettable interactions among couples and how they affect love in the long term. In a fascinating experiment, he designed a lab to look like an idyllic bed-and-breakfast. Then he invited 130 newlyweds to spend a day at the B and B lounging, cooking, reading, and so on. It was after this experiment that Dr. Gottman made a crucial discovery.

He found that some partners make frequent efforts at communication, which he called "bids." These are not direct questions or statements that require an immediate response; rather, bids are subtle cues that one partner desires attention or support. For example, say that Jane and her boyfriend Hiroki are in their living room. Jane is reading a book when

Hiroki mentions he had a hard day at the office. Dr. Gottman would argue that this is a bid for attention—Hiroki, perhaps subconsciously, is hoping for a sign of support from Jane.

From his experiment, Dr. Gottman found that a partner like Jane could respond in one of two ways: She can "turn toward" Hiroki by setting down her book and engaging him in conversation to demonstrate that she is listening and attentive to him. "Tell me all about it," she could say. Alternatively, she can "turn away" from him by not responding at all, or responding so minimally that it is clear to Hiroki that Jane is not interested in what he has to say. During his experiment, Dr. Gottman could easily identify couples in which one or both partners turned away the other's bids, from complete disregard to overt hostility with phrases like, "Please stop bugging me, I'm busy."

Dr. Gottman then followed up with these couples six years later. It turns out that during his original experiment, the newlywed couples who ended up divorcing had "turned toward" their partners' bids only 33 percent of the time. In other words, these couples were not very interested in listening to each other. Meanwhile, couples who did not divorce had successfully "turned toward" each other's bids nearly 90 percent of the time. No matter what the conversation was, these couples responded positively to each other and were attentive listeners.

Dr. Gottman's data tell us that listening matters, no matter the situation. Whether you're in a heated argument or lounging on the sofa while reading a book, *listening matters.* But listening isn't just hearing: you need to demonstrate to your partner that you are engaged, attentive, and that you understand him. Use positive body language. Make eye contact. If you are on your phone or reading the news, set it down to listen to your partner. You don't just want to fully process what he is saying; you want him to know that you are interested.

A great question to ask yourself: "Am I really listening? Or am I just waiting for my turn to talk?" Think about this when you're having a conversation with your partner or if you're on a date. When you're talking, be sure you're talking *with* that person, not *at* him. Even if you're bursting at the seams to say something, take a breath, relax, and *LISTEN.* Resist the urge to interrupt. Once I get over my impulse that I need to say something, I feel relaxed and liberated. I think to myself, *Yes, I have something to say . . . but what's the hurry? What if I don't say it? It's okay. Just be calm and give him the gift of listening.* It's magic.

STAN TATKIN'S MORNING AND EVENING RITUALS

If you are experiencing difficulty developing a close bond in your relationship, the renowned clinician Dr. Stan Tatkin has some wonderful advice: Cultivate morning and evening rituals. As Stan notes, morning and evening often represent the most difficult times of the day. Lying in bed at night tends to make anxious people ruminate while those who are prone to depression often find waking up in the morning very difficult.

Stan recommends developing rituals for these troublesome moments of the day. "In my experience as a couple therapist," Stan writes in his book[35] Wired for Love, "partners who routinely make plans to meet each other in bed at night or put one another to bed (whether or not they cosleep) and who routinely wake together report much more relationship satisfaction than couples who do not."

If you live with your partner, going to sleep together is probably the best evening ritual. Maybe add in a back rub or a good audiobook—anything that you and your partner can do together, every night, and which you look forward to. If you don't live together, talk on the phone or Skype for a few minutes just before bedtime. If you're a worrywart who has difficulty falling asleep, evening rituals can turn what used to be a distressing

> *moment of your day into a safe, comfortable one. Instead of worrying about the future, you will be calm, comfortable, and safe in the moment with him.*

BE CURIOUS!

One way you can mitigate conflict and breakdowns in communication is to be curious. Ask your hubby why he feels a certain way when you sense the tension rising or a disagreement brewing. Ask him to explain when you don't understand (and even if you don't agree). Let him know that you care about what he is saying. By asking questions, you are re-wiring both your and partner's brain for intimacy. For example, a study conducted by psychologists[36] at the University of Buffalo concluded that just forty-five minutes of back-and-forth questioning can generate high levels of closeness and intimacy in the brain.

Of course, I know some women who ask so many questions that they turn their partners off. After all, who wants to be interviewed—or worse, interrogated? Again, watch your tone. There can be a fine line between curiosity and interrogation.

As you're asking questions and trying to better understand him, try very hard to suspend judgment of what you hear. Ask questions without going overboard. Be observant of him and his body language. Demonstrate that you are actively interested in why he feels a certain way. Now here's the harder part: Be sure that you not only listen to the answer, but that you don't summarily reject what you hear, even if you over-my-dead-body, *never-in-a-million-years* don't agree with it. And do be prepared for a response that goes beyond the scope of your original question. You might be opening Pandora's box a bit, but do your best to be patient and listen without judgment.

Sometimes with Sanjay I ask a quick question and expect an equally quick answer. In return I get a monologue, which can then become a lecture. It can be annoying, especially when I'm trying to squeeze in seventeen minutes of yoga in the living room before we have to take the kids to yet another birthday party. (Long gone are the days of ninety-minute yoga sessions in an actual yoga studio!) But I'm taking the long road here. Many times I do learn something new. A helpful, unexpected conversation can be the payoff from being open and curious.

WHAT IS IMAGO THERAPY AND HOW DOES IT WORK?

I am excited to delve into Imago Relationship Therapy, the magical communication framework developed by Harville Hendrix along with his brilliant, beautiful wife, Helen LaKelly Hunt. Harville has more than forty years' experience as an educator, therapist, clinical trainer, and lecturer. Helen is the founder and president of the Sister Fund, which is dedicated to the social, political, economic, and spiritual empowerment of women and girls. She is the author of *Faith and Feminism*, among other books, and was inducted into the Women's Hall of Fame for her leadership in the global women's movement. Together, Harville and Helen are the coauthors of many bestselling books and the cocreators of Imago Relationship Therapy, which helps couples, families, and professionals be more effective partners—whether in business or love. Harville and Helen's nonprofit organization, Imago Relationships International, has trained over two thousand therapists in more than thirty-five countries.

Imago Therapy is a straightforward seven-step process for safely communicating and connecting more deeply with your partner. Ideally you should introduce Imago to him during a low-stress time when you're both in an emotionally safe space together. While it's best to move forward together with Imago, you can use it unilaterally, too (more on that later). Here are the basic steps:

1. During a period of calm, express your desire to have a conversation with your partner. Be sure that he's ready, too. If he's not, ask again later, until he is in a neutral, open state. Be patient but persistent.

2. During the conversation, express your perspective on the situation by focusing on your own feelings. Instead of stating your issues with his behavior as fact, express them in the form of an opinion. For example, let's say he has a habit of interrupting you while you are talking. Instead of declaring "I don't like how you interrupt me all the time," try offering: "I feel that sometimes I don't have a chance to finish my thought before you jump in." Avoid blanket statements like "You're wrong," or "You always/ never do this." By putting the emphasis on yourself, you can preempt his defensive tendencies and keep the temperature of the conversation down.

3. Ask your partner to paraphrase what you said. Don't use an accusatory tone; you don't want him to think you are testing him on his listening ability. Again, bring the emphasis back to yourself. "I want to make sure that I was clear and that I didn't do a poor job of explaining."

4. Affirm when he accurately captures what you're saying. Use positive, open body language. Nod along with him, and try hard not to get upset or frustrated. If he didn't get it the first time, and he often will not, just try to say it again in a different way so he understands. *Do not get impatient with him.* This can go back and forth multiple times—couples have a remarkably tough time paraphrasing each other successfully. Patience and tenderness, please! Once he gets it right, or at least close enough for you, use a positive, affirming phrase like: "Yes, you captured what I was telling you or close enough!"

5. He should say: "Is there more?" In this next step, he should offer

you the opportunity and safety to go deeper. Go back to step 2 above and repeat until you are ready to say "No, that's all."

6. He should offer validation by saying something along the lines of "That makes sense," or "I can see that." Please note: This doesn't mean he agrees! He is just validating your perspective as your perspective. That is okay. This is not about your being right and his being wrong, and try to stress that as much as possible. All you want him to do is acknowledge that certain behavior causes you to feel this way.

7. At this point your partner is welcome to ask or discuss issues of his own. Maybe you occasionally behave in a way that troubles him. Allow him a safe space to bring it up, and don't react. Afford him the same patience and courtesy that he ideally gave you!

Please honor the sanctity of this framework by staying calm, using positive body language, resisting your desire to interrupt, and truly listening to what your partner is telling you. Try to keep your cool, even if what he is saying is very difficult to sit through. Think about opening your heart. Soften your face and try to force a smile. This will positively change your body chemistry and make you more receptive. Breathe deeply as needed.

When I said above that you can use this process unilaterally, I mean that even if you're not having a formal Imago dialogue, you can co-opt key features of the process that can really help your communication efforts. Ask things like, "Is there more?" Also be sure to paraphrase and provide validation. Sanjay and I have adopted these steps with many other relationships, including in our business discussions.

If you or your partner tend to avoid conflict or run away from confrontation, I urge you to push forward with this dialogue, even if it's extremely difficult. I find that so many people who are ordinarily assertive and proactive are the complete opposite with their partners when it comes to conflict. While these couples avoid blowout fights, they have countless "nothing" fights that serve as a proxy for much larger problems in the relationship. If you snap at him for not washing the dishes, are you annoyed because you genuinely hate clutter or are you piqued because he doesn't listen to you? Take a moment and reflect on any "insignificant" fights you've had recently and look for the underlying issue. This is what you need to address with your partner, and Imago dialogue can help.

Imago is wonderful in that it can help you ask for what you want—and offer a means for him to do so as well—in a way that helps foster safety. For example, let's say your partner is highly critical of you. When bringing it up to him, you can say something to the effect of: "I feel hurt by how you constantly criticize me. I would really appreciate if your feedback was more constructive and loving." Or, you can say, simply, "I would really love it if you praised me more frequently. That would feel really good."

Ideally he'll take the message to heart because he loves you, and he'll honor what you have sincerely asked of him—although you may need to remind him of this request several times before it becomes habitual for him. But remember that his challenging behavior is a part of who he is, and it's something you may have to make peace with because it probably will not go away completely.

> **"Peace is not absence of conflict; it is the ability to handle conflict by peaceful means."**
>
> —PRESIDENT RONALD REAGAN

Radical Acceptance is as much about him as it is about getting your own needs met. Asking for what you want, for what you need, and for what will feel great may be scary or awkward at first, but it is critically important. I know far too many women who feel too embarrassed or fearful to ask for what they want or what they feel they deserve. This is extremely common, but with many of us making the effort, it will change. Practice asking for what you want in the safety of your relationship, then bring it to other relationships in your life and be a champion for other women you know so that they, too, can strengthen their voices and build the confidence to become comfortable advocating for themselves.

TAKE THE HIGH ROAD!

I want to conclude this chapter by urging you to take the high road. This is an excellent communication tool that you can incorporate into your life as a mantra. If you remind yourself throughout the day to take the high road, or even invite this phrase into your meditation or journaling, you will reduce conflict in your relationship and promote greater harmony. I know this concept is not necessarily new. That said, it is not widely practiced. I've been astonished by the number of times I have prescribed this approach to couples in conflict and how they later exclaimed its tremendous success. As simple as they are, merely having these four words in your head on a routine basis changes your behavior over time—especially when you are about to lose your cool.

When you experience heated conflict and feel yourself turning into Medusa, when you feel you are heading down a path that will only lead to more hurt and anger, taking the high road will prove to be a godsend. As you learn to do this, you and your partner will communicate better and you will be creating more safety in the relationship. However, there's a good chance that from time to time you will still feel hurt or angry—maybe very angry. Yes, you will likely still fight. Yes, you'll be tempted to hit back. No matter how bad it gets, no matter how obnoxious he acts: *take the high road.*

Eventually calmness will become *almost* as instantly reflexive as a propensity to be bitchy or defensive. By simply ask yourself before you speak or react, "Am I taking the high road here?" You are much better able to respond rationally and thoughtfully. It is a powerful way to minimize hurt feelings and to build a stronger, safer relationship for the long run.

And you want to know what is really cool? Sanjay has also become much less reactionary. This is particularly helpful when I slip up! Instead of pouncing, Sanjay more frequently takes the high road in my stead. This is what being a couple is all about. We can really cover for one another because we much more frequently feel we are on the same team, not fighting a war of attrition over who is more right at any given moment.

Okay, we have just wrapped up step 3 and are officially more than halfway in your Radical Acceptance journey. Well done! Now that you have committed to just love him; learned to Stop, Reflect, Introspect; and embraced a host of tools and insights enabling you to communicate much more effectively (and fight less!), we will now tackle step 4: Love *All* of Him—Even the "Unlovable" Parts. This is a big, exciting step. You are ready. Let's go!

- Take a temporary time-out from an argument if it becomes too heated or consider doing things that say "I love you" when talking doesn't work.
- "Ego-check" yourself when what you're debating is ultimately about proving you're right. What will proving him wrong do for *your relationship*?
- Take the high road! The more you practice taking the high road and not reacting badly, the easier and more reflexive it will become.

RADICAL ACCEPTANCE: STEP 4

LOVE *ALL* OF HIM—EVEN THE "UNLOVABLE" PARTS

A T THIS POINT you have decided to love him. Now the key is to love *all* of him, even his so-called unlovable parts. There is no such thing as meeting him halfway when it comes to Radical Acceptance. There is no cherry-picking the parts of him that are attractive to you and discarding the rest.

I know what you're thinking: *How do I embrace his differences that are unappealing to me? Not to mention those that drive me completely bonkers?! How do I make peace with the parts of him that I find hurtful? How do I suspend judgment?* Maybe you're thinking: *How the hell am I ever going to love that weave of hair that has colonized his back? How can I always have his back if I can't even* look *at his back!*

Don't worry, I will show you.

Step 4 is the heart of the Radical Acceptance framework. This is where the proverbial rubber meets the road. But you're ready for it!

As we explored previously, when you judge him and his unlovable parts, you are most likely reacting to your own crap (to put it indelicately), at least somewhat. You will often find that your own vulnerabilities, fears, flaws, and judgments are being mirrored back to you in your partner's unlovable parts. You may also find that you are eliciting the worst out of him or inciting certain of his unlovable parts. Once you realize (and accept) this reality, you may even have a good laugh ("Ha! Good one, Mother Nature!")

In this chapter we will explore different preferences that may be challenging for you to accept, much less embrace. We'll also discuss what happens when your values differ. Can Radical Acceptance work in those scenarios? The short answer is: sometimes.

And thankfully, mercifully, you will find that it gets easier and easier as you attempt not just to love the challenging, prickly aspects of your partner, but eventually manage to extend them some tenderness and compassion. You will find in this chapter that there is some very compelling neuroscience that underpins the importance of doing exactly this.

Step 4 of Radical Acceptance offers you an exceptionally powerful framework for loving your partner long after you have shelved this book. It's hard work but it is *SO WORTH IT*. Do it for him, do it for yourself. And if you have kids, do it for them. The upside is immeasurable.

Let's start by exploring some of the common menacing, unlovable parts. There are three major categories that are problematic: difficult traits and behaviors, differing preferences, and differing values.

Difficult personality traits and behaviors. So much of the negative, scary stuff shows up here. We touched on some of these in Red Flags, but this is a good time to review them. Difficult personality traits include innate characteristics that are tough to put up with, such as being hypercritical, arrogance, depression, anger, boastfulness, flakiness, anxiety, self-doubt, laziness, hyperambition, obsequiousness, self-righteousness, pettiness, control issues, being overbearing, general jerkiness and negativity, and on and on.

Physical traits include his body shape, weight, height, too much or too little hair, and other forms of attractiveness that may impact how you feel about him. I focus principally on personality traits and behaviors, but knowing that things like back hair and physique can be real issues for people, I give a nod to them, too.

These challenging traits will vary, of course, but be prepared to accept that they will not go away. He's not getting any taller, after all, and that hair isn't growing back in the places you want it to. Meanwhile, that explosive temper can probably be managed, but in all likelihood, the urge for it will always be there. His chronic lateness or sloppiness is not something you can will away through cajoling, nagging, nor negotiating.

For many people, difficult traits and behaviors represent the hardest aspect of Radical Acceptance because they are often the most difficult to live with. Plus, in certain cases, there are seemingly "simple" solutions to many of them: He is always late—*Look! I found you a watch!* He really needs to lose twenty pounds—*We're going vegan!* He has a temper—*Why don't you look at this Xanax pamphlet?*

A lot of us control freaks out there love to find obvious solutions to problems, but it just doesn't work that way in relationships. Chances are that new planner and watch will sit unused and he'll only resent you for trying to change him.

Differing preferences. Differing preferences are, in my opinion, the easiest unlovable parts to accept. Differing preferences range from your typical *He loves sports, I love art*, to *He loves summer blockbusters, I love documentaries*, to *He loves missionary, I love kink.* These are generally the most manageable and the least threatening unlovable parts. Chances are you knew about these a long time ago yet you still stuck with him. They're not going anywhere.

You won't necessarily love his differing preferences, but through Radical Acceptance you can learn to embrace them by not judging them and ideally participating in them. You are showing him that you are both on the same team. You are in it together. In short, by accepting his preferences, you are saying: "I love all of you." And who knows? You might even grow to love pro wrestling. We will talk more in the next chapter about how to handle when his preferences are extremely challenging or perhaps even compromising to you.

Differing values. These can be harder to deal with but they can be manageable. Ultimately differing values can even be an asset in the relationship. Our values reflect who we are as individuals. They dictate how we treat people and how we expect to be treated. For some couples, differing values can mean politics. I once had a girlfriend tell me: "He's great, but he doesn't support abortion. How can I possibly love someone who doesn't respect my right to choose?" I know a couple who can't decide how to educate their children. One parent, an ardent liberal, believes in the importance of public education while the other wants to ensure the best possible education for their children by taking advantage of Houston's excellent private schools.

Differing values are tricky because it can be hard to accept his beliefs without feeling like you are undermining your own. If you accept his pro-life beliefs, does that mean you are abandoning decades of feminist progress? Does sending your kids to private school mean you are a terrible hypocrite? The short answer to all of these questions is no, but the longer answer is that there is a good chance you're looking at a difficult reconciliation process. Dr. Pat Love, the preeminent relationship expert,[37] will rarely tell a couple with conflicting values that the relationship won't succeed; rather, she'll tell them it's a "tough match." Nevertheless, sometimes differing values are just too much to overcome. Pat recently had a client who valued sexual exploration. He didn't fundamentally believe in monogamy. His wife, on the other hand, did. She wanted to have children and she did not want him sleeping with other women. Ultimately the marriage fell apart because these values simply could not be reconciled.

Fortunately, in less extreme scenarios, a person's values *can* be positively transferred to another person without any undermining. For example, I love my family and cherish time with them. But in Sanjay's upbringing, there was even more emphasis on family. After all of these years together, his family values have been transferred positively to me. Not without some challenges and still not to the degree that Sanjay places on them, mind you, but how I think about family has changed and now I prioritize it more thanks to our relationship.

. . .

Now I'm going to ask you to be honest with yourself about what those unlovable parts of him are. Then I'll help you figure out how to make peace with them.

REFLECTING ON YOUR RELATIONSHIP

Some key questions follow that I'd like you to answer in writing. Equally important, I want you to be cognizant about where you may be at fault, or at least exacerbating the problem. I ask you not to just gloss over these, but to really think about them. I want you to write them out, ideally by hand. Putting something on paper, even if you crumple it up and toss it in the trash a few minutes later, really adds insight into your thought process. It's a chance to see or understand something that was not previously apparent or that may seem much bigger in your head than it does on paper. Remember: brutal, beautiful honesty is your BFF in this process!

- What are his unlovable parts, i.e., what are his challenging traits, behaviors, preferences, and/or differences that could use some love or tenderness from you? What does he do that presses your buttons?
- If you were a close friend looking in on your relationship from the outside, what would you honestly say about him and the relationship? (This is a valuable chance to reflect more objectively about him!)

- If *his* best friend were to ask him what *your* challenging traits and behaviors are and how those impact your relationship, what would he say?
- What do you love about him? What initially attracted you to him? What have you grown to love about him more over time?

Okay—you have your list ready. *This is how I really feel about him.* I know how difficult that may have been, but it will ultimately help.

So . . . now what? You've acknowledged the problems, the unlovable parts—how do you actually go about dealing with them? First and foremost: Simply *consider* starting to love all of these unlovable parts, or at least commit to making peace with them. Picture yourself being okay with all of them, as ridiculous or unimaginable as that may seem. (I will eventually ask you to make it your mantra, but for now just sit with this as a possibility.)

You get to decide what you give your energy to. And what you do not. Remember, he is not the opponent. Your reaction is the opponent. When you commit to extending compassion to his unlovable parts and acknowledging that your partner is not the opponent, you will become less reactive. As you endeavor to show a little tenderness and understanding, these unlovable parts will not seem so threatening or powerful.

Many relationships are filled with judgment and resentment, and are thoroughly lacking in trust, warmth, and harmony. In truth, loving his unlovable parts is the only way the relationship will thrive, as tough and demanding as that may be. Sure, you can continue to judge and resist, but where does that get you? By loving his unlovable parts, through all that hard work, you'll build more trust, goodwill, openness, and empathy in your relationship.

If you are simply unable to make peace with his unlovable parts, you are back to step 1: Just Love Him (or Just Dump Him). If you can't love all of him, then you may want to question the viability of your relationship! Why be with someone that you need to judge? Why torture him? Why torture yourself?

Also, please do not gloss over an important part of the message here. If you can truly make peace with traits or behaviors that used to drive you crazy, cause big fights, cause you to withdraw and head for the hills, or cause you to nag or try to control him, the payoff for your own peace of mind and the health of your relationship will be immeasurable.

STARTING WITH YOU: WHERE YOU MAY BE AT FAULT AND WHERE YOU CAN BE PART OF THE SOLUTION!

I'm going to start off with a big ask. During your next fight, can you stretch yourself to empathize with him and try to understand where he is coming from? Even if you see horns sprouting from his head and you're ready to freak out. I urge you to try. Really try.

He's probably not wild about his unlovable parts, either. Sanjay knows he can be reactive; it doesn't give him joy to lose patience with me. I'm grateful when he extends some compassion to my defensiveness, too, for example, because I feel so much more understood and supported. I feel like I'm not alone with this icky, painful thing. Can you start to do the same thing for your partner?

Almost always, there are two sides to every story. Yes, it's true; even when he's doing that annoying thing he does. The ability not to take something at face value and not react to his anger or other repellent behavior, but instead attempt to understand the full picture, is incredibly helpful—not just with him, but with other relationships in your life, from friendships to coworkers.

Sanjay does a great job of this. For example, I'll tell him a story about a friend who is having a relationship issue, and he almost always plays the devil's advocate for the other person. All of a sudden we find ourselves arguing about another relationship we know very little about, one that has nothing to do with our own lives. This used to drive me bonkers years ago, but now I realize how enlightening these conversations can be. Sanjay's point has been that if all of us simply reinforce our friends' views, we are more likely to cause continued deterioration in the relationship, versus helping your friend see the other side (typically that of the absent party).

Believe me, I know it's easy to assume you know all the answers. However, what trips up so many couples is that they forget that there are many valid answers to the same questions. Remember the point that I featured previously about symbiotic consciousness? That we expect, basically, everyone to think like we do? (Oh, symbiotic consciousness: you evil temptress!) Don't fall into this ridiculously common trap—one I've fallen for more times than I care to say. It's a total mystery to me why this isn't more commonly known; it's a failure on so many fronts. But now you get to get it!

The baby's room might look nice in blue, but it also could look fine in green. Both work! You could serve one pancake at a time or you could put them in a stack in the oven and serve them all at once. You could put utensils in the dishwasher with the handles up or down. I use these examples because I know how common it is for tiny issues to be the cause of consternation and the emergence of "The Bickersons" in many relationships. Of course, then there are the actual substantive issues that also have multiple right answers. This has been a big challenge for Sanjay and me, as two controlling people. I have had to train myself to remember that his answer is often equally as valid as my answer—not necessarily what I prefer, but just different (and arguably not worse).

When two people each believe they know all the answers (and have none of the questions!), conversations devolve to talking *at* each other rather than *with* each other. And arguments end up the same way. Does that sound familiar? I can remember so many arguments with Sanjay when it seemed he just didn't *listen* to what I was saying. When I look back, I realize that maybe he did listen. He just didn't agree. Why was that so bad? We don't always need our partners to agree with us, but we do need them to listen and understand what we are saying.

Sure, you may have different ways of approaching situations. Squeezing the end of the toothpaste instead of the middle makes total sense to *you*, or not talking through the movie *would* make it easier for everyone to hear the dialogue. And maybe it would be easier to get your point across if he wouldn't interrupt you every five seconds. But you know what? You've come this far despite all that.

Start small if you need to. Just for today, do your best *not* to insist on your way or the highway. Inwardly, tell yourself that your way is not the *only* right answer. If you can't agree with his idea, try to at least understand his thought process. Then try to do this again tomorrow and then the next day.

Do your best to give him the benefit of the doubt, even with the little things. Lots of little things add up, after all! Trust me, he will feel that you are doing this. This will feel good and affirming to him. Sanjay and I have had a number of disagreements for this very reason. He would tell me that he did not feel trusted on a variety of little things because I would constantly disagree with him. I'd argue adamantly that my disagreeing with him did not translate to lack of trust, often to no avail.

But then I had a big "aha!" moment.

By frequently disagreeing with him, I was not giving him the benefit of the doubt.

What I finally understood was how this felt to him. I realized, in effect, I could be "right" and not continue to argue the point. This doesn't mean I no longer disagree with him. Rather, I try to dial back on disagreeing over the small things that don't really matter. The beautiful irony is that it has been a great exercise for me to cede some control. I feel empowered, wiser, and more loving because I am making a conscious effort to honor his feelings and to put our relationship first. I know to some readers this will raise red flags, that concession will sound a lot like defeat. I used to think like that, too. Now I know better.

CONTROL AND WHERE YOU MAY BE UNWITTINGLY AT FAULT

One of the most common culprits that can lead to negative judgment and conflict is the desire for control in a relationship. It's especially pernicious and pervasive because so many of us are hardwired to seek it. Personally, it's one of my biggest problems.

But here's the truth: controlling a relationship is an illusion. I want you to think about the degree to which you seek control in your relationship—or more specifically, seek control of your partner. For example, do you criticize little things such as how he dresses or how he loads the dishwasher? Do you insist on planning everything in the relationship from what he eats to where you go on vacation? Keep this in mind for now, as micromanaging your relationship can make him feel undermined, not to mention make it more difficult for you to love his unlovable parts.

I asked you to write out and reflect on your own unlovable parts. By being aware of them, you may be able to prevent some of your partner's unlovable traits from bubbling to the surface, or exacerbating them.

For example, do you tend to be controlling? Do you tend to nag him? I hate the word nagging (when in reference to something I am trying to communicate, anyway), but that may be his perception when you repeatedly tell him something. Do you tend to be dismissive or tuned out from him and tuned into your friends, the kids, your work, or anything else? Do you tend to be frequently critical of him (or his friends or family?) Or maybe your unlovable parts are less in relation to your partner but they drive him bananas nevertheless. Maybe you are sloppy? Disorganized? Chronically late? Spend too much money? Stubborn? A perfectionist? Thin-skinned? Easily stressed-out? Fairly negative? Indecisive?

Oftentimes a person will act aggressively or become angry because he feels lonely, emasculated, or that he is not measuring up. This creates a vicious cycle in a relationship, causing some of the most toxic aspects of his personality to surface. He might exhibit some bravado if he feels insecure in the relationship. He may withdraw because he doesn't want to be constantly nagged, criticized, or challenged. It's important to think about the following:

- The degree to which you might be provoking your partner's challenging or offending behavior. Whether it's your control issues or something in your tone, vibe, or body language communicating disapproval, there is a chance that you are a greater part of the problem than you realize.
- The possibility that his flaws trigger a disproportionately strong emotional reaction given your past, your fears, and your insecurities.
- Aside from the black-and-white red flags we talked about in the previous chapter, it's rare that one partner in a relationship is fully "wrong." Even in extreme scenarios like infidelity, there are usually two sides to any conflict.

Remember, Radical Acceptance does not mean swallowing the challenges he presents to you, nor does it mean taking the path of least resistance. You are not his subordinate. It is crucial to underscore that loving his unlovable parts does not mean you are going to be mute, and it does not mean you should not discuss the things that bother or upset you most. I absolutely urge you to be vocal about the challenges in your relationship and the aspects of his behavior you find upsetting.

Learning to make peace with and extend tenderness to his unlovable parts *will make you stronger*. Rather than acting from a place of weakness or scarcity, choosing to love all of him is a choice that comes from abundance, from wisdom, from compassion. Since this means letting go of judgment, control, and ego, it may feel like the exact opposite of that in the beginning. But it does get easier. You will feel a positive difference in your heart, your mind, and your body. You'll feel lighter, and you'll feel stronger. But as with training for a marathon, you won't get the high and the tremendous sense of accomplishment if you don't show up and do the work.

If you find that you're not able to come from a place from abundance, it is worth asking yourself why. Perhaps it's because, ultimately, you are not compatible—either because of any number of red flags or more minor deal-breakers that are preventing you from being energized by the relationship. That you must not ignore. Or maybe you're in a rough patch due to some external factor that you can reasonably see getting resolved and it's just a matter of hanging in there.

Perhaps it dates back to attachment issues from childhood or the fact that you lack role models for healthy partnership? If so, you may need to seek out professional therapy and/or other forms of healing to come to terms with this obstacle. Or perhaps it is because you are simply too stressed or too depleted due to other factors in your life. Do you feel burned-out or overextended at home and/or at work? If so, seriously think about what you can do to change this.

Whatever the answer, do your best to be honest and ask for the help you may need.

WIRING THE BRAIN FOR LOVE

I promised some more clarity for how you can love (or at least make peace with) his unlovable parts. Thankfully, neuroscience backs up this crucial component of Radical Acceptance!

During the introduction to this book we talked about some of the incredible research conducted by the one and only Dr. Helen Fisher. Using

MRI, she scanned seventeen people who had remained happily in love for an average of twenty-one years, seventeen who had recently fallen madly in love, and fifteen who had just been dumped. After comparing all of the participants, Dr. Fisher discovered that the most loving, long-term couples shared three common traits that weren't present with the other two groups.

First, she found these loving couples had numerous brain regions associated with the ability to control emotions, e.g. they don't freak out easily. Second, Helen found activity among the mirror neurons linked with empathy. Third, among the happiest couples, Helen discovered brain activity in the frontal cortex—an area of the brain that enables us to overlook the negative and accentuate the positive in other people. This is a phenomenon she calls "positive illusions." So what does her research tell us about how to practice Radical Acceptance, and more specifically, how to love unlovable traits?

Let's start with emotional control. I know this can be super hard, but as we talked about in depth earlier, your job is to *NOT REACT* to that annoying thing he says or does. Let's say he talks over you incessantly. You're having a discussion and he has this persistent, annoying, *infuriating* tendency to cut you off before you've made your complete point. You want to reach out and stuff a napkin in his mouth and shout, *"Let me finish!"*

It's true: you'll never love this part about him. But your job right now is to not freak out or appear injured, nor withdraw from him every time something like this happens. Stay calm; stay positive. Instead of yelling at him or being sarcastic, say: "I know you wanted to make your point right away, and I know that is the way you are. But I wasn't done making mine yet. Please give me a moment to finish." You may get to a place where you can even gently poke fun of this propensity and it can be something that unites you two rather than pushes you apart. You know you have made major progress when you're both so comfortable with the scary stuff that you can laugh about it together!

Remember, he may never change this behavior. You should assume he will continue to interrupt or be late or buy the wrong kind of detergent despite your very specific shopping list. He is wonderful in other ways, after all. This is a great time to reflect up on that list you composed of what you love about him—a good way to reinforce positive illusions! Think about how his lovable and unlovable traits are linked. It may be infuriating, but that knack for interrupting probably influences the aspects of his character you admire. He thinks quickly, he's decisive, he has strong opinions, he doesn't back down. In Sanjay's case, he is an extremely successful business leader who has achieved an enormous amount, in part, because that critical, exacting side of him provides energy and focus; it fosters progress and positive outcomes that would otherwise be mediocre or nonexistent. Plus, he's a Virgo. He can't shake his critical nature, even if he wants to! But his critical comments come from a good place of trying for a better outcome for both of us, although it may not seem like that at first glance.

In Helen's MRI studies, the happiest couples had the most activity in the brain regions linked with empathy, which lead to Helen's second revelation. Not only can the happiest couples exercise restraint when tensions rise, they can *empathize* with their partner. These couples can listen to and identify with their partners, even during arguments. One of Helen's colleagues,[38] the psychologist Mona Xiaomeng, took this research further when she conducted her own study, and scanned the brains of seventeen young men and women who were passionately in love. The same regions of the brain associated with romance lit up again, but then Xiaomeng returned four years later and repeated the experiment. Eight of the participants were still with the same partner, and this time the brain scans revealed something new: the ability to suspend both negative judgment and the tendency to overevaluate a partner. The couples who stayed together, in other words, had a heightened ability to let things go, empathize, and accept each other as they were.

Third, couples who remain "in love," for as long as several decades, also maintain positive illusions, or the ability to overlook their partners' bad parts and focus on the positive parts. The term sounds a bit like an oxymoron—doesn't *illusion* suggest something negative, that you are wrongly perceiving something that isn't there? Well, yes and no. The key is to develop the ability to overlook the negatives and focus on the positives. Train yourself to always search for his best parts. You may not be able to ignore that explosive temper, but you can still find the kindness in his eyes, or that he would go to the end of the earth for you, or that wicked sense of humor.

Helen told me about a man she was with for eighteen years. "He was really slow," she likes to deadpan. "Big-time slow. I spent my life looking over my shoulder wondering if he was there. He thought slowly, he talked slowly." Everything he did took ages and ages. As a New Yorker accustomed to operating at a million miles per hour, Helen found that it drove her crazy. But over time she realized that his leisurely nature brought out something beautiful:

> We'd go to the Metropolitan Museum [39] and he would look at a picture for the longest time. Then we'd go out to dinner and he would (slowly) describe to me so many things that I had missed in that painting.
>
> And almost every night for eighteen years he read to me out loud. More than two hundred books. Almost all of Shakespeare, Gibson, Chekhov, Shaw. The great books—everything from The Magic Mountain to Dickens. When we'd go on vacation we'd always discuss first what books and poetry we'd bring. So, I would say to myself: "Okay Helen, he's walking slowly now, but look what I get from that slowness."

This is where neuroscience is a godsend. Through practice, by regularly attempting to focus on his positive traits and not dwell on the negative ones, it gets easier. By practicing something again and again you effectively rewire your brain, creating new, desirable neural pathways.

Indeed, when Helen put couples into the brain scanners, she found that couples who scored the highest in marital-satisfaction questionnaires also exhibited deactivations in the ventral medial cortex, which is the brain region linked with assessing negativity. Meanwhile, couples who scored lower on the marital-satisfaction surveys had much higher activity in the ventral medial cortex. In other words, they were wired to focus on the negatives.

I know what you're thinking: It's all a matter of genetics, or simply a matter of those lucky ducks who magically found the perfect partners. (Don't believe that Disney myth!) Either you're wired to succeed in love or you're wired to fail at it, right? How can you *possibly* rewire your brain?

It has to do with neuroplasticity—your brain's ability to reorganize itself by forming new neural connections throughout your life. In other words, your brain changes itself based on how you train it. It's the same way stroke patients and victims of catastrophic head injury can regain the use of their mental and physical faculties with therapy, or how students who study intensely for long periods of time enlarge or activate a specific part of their brains. In one study, researchers at the University of London analyzed individuals studying for possibly the most difficult test in the world: the London taxi-driver certification. Prospective cabbies must study "The Knowledge" for months or years, memorizing London's twenty-five thousand labyrinthine, tangled roads and all businesses and landmarks on them. Flower shops, Laundromats—everything. The research team found that these drivers not only improved their memories, but the physical size of their hippocampi—the center for memory and emotion—actually got bigger. And those who had been driving the longest had the largest increase in size. Similar studies have been performed with medical students and other people required to memorize a large amount of information.

Aside from memorization, learning new behaviors can change your brain in many ways. But don't worry, you don't have to become a London cabbie to learn to put up with his chronic lateness or his infuriating obsession with professional wrestling. Neuroplasticity studies demonstrate how the brain can adapt to a wide degree of stimuli, even psychological disorders.

While partnering with someone and hoping to change them is a recipe for disaster, you must be willing *to change yourself*. Practicing Radical Acceptance, and learning to love his unlovable parts, means you are going to change yourself in positive, powerful ways. You are going to stretch and grow, big time.

While your heart clearly needs to be in it, your brain is a powerful resource in your relationship. Neuroscience is on love's side, after all. It doesn't matter how old you are. You can do this. That said, it is going to be a process. You're going to need to summon your highest wisdom and cultivate a strong emotional maturity within yourself.

Learning to love his unlovable parts is not a quick fix. You'll mess up and you'll overreact. You'll get angry or upset. You may even feel hate toward parts of him along the way. That is natural and okay. The key is to know you're in it for the long run. In fact, the hard work you're doing is paving the way for a loving, happy long run together.

Remember to extend lots of compassion to yourself, too, along the way! Remember when you examined his unlovable parts and then linked them to traits you admire and love? Do the same with yourself! I know my unlovable part is a tendency to be overly defensive. But you know what? I also stand up for myself and for others, and I never back down when the going gets rough. Now think about your unlovable parts. What positives can you extract from them? You'll find it much easier to accept his unlovable parts if you can learn to accept your own!

AT LAST: READY FOR ACTION!

Drumroll please . . . the time has come. I want you to commit to the overarching Radical Acceptance framework and make this your mantra:

I radically accept you. I love all of you, even your unlovable parts. I have given you a bunch of tips leading up to this point, and more will follow, but it's time to cross the Rubicon and simply start loving all of him. That's really where the magic and power lie.

I want you to say this to yourself again and again. Say it out loud. Write it down. Sing it in the shower. Commit to making Radical Acceptance your default mode. You are, in effect, saying, "Okay, bad temper or critical nature or obsession with sports or hypersensitivity or whatever the heck 'it' is, I'm going to extend some compassion to you. You are no longer going to have the power you used to have. Now sit the f*ck down because you're being radically accepted."

Go back to the list you made at the beginning of this chapter and go through every negative point. Tell each and every one, "I have the upper hand now." Think about how those negative points have a beneficial side. Then go through every positive trait, everything you love about him, and prepare yourself to focus much more on those wonderful things. You are creating positive illusions. Overlook the negative and accentuate the positive. Even during the worst fights, look for these positive traits. They are always there, even if you have to dig deep for them at times.

This is your task right now. Don't pretend his horrible snoring or his occasional indecision or his juvenile jokes do not exist. Don't delude yourself that they will go away magically or that one day you'll wake up and love it all. Instead, say to yourself that you will make peace with them. Fighting his unlovable parts—including resisting or resenting them—will only make you feel worse. Let go of them so they can let go of you.

No, you don't like his stubbornness, and you never will like his stubbornness. Instead, I urge you to get to know it, to know what might be behind it. I urge you to show this part of him tenderness and compassion rather than resent and reject it. Extend empathy to his stubbornness by accepting that it's a part of who he is. Then create a positive illusion by linking that stubbornness to a positive trait you love—maybe his loyalty or unwavering commitment?

. . .

In my and Sanjay's case, our individual shortcomings have not miraculously gone away, but they have become greatly diminished and they no longer have the power to push us apart like they used to. In fact, what's amazing about our Radical Acceptance journey is that it has enabled us to have much more of a sense of humor about where there used to be so much conflict. We know we are on the same team.

By continuing to practice emotional control, we have learned how to do a much better job keeping our cool when either one of us irritates the other. By learning to be more empathetic, we have become more adept at seeing the other's side of the argument and understanding how the other feels. We both practice positive illusions: I focus on the parts of him that have never gone away, the parts I was so head over heels in love with and still am—his brilliant mind, his big heart, his endless charisma, his generous spirit, his wonderful sense of humor. And he will tell you that he still loves my honesty, perseverance, sense of fun, and love of life. Yes, of course, we still do fight sometimes. But these instances are much less prevalent. What is much more dominant is how we love each other—flaws, shortcomings, and all.

I noted at the beginning of the book that Radical Acceptance is not about instant gratification, that you should not expect rapid reciprocation. That said, you should expect to eventually experience greater harmony in your relationship. There may be some rough edges that persist, but generally you deserve to feel more loved. I am grateful to share more about how Radical Acceptance has managed to bring out the best in Sanjay. His kindness, generosity, sense of humor, and fun-loving nature are in abundance more than ever. These traits were always there, of course, but now they routinely dominate our interactions. I have seen more patience and even more compassion and understanding emerge from him—with me and with others he interacts with. Indeed, I believe the improvements in our marriage have had a meaningful ripple effect elsewhere in his life. They certainly have in mine.

As a result, he is much less critical of me. He is more affectionate, more complimentary, and more supportive. We experience more emotional and physical intimacy. He is less judgmental and more tuned in. Sanjay may never totally understand my hang-ups, but he is more sensitive toward them—and that's what matters. He is also more appreciative of my efforts. We love being together. It feels great.

Thankfully, our increased harmony positively impacts our little boys. Like Sanjay and me, our kids are hams, so there's tons of goofiness to go around. They see our affection and kindness and are drawn into it. I know that one day they will offer the same gift to their own significant others.

To wrap up this chapter I want to tell you a funny story. I was leaving an event that I was attending with my friend Heather, and we began saying our good-byes. Then Heather looked at me and put her hands together in the prayer position. But instead of saying "namaste"—the Hindu greeting meaning, roughly, "the peace and god in me sees the peace and god in you"—she said, "namascray." Then she gave a solemn bow and said: "The crazy in me honors the crazy in you." We laughed our heads off.

It was a brilliant twist on the ancient Hindu greeting, which is meant to be respectful of everyone you meet, no matter what. I love this twist because everyone has a little crazy in them. Your crazy is okay and you don't have to hide it. That's one of the things that I have sought for YourTango to do as a media company: to help our audience feel like their crazy is okay and to love one another (and themselves) despite—or maybe even because of—their own personal crazy.

And it's the same way I want your relationship to be. Embrace his crazy, embrace your crazy, and love him without judgment. It feels great. Why? Because judgment and negativity are toxic. Worse, they are contagious. They fester and snowball, especially in the absence of praise and appreciation. To suspend judgment and negativity is to liberate yourself. You are no longer suppressing. You are accepting. I cannot adequately describe what a beautiful feeling that is.

If everyone could do a little more of this for each other, the world would be a better place.

- Actively give him the benefit of the doubt, especially during fights. Reflect on what may be causing you to feel especially sensitive or vulnerable. Most likely, he is not trying to push your buttons on purpose.
- Embrace positive illusions! Focus on your partner's best parts and learn to overlook the negative. Also, try to see how his negative parts help make his positive parts so wonderful (and vice versa).
- Extend compassion and empathy to yourself, especially to your unlovable parts. You deserve tenderness and understanding. The more you can love yourself, the more you'll have to offer everyone else in your life that is important to you.
- Remember: Radical Acceptance of yourself and your partner springs from abundance and grace. It makes you stronger and more resilient. Choose to replace judgment with compassion. You get to decide what you give energy to!

RADICAL ACCEPTANCE: STEP 5

APPLY THE PLATINUM RULE AND MAKE HIM YOUR PRIORITY

WE'VE ALL HEARD of the Golden Rule: "Treat others as you wish to be treated." It's a solid, catchall code of ethics that provides a reliable frame of reference for how to treat others. But when it comes to love, romance, and long-term relationships, the rule of reciprocity only governs half of what matters in a relationship. Well, now we're going to take that rule one powerful step further. Behold! The Platinum Rule: "Love others as *they* wish to be loved." Most of us practice the Golden Rule with the best of intentions. It makes total sense. The Platinum Rule, however, is even more effective because it is predicated on knowing what makes your partner tick—and then acting on it. After all, what you need from a relationship isn't necessarily what he needs. The Platinum Rule flips the Golden Rule on its head, and demands that in order to get the most out of your relationship, you've got to love your partner the way *he* wants to be loved, not just the way *you* want to be loved. (Aha! Big difference.)

You may feel the most loved when you're showered with gifts, fancy dinners, and compliments, but he may feel loved with a home-cooked meal and movie night on the couch with lots of snuggling. Remember, *love* is an action word—the Platinum Rule is that maxim on steroids. It asks, "What does your partner want? What makes him feel loved?" Practicing the Platinum Rule means you are grounded in abundance. But you may find yourself feeling introspective, looking within to understand where your resistance to his desires is coming from. This can be hard at first, but it gives you a wonderful chance to let go of the hurts, feelings of scarcity, or misconceptions that only damage your relationship. You become *more* empowered as you practice the Platinum Rule.

In this chapter, we'll explore lots of ways to practice the Platinum Rule, including how to be more in tune with his wants and needs—without feeling like a feminist's nightmare. We'll touch upon your different "love languages" and help you realize that what makes him feel loved may be very different from what makes you feel loved. These differences may be quite considerable, so practicing the Platinum Rule may involve something much more dramatic than, say, agreeing to watch baseball during the playoffs or cooking at home on the weekends.

The Platinum Rule will ask you to consider doing things with a good attitude that you may not like or agree with. Most of us have to work really hard to stretch beyond our own understanding, preferences, proclivities, and, let's face it, selfish inclinations. Translating these into action on behalf of another adult is even harder. But this is what makes the Platinum Rule so powerful.

Please note that I would *never* advocate that you do something that goes against your morals or makes you very uncomfortable. No one who truly loves you should ask this of you.

It must be said way up front: initiating sex, or at least not rebuffing his advances, is often a key Platinum Rule ingredient. Okay, time for a huge, sweeping generalization: Many women can go without sex relatively easily, especially as they get older and feel considerable stress and exhaustion due to life's endless demands. Most men cannot, especially when they are younger. Men's testosterone drops as they age, typically curbing their libido. But, independent of gender and age differences, unless both of you are record-winning low-libido people, having sex regularly is really, really important to maintaining a close bond. Yes, even when you feel tired, grumpy, bloated, or bored. We'll talk about tips for improving your sex drive in part 3 of the book.

You might also find yourself wondering: *Can I go overboard with the Platinum Rule? What if he does not reciprocate? At what point is he just taking advantage of me?* I will address these concerns and lay them to rest.

The Platinum Rule implicitly means making him a priority. Your partner needs to feel highly valued by you and believe, with every fiber of his being, how important he is to you. It is easy to say "I love you," but actions speak louder than words. This is your chance to prove you mean what you say. And be honest with yourself: Isn't this what you want and expect from him?

If your inner feminist is seeing red lights flashing right about now, please just trust me here for a second. I have done considerable research on this topic. Not feeling valued or prioritized by one's partner is among the top two causes for discord, marital dissatisfaction, and divorce. (The other is faulty communication.) Taking each other for granted in a long-term relationship is practically an epidemic. Conversely, the couples who mutually feel highly valued and prioritized experience much more fulfillment from the relationship.

I am often asked about how married, working mothers find balance and keep their marriages strong. My answer is simple: Put your husband first! And then I wait for the aftershocks to wear off before I explain that it is not a zero-sum game, nor am I advocating for submissiveness or a return to 1950s-era gender roles. Rather, prioritizing your partner is based in sound logic—and science! Think about how you devote yourself to master the piano, earn a promotion, receive an advanced degree, or take care of your kids. Doesn't your partner deserve to be in the same league? Sanjay would grouse that he's tenth on my list—always with a smile—but I also knew there was hurt in this tough-to-hear truth. I do a much better job of making him feel he is my priority, along with our family, my business, and (it must be said) this book!

An ongoing stream of small gestures goes a million miles toward bridging the priority gap. Commit in your heart and in your mind to make him a priority—and to think about how you can communicate this to him regularly through your words and actions. Regular words of gratitude and appreciation also go a very, very long way.

Men often need to be needed. Most women have an innate capacity to be nurturing and caring. John Gray agrees.[40] "Women are the best appreciators," he told me. "They're the fans. They're the support. That's the female side. When women can provide Radical Acceptance, a man knows he can feel safe, that he can be himself, and that he will be loved just the way he is. That's what brings out the best in a man."

Traits that are typically considered "feminine"—the instinct to nurture others, for example—has enormous value in the relationship. This may be hard to hear because we are conditioned to believe that acting female is somehow lesser, that caretaking, and being warm and supportive, signals weakness. No. Those impulses should not be suppressed in an effort to prove you are equal, or to avoid becoming calcified into a stereotypical, patriarchal arrangement wherein he is dominant and you feel a duty to cater to him. *Nooooo.* By embracing your propensities to be compassionate and attentive, *you* are making the relationship stronger. Needless to say, there is WAY more to you than this!

Here's the thing. If your partner feels valued—really and truly—your relationship will have a strong foundation that can withstand many other weaknesses. Not only will this enormous display of love likely come back in a big way to you, but you will feel *REALLY GOOD* when you practice the Platinum Rule.

Before we go any further, let's find out how you're doing with the Platinum Rule. You know what that means: Time for a quiz!

THE PLATINUM RULE QUIZ

This quiz will help call into focus the ways in which you are already living in tune with the Platinum Rule, and the areas where you may have opportunities to improve. Note that not all of these possible answers are likely to describe your response perfectly, or constitute a scenario that readily applies to you. I understand that your response to each question may differ based on the circumstances, but I ask you to please choose the answer that is most representative of how you would likely behave in that particular situation.

- If my partner wants to do an activity that I don't like (for example, bowling, watching a "guy movie," shopping for electronics, a pub crawl, sports event, concert, dinner with his friends, etc.), I:

  1. Suggest he do it without me. Really, do we need to be together *every* day?
  2. Probably go along with it, but I'd have a hard time not reminding him that I don't want to be there.
  3. Put up a degree of resistance at first, but come around to the idea eventually. That said, I'll probably spend most of the time on my phone.
  4. Go along with a good attitude and have fun. After all, it's time together.

- If my partner and I have a free weekend, I:

  1. Suggest a few things I want to do, and try to persuade him to do them.
  2. Go along with what he wants, per usual, feeling kind of annoyed the whole time.
  3. Offer my ideas, listen to his, and then try to find a compromise so we both get what we want.

4. Suggest something that I know he'll enjoy, even if I would pre-fer to do something else. I know this will make him happy.

- When he tries to talk to you, what is your typical response?

  1. He often tries to talk with me while I am busy, so I often find that I have to ignore him.
  2. It depends on what I am doing and what he's talking about. I probably tune in to him about half the time.
  3. If he is talking about something I'm interested in, I politely ac-knowledge what he is saying and go back to what I was doing
  4. I readily tune in and show genuine interest in what he is saying, even if I am trying to focus on something else.

- I love my Sunday morning yoga routine, so when my partner says he wants to stay out extra late on Saturday night, I:

  1. Smile and say, "Have fun!" and leave him out with our friends. I need the shut-eye and he should understand.
  2. Agree to stay out, but I'll probably spend the whole time think-ing about getting home.
  3. Agree to stay out for an extra half hour, but then make it clear that I need to get to sleep.
  4. Smile and offer to buy the next round of drinks. I'll either blow off yoga or go with a lot less energy than usual; either way, we had fun together.

- How would he rate how kind I am to him?

  1. He would say that I'm rarely kind to him.
  2. He would say that I'm sometimes kind to him.
  3. He would say that I'm frequently kind to him.
  4. He would say that I'm always kind to him.

- It's holiday time and our families live far apart. This year he wants us to go to visit his family as they are also celebrating a special birthday or anniversary. How would I handle his request?

  1. I would pick a fight about why we should visit my family and insist that we find a way to see them regardless of any other traveling we choose to do.
  2. I would do what matters most to him, but make it clear that this wasn't my choice and that I'm not happy.
  3. I will do what he wants and be a good sport to him, but you can bet that behind closed doors I'll be complaining about it to my closest friends.
  4. While I would prefer to be with my family, I'll go with a good attitude, bringing gifts and trying to have fun with everyone while I'm there.

- Do I know what he wants from me and if so, how willingly do I give it?

  1. No, I really don't know what he wants from me. He can be so difficult.
  2. I don't think about it much. I just try to get along with him!
  3. I have a decent idea about what he wants, and I try to give it to him when it works.
  4. Yes, I have a clear picture of what he wants from me and I give it to him readily.

- How often do I either initiate sex or readily accept his advances?

  1. Never
  2. Sometimes
  3. Frequently
  4. Always

- How do I rate myself in terms of the active steps I take to express my love to him?

    1. Does doing his laundry count?
    2. That's what birthdays, anniversaries, and Valentine's Day are for!
    3. I try to do special things for him when it's convenient or when I am inspired.
    4. I express my love for him in all sorts of ways, regularly and with a full heart.

- If he does or says something I don't like, how do I respond?

    1. I roll my eyes and tell him what an idiot he is.
    2. I make a face and think he's an idiot but don't share my feelings completely.
    3. I feel my blood pressure rise and feel hurt or defensive, but don't make a big deal about it.
    4. I pause, take a breath, and think about whether I want to engage with this. Then I either let it go or say something to the effect of, "Honey, I can see your point of view but I would love to share my perspective on this."

- When it comes to chores or responsibilities we both have a stake in (financially or in terms of time/energy required), I:

    1. Keep track of what he's done and remind him when I have done more.
    2. Keep an eye on what each of us is doing. I try to keep it even but I don't make a big deal out of when he's not pulling his weight.
    3. Mostly step up to the plate and even go the extra mile but occasionally will remind him that he needs to do more.

4. Willingly do what is required of "us"—I trust he'll never take advantage of me. We are a team.

- Which sounds most like a conversation I've had with your partner in the last twenty-four hours?

1. Why didn't you put the kids to bed on time? Take out the garbage? Put away the milk? Pick up your dishes? Pay the cable bill? Why do I have to do everything myself?
2. Thanks for picking up those groceries, but you always forget to get the right brand of coffee. Please try to remember next time.
3. Thank you, honey, for putting the kids to bed/making dinner/fixing that lamp, etc. I really appreciate that.
4. You are brilliant/handsome/wonderful/hilarious . . . I love you dearly and am so grateful to have you in my life.

Now it's time to tally it up. Score yourself by adding together the numbers that precede the answers you chose.

12–20: You are "Platinum Rule challenged." There are a variety of thorny issues in your relationship and possibly other ongoing challenges in your life. Be very honest with yourself and determine whether these issues in your relationship lie with him or whether you play a significant role. It's possible you are with the wrong person, which is why it is so hard for you to practice the Platinum Rule—you don't feel he deserves your love. Think about whether you truly want to commit to him. If the answer is yes—wonderful! But you have a lot of work to do. Take small steps every day to practice the Platinum Rule. A little goes a long way, especially if he isn't used to your going the extra mile for him. It gets easier. If you are not committed, I urge you to give yourself a finite period of time to determine whether you can commit. If you cannot, you should part ways. Remember: just love him or just dump him.

21–30: You appear to be dealing with some issues around how you express your love, and you and your partner may be slightly disconnected. It is worth looking in your heart and asking whether you are truly committed to this relationship. If the answer is yes, hallelujah! That's a great start, but you have some real work to do to. When you feel there is friction, judgment, and resistance with your partner, I urge you to ask yourself, "What's really going on here?" Is it your partner, or is it you? Has doing your best to love him the way he wants to be loved simply not occurred to you? Or is there a frustration that has prevented you from practicing the Platinum Rule more regularly and easily? You may love him, but you're not necessarily showing it with your actions. Start with being kind and tuned into your partner every day, then over time build up to the more generous forms of the Platinum Rule.

31–40: You are doing well—nice job! But as you probably are already aware, there's room for improvement. Think about how you can be more generous and more aware of your partner and his needs. Then ask yourself, "Where do I feel resistance when practicing the Platinum Rule?" You are good at compromising and doing your part to make the relationship equitable. You may be in a bit of an accounting mode—that is, keeping score to make sure both partners' desires are met. That's not a bad thing, but try to let go of the need to have that balance and control, even just a little bit. Over time, keeping score can lead to resentment or feelings of obligation. Love him and do things for him because you want to, not because it's your turn. Commit to small measures every day, but also commit to some bigger ones—especially where you are feeling reluctant. When you overcome that a time or two, you will feel liberated and empowered—and your partner will too!

41–48: You are rocking the Platinum Rule—well done! You clearly get the value of prioritizing your partner, tuning in to him, and going to great lengths to treat him with kindness and as he'd like to be treated. (Do you want to help me write my next book?) You're in the zone! Keep that love flowing. Just make sure you're also being prioritized by him and that you aren't afraid to ask for what will make you feel loved and valued.

If you don't love what these answers reveal about how you treat your partner or the state of your relationship, the good news is that with greater awareness comes a powerful opportunity to make better, more loving, more expansive choices.

GETTING STARTED WITH THE PLATINUM RULE

Without the underpinning of Radical Acceptance, the Platinum Rule will offer only a fraction of its full potential to your relationship. Even if he loves a home-cooked meal, your special rigatoni recipe will have a tough time going the distance if you are regularly judging him, nagging him, avoiding him, fighting with him, or dismissing him.

Applying the Platinum Rule means being proactive, generous, and flexible in your relationship; it means practicing kindness and minimizing negativity and criticism; it means doing things for him that you don't necessarily love to do but you do for his sake; it means really trying to understand your partner and honoring your differences. When you are truly living the Platinum Rule, you don't just passively go along with whatever your partner wants and become resentful, either—you communicate without judgment or criticism when something isn't working. You also don't have an obligation to do everything he wants to do, nor must you honor his every whim. Prioritizing him DOES NOT mean subordinating yourself!

In step 3 we looked at the "masters versus disasters" research conducted by John Gottman, which explained how kindness and empathy are paramount in successful relationships. But the key is that being kind doesn't always mean being sweet and perfectly happy. "Kindness doesn't mean that we don't express our anger," John's wife, Julie, also a psychologist, explained to *The Atlantic*, "but the kindness informs how we choose to express the anger. You can throw spears at your partner. Or you can explain why you're hurt and angry, and that's the kinder path."

John and Julie's research, along with countless other studies, consistently demonstrates that simple kindness is the glue that holds relationships together. As the Gottmans' research shows, kindness can take the form of giving your partner the benefit of the doubt—such as chalking his tardiness up to bad traffic instead of an inherent disregard for you—as well as sharing in his delight. That last point is very important. As Emily Esfahani Smith points out in *The Atlantic,* being there for each other when things are going well is actually more important for relationship quality than being there when things are bad. How one partner responds to the other's good news can greatly impact the relationship.

So, if your boyfriend shares good news with you, be sure to *actively engage with* his joy. Let's say he aced his LSAT for law school. Clearly, that high score is a milestone for him. Instead of passively congratulating him while texting on your phone, set aside whatever you are doing and give him a nice big kiss. Demonstrate that you care about what brings him joy. Take him out to dinner to celebrate. It doesn't matter what the achievement is—if it's a big deal for him, then make it a big deal for you.

As is the case in the previous steps, someone has to take the lead. Let it be you who goes the distance and introduces the Platinum Rule into your relationship. Unless you (or he!) are already doing a bang-up job with applying the Platinum Rule, you get to take true initiative to bring this enlightenment into your relationship.

WHAT MAKES HIM FEEL LOVED?

In *The Five Love Languages*, Gary Chapman writes beautifully about how different people speak and value five primary expressions of love. Expressing love through gift-giving is one of these five love languages, along with the gifts of physical touch, affirming words, quality time, and acts of service. Knowing which of these languages are most important to your partner will help you successfully practice the Platinum Rule. Within that framework, here is a sample list of things that can make a big difference:

Physical touch: Snuggling; holding hands; stroking his hair; touching his face; having sex; a hand, foot, shoulder, or body massage.

Quality time: Going to a sporting event, concert, or other form of entertainment while being genuinely engaged; leisurely sharing a meal or drink—just the two of you; going for walks or a drive together; doing a project together; playing cards or another game together; anywhere you can be together—and not distracted—tuned in to one another.

Gifts: Homemade gifts of course have their own special magic, but plenty of love can come from gifts thoughtfully procured from Henri Bendel, Macy's, Tiffany & Co., or that wonderful boutique or sports store down the street.

Affirming words: Sharing words of love, praise, confidence, gratitude, and appreciation. You can write him a love letter, sweet text, or original poem. Better yet, draft a list of fifteen specific things you love about him and read it out loud to him!

Acts of service: Doing his chores when it's not your turn; organizing his closet; cleaning out his home office; putting together a photo collage; detailing his car; packing his lunch; ironing his suit; running his errands. If he is religious or spiritual, going to church or temple without grumbling. (Bonus points for asking questions and really engaging.)

Here are some more ideas for practicing the Platinum Rule:

- Giving him his own space without making him feel guilty or bad about it.
- Spending focused time with his parents, siblings, and other family members.
- Flattering him in front of his friends or colleagues in genuine, authentic ways.
- Planning something special with his friends or family—or just for the two of you.
- Going shopping to help him pick out some clothes that look good on him.
- Picking up his favorite beer or wine on the way home and drinking it together.

Remember that the smallest gestures and kindnesses matter. They cost nothing or next to it, but they are immeasurably valuable for both of you. What can you do to make him feel truly loved? Is the way to his heart through his stomach? Through listening to loud alternative music together? Through physical activities? Of course, you don't have to do everything he would love from you. That would likely be impossible and exhausting. The key is to know what will make him feel loved and to do it with enough frequency.

Remember: when you provide love and kindness to him, you provide it to yourself. If you have children, they'll also take note of the small ways you care for one another. You're setting an example that will positively impact how they interact with their future significant others.

Hanna, a close friend of mine, has a tradition with her boyfriend, Gerald. Every Christmas he comes over and she makes him dinner. Then he reads literature to her for hours. They have read everything! It's an important tradition to them both, but especially for Gerald. She recounted to me that there have been a few Christmases in which she had been so exhausted from work and travel that she was nearly cross-eyed and just wanted to sleep. But she knows that this tradition is very important to Gerald, and so she has always made it a priority, even when she'd prefer to pass out in bed.

I can easily connect with Hanna's story. Sanjay loves my homemade pesto pasta, which, frankly, is a real stretch to call "homemade"—it's a package of pasta and a jar of store-bought pesto tossed with fresh spinach. (I lovingly call it "assembled.") I'm not the world's greatest cook. In fact, the kitchen is just about the last place I want to be. But I know the way to Sanjay's heart is through his stomach. When he raves about how my pesto pasta is his favorite meal, I feel good. I know it's not because it's the most gourmet meal he's ever had. Rather, it's because I put aside the 342 other things on my to-do list to create something I know he loves. I used to laugh and wave away his compliments—after all, almost anyone can boil a box of pasta—but then I realized this wasn't about the food so much as the gesture. Sanjay was thanking me for the love, care, and attention I was feeding him.

Plus, I always get to say, "This was made with love." Because it was.

. . .

Okay, so how can the Platinum Rule be pivotal? Here's one of my favorite Radical Acceptance stories. It is from my friend Rachel, whom I referenced previously.

Rachel was dating Ethan at the time, who, as you may recall, was a practicing Orthodox Jew. Rachel was not. Rachel had fallen deeply in love with Ethan and had told him as much, but he had never said "I love you" back to her. Rachel was a bit put off by this but was taking the long-term view and just kept doing her part in the relationship. She wound up reading an essay I had written about Radical Acceptance. I am glad to say that Rachel took the Platinum Rule to heart, big-time!

Rachel decided that she'd proactively plan to go to the temple and seek out activities within the Orthodox community as a way to get to learn about Ethan's faith and get to know people in his community. After doing some research and planning a couple of these outings, when Rachel told Ethan she loved him, he (finally!) said it back.

Such a beautiful story. Kind of lays down the gauntlet, doesn't it?

. . .

While Sanjay does appreciate my, ahem, "cooking," this is relatively easy for me to do. It still counts, of course, but practicing the Platinum Rule in the face of differing values can be a whole other ball game. It may fundamentally come down to understanding his needs and values—and how they may be different from yours. When your values differ, to practice the Platinum Rule will most likely mean overcoming some stiff internal resistance.

I'd like to share a story that demonstrates the power of the Platinum Rule when one partner is willing to look within and understand that a huge obstacle in her relationship can come down to differing values. In this case, it was a fundamental difference around money and spending.

My longtime friends Ruth and Beth are lovely, smart, caring, fun, fabulous people who've been together for about twelve years. They have a great deal in common, including, recently, a baby daughter. But they come from the opposite ends of the spectrum when it comes to money.

For Beth, a penny saved is a penny earned. She was raised by fiscally conservative, middle-class parents from Ohio. She worked her way through middle and high school with various odd jobs, from paper routes to mowing lawns. She paid for her own college and began a successful career as an IT expert after graduating from the University of Chicago. Now a successful executive, she does well, but never misses an opportunity to save money, such as refilling her old water bottle rather than buying a new one, seeing movies early in the morning, and so on.

Ruth was brought up by a family that spent lavishly on cars, jewelry, international trips, and dining out. Her parents, both successful lawyers, paid for Ruth's private-school education and never pressured her to make money. They had scraped and clawed and wanted to give their daughter an easier, more fun-filled life in which she could pursue what she enjoyed rather than feeling pressured to make ends meet.

Ruth found Beth's conservative nature difficult to accept. Ruth was accustomed to being pampered by her parents with expensive gifts. She grew up observing her father giving her mother fine jewelry and other luxuries. Thoughtful gift giving meant a lot to Ruth.

While the two women were truly in love, this difference in spending and gifting had become a painful wedge in their relationship. Beth could not fathom why Ruth would want to spend so much money on expensive restaurants and other luxury items, and Ruth did not understand why Beth wouldn't want to spend the fruits of her labor on the woman she loved, or at least in ways that they could both enjoy.

This had always been an area of some tension, but it was getting worse. Beth held the purse strings and thought Ruth was being childish. Ruth felt Beth was cheap. What pushed Ruth over the edge was Beth's flat-out rejection of her desire to visit Madrid for their once-a-year vacation. They ended up renting a cabin in Michigan instead. Not surprisingly, the trip was a disaster. Both of them returned angry and hurt.

Ruth called me soon afterward, still very upset. I told her she had to accept this difference between them, and that it didn't mean that Beth didn't love her deeply. It's just that Beth was wired to save and didn't value the experiences and luxury items as Ruth did.

Still upset, Ruth suddenly accused me of taking Beth's side. But as we spoke, the concept of Radical Acceptance really began to sink in. Ruth started to understand that Beth wasn't deliberately trying to deprive her of love by withholding material items. Rather, Beth was attached to another idea of what a partner does in a relationship, based on her own upbringing. There was no question Ruth loved Beth—and she recognized that her partner was amazing, fun, and fascinating to be around.

Ruth also realized that by continuing to pine for these things, she was creating more conflict in the relationship. She decided to accept Beth's penny-pinching ways and to stop punishing her for having a different spending philosophy. It was hard for Ruth, but she agreed to try. I also talked to Beth, who more than anything wanted the relationship to succeed. Both of them soon committed to trying out "this weird idea of yours," as Beth put it.

Three months later I got a call. "It's working!" Ruth said. She explained how she had very much wanted an expensive piece of jewelry for their anniversary. At first Beth said no, but when she realized how much this gift meant to Ruth, she relented. Ruth was shocked and over the moon!—yes, partly about the necklace, but even more about what it symbolized: Beth had overcome her own long-held beliefs over what was worth spending money on and chose what would make Ruth happy. For her part, Ruth had made meaningful strides in accepting Beth's conservative nature.

Beth opened up her heart to understand the true significance of what having an expensive necklace from her meant to Ruth. And Ruth understood this wasn't a change in Beth's belief system, but the willingness to place her love for Ruth over the values that she had been clinging to rigidly. This was a huge breakthrough.

. . .

One inherent challenge many of us face is that we are attached to our own experiences and expectations, which makes it hard for us to truly empathize with our significant others. This can be downright painful if you are not feeling like you are getting the love you need from your partner, as though they are deliberately withholding love or affection from you. Coupled with the first four steps of Radical Acceptance, practicing the Platinum Rule will take you and your partner miles—it will make you stronger and more empowered—especially when you're both feeling hurt and underappreciated.

At the outset, you may have to suspend what you want from your partner—I promise this is a temporary measure—and just focus on what makes him feel loved. As we have addressed previously, if your partner doesn't eventually step it up, you'll have to reassess the viability of the relationship. And as we have also addressed, exercising courage and leadership in your relationship is one of the best—if not *THE* best— places in which you can make a big difference in your life and for others.

OBJECTIONS: WHAT PREVENTS YOU FROM PRACTICING THE PLATINUM RULE?

At the risk of sounding like a schoolmarm, you will be very well-served by occasionally going to have to do things for or with your partner that you don't feel like doing. Whether it is having sex, calling his mother, going to a Jethro Tull concert (this is *NOT* a theoretical example, by the way), or going to RadioShack to "look around" (also not a theoretical example—thank God it went bankrupt), just know this is part of the deal and is key to practicing the Platinum Rule. As I discuss in greater detail in the last chapter, I would put having sex in this category. Let's be clear: you should never ever feel compelled to have sex, but an active, healthy sex life is important for the well-being of your relationship over the long run.

You want to master piano? Excel in your career? Earn an advanced degree? You work at anything you care about achieving—even when you don't feel like it—often when you're tired, hungry, or stressed out. You give up other things that you care about and enjoy as needed. Relationships are the same way. It's a choice you deliberately make, and keep making.

I emphasize this because I know numerous people who feel they don't have a responsibility to do unappealing things with their partner. This is a common perspective, especially among ultraindependent, superbusy, empowered women.

Rather than resist or be resentful, I ask that you simply do what your partner will truly appreciate from you—with a good attitude. In fact, take it one step further: you can suggest things from time to time you know he'll love doing, even if you don't. It might feel really hard at first but eventually it won't seem like a big deal. Moreover, surely he knows that you don't enjoy *Lord of the Rings* marathons or watching the Ultimate Fighting Championship, but he will love you for trying. These efforts to suspend your judgment and suppress your preferences show a meaningful degree of generosity and care for him. Putting his interests first from time to time has a lasting effect. As we all know, actions speak louder than words.

We have all heard the phrase, "It's better to give than to receive." (If it involves anything resembling a chocolate croissant, I beg to differ. But I digress.) I think about the times I am hopped up on the excitement of doing something special for Sanjay that I know he'll appreciate. His happiness makes me feel so good. I know that the aftermath creates a ripple effect where we're both extra attentive and loving toward each other. The experience is the same when he does something special just for me. He wants me to feel happy and loved. This is also why I emphasize that having a good attitude and full heart when practicing the Platinum Rule is so important. It truly feels good to be giving and generous to someone you love.

Practicing the Platinum Rule should never cross your ethical or moral line, nor should it cause you to feel obligated to do anything with which you are genuinely uncomfortable. What this could do is open your mind to trying something that you previously may have rejected outright, because it didn't appeal to you, or was outside of your comfort zone.

Going to an electronics store that makes you painfully bored or listening to a live rendition of "Aqualung" is one thing. Trying BDSM or an extreme sport might be another. If there is something new he really wants to do with you, open your heart and mind to consider it. If it would still compromise you, then you should explain to him in a kind and nonjudgmental way how you feel. Maybe there is something else that you can do that would be a small but helpful step in bridging the gap. Say, in the case of BDSM, rather than inviting a dominatrix into your bedroom, you can start with a mask or some toy handcuffs. Say he loves porn and that really turns you off. Maybe there's something that's much softer and sexier that you could suggest watching together. Or you could pick up some *verrrrry* sexy books or magazines and read them out loud to him.

We touched on this in the fourth step of Radical Acceptance. I asked you to accept aspects of your partner that were different and potentially objectionable to you. I am asking you now to go a step further to consider participating in activities with him that, rather than compromising your comfort zone, ideally expand it. After all, you might—just might—actually enjoy it.

. . .

Now that we have addressed some of the common hurdles, what else is preventing you from practicing the Platinum Rule? Ask yourself: What holds you back from loving him how he wants to be loved? What prevents you from going the extra mile for him? Fear? Laziness? Selfishness? Lack of information? Apathy? Never thought about it, like this? Too busy? Look into your heart and mind and figure this out. Take another look at step 2, in which I asked you to stop and introspect upon your own hang-ups. Similarly, it's now time to reflect on why you are holding back. Once you come to acknowledge these answers, practicing the Platinum Rule will be infinitely easier. I promise it will become more reflexive to you—and more rewarding—the more you practice.

Most likely, practicing the Platinum Rule regularly will lead to many small (and large!) spontaneous acts of love. It has for Sanjay and me. For example, Sanjay handles Costco trips for our family. I avoid Costco like the plague. Recently, when we were out on a ski vacation in Beaver Creek, I took a short afternoon nap. I awoke to find he was just about to leave for Costco. I quickly called his cell to ask him to wait in the garage for me. He knows I don't enjoy going, but I wanted to help with the shopping and to spend time with him. It was a tiny gesture, but he appreciated it.

PUTTING THE PLATINUM RULE TO WORK IN YOUR RELATIONSHIP

Now that you know what the Platinum Rule is all about, I'd like to help you put it to work in your relationship proactively. You may think you already know best how to make your partner feel loved, but I urge you not to make assumptions. Here are some ways you can ensure the Platinum Rule really works its magic in your relationship.

Do a little research. For a week or two, play the role of romantic anthropologist and just observe your partner. No judgment, no comments. Notice when he's most excited, most tuned-in, turned-on, most calm, most affectionate—most *anything*. Does his emotional temperature change based on your interactions? The answer will likely be *yes*. From there, it's your job to turn the tables on yourself and take note of what you did or said to encourage that change in temperature—again, without judgment. The trick is to remain as objective as possible. You're an outsider looking in, acknowledging things as they exist now, not proffering advice for how to make them better.

Ask the all-important question. It's the easiest question to ask because it's the most disarming question in the world: "What can I do to make you feel more loved?" Ask it during a quiet moment together, and don't joke. If he laughs, ask him to be serious. Let the question hang in the air, and listen. And wait. Just by asking, you're doing an incredibly loving thing. You're asking him for an honest answer, not just to hear what you want to hear. It might take a few attempts before he's ready to answer seriously. If you're feeling scared or apprehensive, engage in a healthy relaxation technique—try meditative breathing or visualization—or even try drinking a glass of wine before you ask. Of course, there's no reason to be afraid, but somehow, asking this question can make people feel nervous, silly, and maybe even vulnerable. And he may feel the same way when he tries to respond.

Be prepared for the response. It's not likely he'll be expecting such an earnest question, and so there may be a knee-jerk response that's funny, snarky, even angry. But push past it. You may get jokes ranging from cooking to sex, but whatever you do, don't get defensive—"Well, *you* try crafting meals from scratch when you've got a full-time job and three kids!"—or apologize—"You're right, I'm terrible." You are not on trial. You are simply asking for guidance so you can put the Platinum Rule to work. In any case: do *NOT* react! You may never have asked this before, and so he likely hasn't had time to think of a good answer. If you give him a safe space to explore his answers, you'll be amazed at what you may discover.

Remember, this is not a rub-the-magic-lamp moment: you don't *have* to grant his every wish. You aren't contractually obligated to do everything he mentions. This isn't about what would make *you* a better person, nor is it an invitation for him to critique you—although you should be prepared for that, especially if your relationship has been rocky. This is an information-gathering mission to seek out the areas in which you could be practicing the Platinum Rule more effectively. It is a powerful opportunity to bring to light sides of him you might have overlooked or never knew in the first place. You aren't expected to change who you are (say, becoming an Iron Chef, when you in fact rarely cook), but you have a powerful opportunity to listen, reflect, and take steps to make him feel more loved by you.

For example, say he is heading to the game and wants you to join him. You don't like baseball. Instead of reluctantly agreeing to join him, look at it from another viewpoint: he asked *you*, and not one of his friends. Go with a great attitude, and use this time as an opportunity to show him love in a way you hadn't previously. Nope, it's not quid pro quo, with the hint that maybe he'll join your Sunday night book club. It's giving a bit of yourself, and your time, in the name of love.

Be ready with your own response as well. Voicing what you'd like from him is not the goal of this conversation, but such a loving question may well be reciprocated by your partner. If the question comes back to you, that is, if he asks, "What would make *you* feel more loved?" do you know what you'd say? Be prepared with a response; this way you can offer a thoughtful answer that moves your conversation, and relationship, forward.

Eventually, if he doesn't ask or doesn't seem to understand how he should apply the Platinum Rule to you, you should tell him what he can do to make you feel more loved. Sure, it would be preferable for him to take the initiative, but it's far better to take responsibility and ask for what you want than to feel disappointed by him. (Remember that scene from the movie *Jerry McGuire*, in which Tom Cruise says to his client "Help me help you." In this case, it's more like "Help him love you."

There is great power in asking for what you want—even though it can feel scary. It'll make you and your relationship stronger. If he puts you down or shames you, it may be a very tangible signal that he's not the right partner for you in the long run. Never feel embarrassed or fearful of asking for things. You deserve it.

There's a little bit of muscle memory in practicing the Platinum Rule; by doing it often and mindfully, it becomes easier. With practice comes habit, with habit comes confidence, and with confidence comes expansiveness. There are endless examples of how you can honor what your partner values most when it comes to your love. Some will be easy. Some will be hard. Some will be big. Some will be small. What follows are relatively easy examples, followed by relatively more challenging ones.

The question is, how far are you willing to go to love your partner as he wants to be loved?

SOMETIMES LOVE COMES AT TOO GREAT A COST

Sometimes, no matter how much you try, a relationship doesn't work out. With the Platinum Rule, as we have discussed at length, you've got to be willing to put in the work and to go 150 percent of the way for the person you love. That's what deep, committed, transformative love demands of you. Yet if you make this kind of investment and the relationship still fails, you naturally may be heartbroken, hurt, and angry, but in a powerful sense, you are free. You are free of the guilt and doubt of having not given the relationship your all. Even if you feel wrecked by the end of a relationship (and who hasn't felt that way?), knowing you did everything you could to make it succeed is liberating in a powerful, Zen Buddhism kind of way.

You may be tempted to ask yourself why you chose him, why you stayed with him as long as you did, or why you ignored the red flags, and so on. I am not suggesting you deny yourself an honest analysis of what happened. But I want you to be encouraged by how you gave love a chance, and how you gave fully of yourself—you did everything you could. Despite all that, the relationship did not work out. After all, love is not an exact science. There often are not easy answers. But you can derive strength knowing you practiced Radical Acceptance and specifically, the Platinum Rule; you loved him how he wanted to be loved. If you have given it your all and your relationship still fails, resist the urge to regret. You've gained valuable tools to help you with the next one. Relationships may not last, but real love is never wasted.

Annie, a woman I have known for many years, described how after she gave her all to her marriage with James, she came to realize that loving him came at too great a cost.

My husband and I had been together for three years. I loved him; however, we fought all the time. We tried counseling; however, our disconnect was not getting bridged. He yelled. A lot. I shut down, pulled away, or yelled back. The tension between us grew; I felt like I was falling apart. We decided to separate. He moved out. I told myself I would focus on myself to try to detangle the turmoil I was drowning in . . . that then he and I would have a chance.

Living apart was painful. In my heart, I knew he was not a good match for me; however, I could not mentally go to a permanent split. One evening I spent the night with him; however, I felt that I had betrayed myself by doing so. I felt ashamed when I left the next morning; I told myself: It's okay to sleep with him, he's my husband! But part of me knew that in fact, it was not. Not too long after that, we met for lunch; it was in January. We started arguing about money. I was trying to defend myself while he was telling me what I was doing wrong. We continued to go back and forth as we left the restaurant. I was dressed for work in a skirt and heels; I had left my winter jacket in the car. He, however, was wearing a long wool coat. We were standing outside; I was shivering. He continued to berate me, going on and on and on.

In a moment of clarity, I realized that he was not going to ever be aware that I was freezing, that he was caught up in his own pain. I knew a life of constantly defending myself was ultimately one that I did not want. I accepted that this relationship, though heartbreaking to lose, was not in my best interest. I knew I needed to move on.

I put this story here to say that Radical Acceptance cannot guarantee an outcome. You may do everything you possibly can to love him, including prioritizing him and practicing the Platinum Rule. But it still may not be enough. And that is crucial to understand if you think you're at this point or close to it.

Nothing is guaranteed in life—not a husband or girlfriend, not a job, not an apartment, not even the chance to live until tomorrow. You may end up loving someone more than they love you, or giving to someone more than they give back to you. And you may even have your heart broken in the process. But I promise you that the upside to practicing the Platinum Rule far outweighs the downside. Don't be afraid to be the one who loves the most. Don't believe for a second that loving someone deeply and passionately and putting your whole heart into a relationship puts you in a position of weakness. Don't believe that you have to keep score to ensure you get what you deserve and that you're a sucker if you give more. You are worthy of tremendous love. You deserve tremendous love. But don't hang around waiting for it to sweep you off your feet and knock you over. You are one thousand times more likely to get love if you are truly willing to give it.

As Wayne Gretzky put it, "One thing is certain, one hundred percent of the shots you do not take will not go in." Practicing the Platinum Rule ensures that the relationship you're in now—and, yes, possibly the next one—receives an abundance of love and care and that you give it your very best shot to make it succeed.

- Get ready to practice the Platinum Rule. During a quiet moment, ask him: "What can I do to make you feel more loved?" Try to accommodate as best as you can, but do not feel you have to grant his every whim. Ideally he will reciprocate, too, but if he doesn't, let him know what makes you feel most loved. Asking for what you want can strengthen your relationship.
- Practicing the Platinum Rule means understanding his love language and accommodating him to the best of your ability with a

good attitude. Do not compromise your morals or feel compelled to do anything deeply uncomfortable, but do see where you can stretch yourself to show your love.

- Kindness is crucial to the health of your relationship. Look for small and large ways to simply be kind and attentive.

PART 3

BEYOND RADICAL: LIVING HAPPILY EVER AFTER

AMAZING, GLORIOUS YOU: IT IS AS IMPORTANT TO *BE* THE RIGHT PERSON AS IT IS TO *FIND* THE RIGHT PERSON

WHEW! WE'VE TALKED *A LOT* about your partner and your relationship. Enough of that, already! Now I want to focus on the amazing, glorious *YOU*. I have long trumpeted that it is as important to *be* the right person as it is to *find* the right person. This is because in order to be at ease with radically accepting your partner's flaws, you have to make peace with your own. Where can you improve? Crucially, for you to practice Radical Acceptance with gusto, it helps to have sufficient confidence, fortitude, and emotional resilience. It's a little like when the flight attendant reminds us before takeoff: "Put the oxygen mask on yourself first." If you can't breathe, you can't help others. But let's amend the analogy a bit. If you don't take care of yourself and develop your best self, how can you give your best to others?

From taking care of yourself physically to managing your stress to showcasing your unique interpersonal skills, your relationship will benefit from your being strong, happy, and empowered. Don't worry, I'm not about to introduce you to Radical Pilates or Radical Dieting. This is about being your *authentic* best self. Your kindness, humor, joy, grace, knowledge, patience, passion, fun, curiosity, sense of adventure, and open-mindedness are traits that make you you. And these special traits and attributes have a powerful, affirming role to play in your relationship.

What makes you attractive, admirable, unique, strong, irresistible, and funny? How can you ensure that you are the right person—and then remain the right person? We will discuss examples and ideas from others who do this naturally and beautifully. I will encourage you to do things that you love to do, activities that make you feel happy and confident. This includes cultivating and maintaining strong relationships outside of your love life. Carving out regular QT with some of your close pals is a powerful tonic.

I will ask you to observe the traits and skills that you admire in other strong, kick-ass women and take steps to embody them yourself. No need to be jealous! Use the observation of their gifts as an opportunity to do something good and positive for yourself. I recently ran across this lovely meme: "Admire someone else's beauty without questioning your own." Great advice. If I find myself feeling that yucky sting of jealousy, I instantly ask myself: "What's going on here? Am I coming from a place of scarcity? Or a place of abundance?" I always aim to operate from a place of abundance. There is room in this world for lots of beauty, success, love, and badassery, after all.

Also, crucially, being critical of yourself and judging yourself negatively are verboten. Life is too short. I know that's easier said than done, but radically accepting your own shortcomings is every bit as important as radically accepting your partner's.

While we touched on mindfulness in step 2, I will urge you here, too, to slow down and be mindful. I mean that quite literally, as in walking and talking slowly, especially if you tend to always be in a hurry. Throughout your day, give yourself a moment to pause and be present wherever you are, rather than rushing from one activity to the next or perpetually multitasking. If you're like me, you want to be productive nearly every minute of every day. The degree of stress with which we have become accustomed to living is insane. Slow down, take two to three long breaths, and tune in to what's right in front of you.

Finally, I encourage you to be brave! To be bold! To pamper yourself, to give yourself a break, to be a friend to yourself. In some of my most challenging moments, when I've felt alone and as if I were carrying the weight of the world on my shoulders, I ask myself, "What would a kick-ass, ultrawise coach say to me right now? How would she help me channel my inner resolve and resiliency?" While I also turn to my actual friends for similar advice and support, these little conversations with myself have been a source of great strength.

I remind myself of the following and ask you to remember this, too: you have great wisdom and can trust yourself to find the right answers from within.

. . .

Let's start with a little quiz. Please be very honest with yourself!

1. What makes you feel really good about yourself?
2. What are your three best traits?
3. What sounds exciting and fun? Or, what is something you'd love to do but might have been too afraid to try? (Until now!)
4. What are you passionate about?
5. What are you interested in learning?
6. What feels like an indulgence that you'd love to do more frequently?
7. What are the negative messages that are on auto-play in your head? I'm talking about the ones that your closest friends would

tell you to immediately disavow and then proceed to persuade you how kick-ass you are?

Finished? Good. Now what?

For questions one and two—What makes you feel really good about yourself? What are your three best traits?—savor these answers and reflect on them with gratitude every day. Appreciating yourself is so important! You've heard this before, but it's worth saying again because so many of us don't follow it: If someone compliments you and your knee-jerk reaction is to downplay or brush off the compliment: Just. Stop. All you need to reply to a compliment are two simple words: "Thank you!"

For question three—What sounds exciting and fun?—I want you to commit to acting on this within the next two months. Plan it. Do it. Skydiving? Skiing? Climbing a mountain? Going up in a hot-air balloon? Deep-sea diving? Tango lessons? An improv class? Asking that cute guy in the gym to go for a hike with you? Or maybe it's more like getting that ultrasexy Robin Wright haircut, getting a tattoo, or dyeing your hair a bold new color. Think of whatever it is that sounds fun, exciting, or even scary, and then make it happen. You may be thinking: *What does any of this have to do with Radical Acceptance?* You are teaching yourself to go outside of your comfort zone. By trying new things, you are learning expansiveness and you are opening yourself up to new possibilities. Moreover, these kinds of things can enhance your self-confidence and thereby add to your allure. Forget a perfect body or beauty-pageant face. The key to being magnetically attractive is feeling great about yourself! It's all about confidence and that inner glow and bringing your best self to your relationship.

I just learned that my friend May, mother of two and a super-smart, tough-as-nails senior leader at a top pharmaceutical company, has been taking belly-dancing lessons! She just made her onstage debut, fully decked out in a very sexy midriff-baring white costume with the full regalia of jewelry and swords. Not surprising, she's glowing from head to bejeweled toe.

The ability to identify a desire, no matter how small it is, and then following through with it is such an amazing confidence boost. It's saying YES to yourself. Try doing something along these lines at least two to three times per year—or more!

For questions four, five, and six—What are you passionate about? What are you interested in learning? What feels like an indulgence that you'd love to do more frequently?—I want you to commit to acting on at least one of your answers within the next two weeks. Plan it. Do it. And then keep doing it. Even if you can only spare a little bit of time, taking action is powerful! I think of these as feed-your-soul projects.

I know what you're thinking: *I can hardly get a good night's sleep as it is. How am I going to squeeze in a feed-my-soul project?!* Whatever it is you'd like to learn more about, commit to getting started, even if it's just fifteen minutes per week. Maybe you can even entice your partner or kids to do it with you.

Rather than listening to music on your commute, why don't you listen to Rosetta Stone if you have been longing to learn Italian? Interested in pottery but haven't touched clay since sixth grade? Try taking a beginners' pottery class! One of my closest friends, Brenda, and I took a pottery class together years ago. We also tutored two young girls when we were both living in Houston. We fed our souls and our friendship through those memorable, endearing activities.

There is so much power in learning something new or indulging in your passion. It's an investment in yourself. This is why I have pursued karate with such ardor. Of course I'd love to lounge in bed on Sunday mornings reading the *New York Times* rather than getting my butt out the door and into the dojo. But I always feel so much better after training. Beyond the physical rewards and increased mental toughness, the amazing community of people I train with, led by the august sensei Mori, have added meaningfully to the value of karate in my life.

Finding rewarding activities to do will bring you joy and revitalization. In my case, they have made me a better wife, friend, mother, business leader, and entrepreneur.

REALIZE HOW AMAZING YOU REALLY ARE BY MAKING CONFIDENCE A PRIORITY

You may be well aware of how amazing and glorious you are. However, my research on female confidence demonstrates that many women suffer from the same insecurities. We've been told that if we keep our heads down and work hard, we'll be rewarded. But the rewards don't always come, and when they do they're usually less than men's. We earn more degrees than men do and studies show that the more women a company has in leadership roles and on its board, the more profitable it is. But still we lag behind, and this has a draining effect on our confidence levels.

For example, an Institute of Leadership and Management study[41] found that just half of female managers felt confident in their job performance while more than two-thirds of male managers did. Meanwhile, women ask for 30 percent less money during salary negotiations. In another fascinating study,[42] Cornell University psychologists had men and women estimate their scientific ability on a one-to-ten scale before taking a quiz. On average, the men ranked themselves at 7.6 and the women ranked themselves at 6.5. Even though the women were less likely to perceive themselves as knowledgeable, on the actual quiz they scored nearly exactly the same as the men did.

I spearheaded research on confidence at YourTango, in which we asked 587 women, "On average, how would you rate your self-esteem?"

Brace yourself for some disappointing data.

A mere 13 percent of ladies answered "High." Forty-three percent said "Mostly good." Finally, 44 percent said there was room for improvement or that their self-esteem is low.

This is a big problem, people. Unfortunately, it gets worse.

A remarkable article in *The Atlantic* goes in depth to explain what's happening. It is called "The Confidence Gap: Evidence Shows That Women Are Less Self-assured Than Men—and That to Succeed, Confidence Matters as Much as Competence" by Claire Shipman, a reporter for ABC News, and Katty Kay, the lead anchor of *BBC World News America*.

"In studies, men overestimate their abilities[43] and performance, and women underestimate both," the article explains. "Their performances do not differ in quality." In one study, for example, a review of personnel records at Hewlett-Packard found that women only applied for a promotion when they met 100 percent of the qualifications, whereas men applied when they met a mere 60 percent. In short, men often do not have any problem asserting themselves in business, even when they are brazenly underqualified, while women only advocate for themselves when they are positive they are deserving.

As Kay and Shipman write, "Women feel confident only when they are perfect. Or practically perfect." The strive for perfection is a common female trait. While it's certainly admirable—who doesn't want to be the best they can possibly be?—perfectionism can be extremely detrimental. As the authors note,

Study after study confirms that [perfection] is largely a female issue, one that extends through women's entire lives. We don't answer questions until we are totally sure of the answer, we don't submit a report until we've edited it ad nauseam, and we don't sign up for that triathlon unless we know we are faster and fitter than is required. We watch our male colleagues take risks, while we hold back until we're sure we are perfectly ready and perfectly qualified. We fixate on our performance at home, at school, at work, at yoga class, even on vacation. We obsess as mothers, as wives, as sisters, as friends, as cooks, as athletes. Bob Sullivan and Hugh Thompson, the authors of The

Plateau Effect, *call this tendency the "enemy of the good," leading as it does to hours of wasted time. The irony is that striving to be perfect actually keeps us from getting much of anything done.*

Now, I'm sure many of you have read *Lean In* by the ultra-accomplished COO of Facebook, Sheryl Sandberg, but even she admitted that "There are still days I wake up feeling like a fraud, not sure I should be where I am."

Oh sweet Jesus. If that's how one of the most accomplished and influential people on the planet feels, what does this mean for the rest of us? I know I am *SO GUILTY* of falling prey to insidious, self-defeating perfectionism. But I'm glad to know it's a thing and that I am now more empowered to send those negative thoughts to the curb! I hope you are, too.

One important way we can do this, which is partly the point of movements such as Sheryl Sandberg's *Lean In*, is to keep it real with one another. Let's do what we can to build one another up, yes, but let's also not pretend we all have it figured out. I admire how Sheryl and some of the strongest, most kick-ass women on the planet share their vulnerabilities. Being accepting of vulnerability makes these women and everyone around them stronger.

I can hear some of your cries of dissent: "But why do women have to do this? The guys sure as hell don't actively share their vulnerabilities." Yes, but the guys are also not the ones suffering from the same confidence gap! The data do not lie, and we would be foolish to pretend everything is hunky-dory. Strong, confident women need to help other women become equally strong and confident. Why? Because endless evidence shows that having more strong, powerful women is good for the economy, good for business, good for societies across the globe, good for raising strong boys and girls, and it's just so much more *fun*!

I love being among groups of powerful women who don't hesitate to identify themselves as so-called girly-girls, but who are also badass feminists and ultrasupportive of other women. Take Shelley Zalis, the ultimate girls' girl. Shelley is chairwoman of TFQ Ventures and founder of the Girls' Lounge, which supports and mentors women to stand out with their unique leadership powers and transform corporate culture.

In an interview with the *Huffington Post*,[44] Shelley was asked this question: "What do you want the Girls' Lounge to accomplish in the next year?" I loved her response: "I want to continue moving from conversation to activation, and keep helping women along the continuum from insecurity to confidence. I'd like to help transform corporate culture from rigidity to generosity."

It has been a great gift observing and spending time with warm, wonderful women such as Shelley who are committed to helping women advance. I encourage you, too, to hang around with women (and men!) who are supportive and who make you feel great about yourself. Seek out people you admire who also keep it real and don't pretend that they have it all together. No one does, unless they're some sort of bot or automaton. And those types? They are *NO FUN*.

. . .

Is it possible to do an about-face and drastically change your confidence levels? Sure! Perception is reality. As you perceive yourself to be the best, most authentic version of your true self, this will become your reality. The key is to ensure your thoughts, words, and actions align around the traits you most wish to cultivate and project.

I recently attended the incredibly inspiring MAKERS Conference, which brings together some of the world's most impactful female leaders and innovators under one roof. We were fortunate to hear from one of the most powerful people on Wall Street: a kick-ass woman named Carla Harris. Carla is vice-chairman of wealth management and senior client advisor at Morgan Stanley—and so much more. She recounted a wonderful story of how, midway through her career, her boss told her: "Carla, you're smart and hardworking, but we're not sure you're tough enough." Carla is the epitome of a self-made success and has hugely thick skin, so her response was: "You can call Carla Harris a lot of things, but 'not tough enough' is not one of them!" (Though Carla was the first in her family to go to college, she graduated magna cum laude from Harvard University. This just scratches the surface of her many hard-fought and hard-won accomplishments.)

Carla realized she needed to change others' perception of her. She decided to "walk tough and talk tough." For weeks, she focused on how toughness was an essential part of her being. She would go so far as to say to colleagues who sought her assistance with a pitch to a company, "Yes, I am happy to help you, but tell me about the CEO. Is he or she thin-skinned? I am really tough on people, you know!" Soon after that she was following a team of colleagues into a conference room who had put together a presentation for her. Then Carla heard a manager alert an associate that he had better be ready and super buttoned-up. "Carla Harris is very tough!" he warned.

Carla knew she had won. She had changed her narrative. She felt stronger and tougher than ever! Carla offered professional advice to the attendees of MAKERS that works just as well on the personal front. She asked the audience to think of three key adjectives that both they and their organization valued about themselves. Carla said to focus on those three amazing traits and truly own them, to allow them to be fully imbued into your mind, body, and spirit. Let them influence how you move, speak, think about, and talk about yourself.

Here's my slight twist to Carla's advice: What are three powerful adjectives that you value in yourself, but that you would also love for your partner to value? (I know he might not exist yet, but the key is you want to telegraph the traits that will attract the right person!) Think about attributes that are authentic and that you admire, and pick the three that you most want to project to him and to the world. Let them be empowering and beautiful, characteristics that you feel great about— with or without a man. Write them down. Now live them. Project them.

Make sure that you believe them, that you own them. Do you want to be perceived as confident, passionate, and trustworthy? Maybe you value being perceived as kind, strong, and adventurous? Or creative, fun, and powerful? Or centered, loving, and filled with abundance? The choice is yours!

. . .

Even if you have your fears and doubts in check, and even if you know about those characteristics that make you beautiful and unique, there is something that can still upend all of it: stress. Stress is such a killer—it insidiously warps and heightens emotional reactions, fear, and negativity. This feeds a vicious cycle in marriages, especially when children are in the mix. You might even be accustomed to a high level of stress, especially if you have a pressure-cooker job or a house full of young kids—or both! As a result, you're unaware of how much impact stress is having on you and your relationship. There are times when Sanjay and I have taken our stress out on each other. Stress is incredibly contagious: if you're full of anxiety and lashing out at your partner, it will only increase his own anxiety levels.

There are many things you can do to mitigate stress and the anger that it often foments. Here are a couple of the things that I do to limit my stress level.

COMMIT TO SLOWING DOWN

Slow down. Even just a little bit—especially if you tend to be high strung and feel the need to go, go, go. If you're a hard-driving type AAA (not a typo nor my bra size, but close) like me, slowing down your life is like telling a shark to swim less. The truth is, this go-go-go lifestyle isn't very healthy—especially for your partner, who perhaps feels like he has to email you a calendar invite just to find time for a hug and kiss.

If this describes you, try to keep more of your schedule open for down time with your partner and with yourself. I don't mean rushing to squeeze a much-needed yoga session or SoulCycle class—although those are good to add to the mix—I mean good old-fashioned lazy, hang-out-in-your-PJs time, especially with your significant other. Or maybe he'll take the kids out and give you some time to not organize closets, but to savor a book you would love to read. When you are in the middle of the hustle and bustle, take a few moments to stop and look around you to get present. Or perhaps sit at your desk and close your eyes and take a few deep breaths or maybe even listen to a favorite song. If you can take a short walk, even better! By slowing down and being present, even for just a pinch, you de-stress your system and become more tuned to those you love.

PRACTICE REGULAR MEDITATION

Even if it's imperfect and it's only ten minutes a day, regular meditation is a wonderful addition to your routine. And don't worry about mastering a perfect lotus pose—you don't have to sit cross-legged with your hands upturned on your knees. Just find a position that is comfortable for you.

The science is all over this one, guys. A Harvard University study[45] noted that mindfulness meditation enlarges the hippocampus, which controls memory and learning, while shrinking the amygdala. Everyone remember the amygdala from steps 2 and 3? It's that pesky region of the brain that's responsible for stress, fear, and anxiety. After meditating for just eight weeks, the Harvard study participants felt happier and less stressed out. Finally, a UCLA study[46] found that long-term meditators—those who have been doing it for more than twenty years—have better preserved brains as they age, meaning they have a stronger chance at remaining sharp into old age. Live longer, and live happier! There is a truly endless amount of additional compelling data that shows meditation and mindfulness improve health.

Now, it might take a while before you're comfortable with meditation. You might feel bored or like you have ADD, as your brain wanders to a million different places at once. This is okay. Dr. John Gray spent nearly a decade studying with the master of Transcendental Meditation, the Maharishi Mahesh Yogi. Based on his experiences, John agrees with me that it can take a little while for women in particular to become acclimated to meditation:

For women, sitting still[47] *increases brain activity. So quite often the thought process increases and it can be hard to follow a meditative process. The key is to understand that the practice of meditation is simply to relax, to repeat some uplifting thought, or even a sound.*

Your objective is not to stay focused on the object of meditation. Rather, your objective is to strengthen your mental muscles to notice when you are off that uplifting thought or sound and to bring your attention back. This strengthens the mind.

For many people, to meditate is an extremely boring practice. This is because it's actually helping the brain restore balance whenever it is overstimulated. The brain needs to relax and basically feel bored in order to rebuild. Without being a master meditator, it's of great benefit to simply quiet the mind and produce the antistress hormones. It's proven to work.

When you're first starting out, even five to ten minutes of meditating daily can have a tremendous effect. If you don't have access to a quiet place, similar results can also be found from simply going for a walk.

You don't have to be on the level of a Buddhist monk to experience the wonderful benefits of meditation. For example, a study conducted jointly by the Wharton School[48] and INSEAD found that a single breathing-focused fifteen-minute meditation session like the ones John recommends can help people make wiser decisions. By being in the present and letting go of our thoughts, we are more likely to admit when we are wrong and, according to the study, "make more rational decisions by considering the information available in the present moment." You can even take advantage of meditation apps—I've been using an app called Headspace, which has features for newbies and pros alike.

NEGATIVE THOUGHTS AND BAD HEALTH

Simple relaxation techniques have been shown to drastically reduce the incidence and severity of migraines and muscle pain. And perhaps most important is having a positive outlook: a 2013 study of more than six hundred heart-disease patients[49] found that people with the most positive moods were 58 percent more likely to live at least five more years.

While soothing, positive thoughts can improve our physical well-being, negative thoughts can do the opposite. Here's an eye-opening study: numerous studies following medical students[50] have found that as many as nearly 70 percent of students began developing symptoms of the diseases they were studying. These negative thoughts were like a self-fulfilling prophecy: the more paranoid the medical students were about catching a disease, the more likely their body was to become sick.

If you've been feeling down, don't ignore it! Learn to meditate, try some stress-reducing techniques, or see a professional. Your overall health, like your relationship, will be impacted by your mood. Stay positive!

SLEEP MORE

We don't sleep enough! Seven out of ten adults say they suffer from some degree of stress or anxiety every day. Meanwhile, seven out of ten adults say they have difficulty sleeping. When you feel stressed, you often have trouble sleeping, and when you have trouble sleeping, you feel more anxious, depleted, and stressed out. Ack! It's a vicious cycle!

I love this quote from Arianna Huffington,[51] the high priestess of sleep, "I studied, I met with medical doctors, scientists, and I'm here to tell you that the way to a more productive, more inspired, more joyful life is getting enough sleep." Arianna makes a cogent, extremely compelling case[52] for the power and importance of sleep in her book *The Sleep Revolution: Transforming Your Life, One Night at a Time.* She writes: "You need to be able to nurture yourself in order to be a good mother, good at your job, good at servicing your community. I really believe women can do it all, but they can't do it all at the expense of their health, their sleep, and their sense of well-being." Arianna is also urging everyone to sleep their way to the top. Hah!

It's a little sad that we need someone to give us permission to get a decent night's sleep, but in a way it's also not surprising given the endless demands on our time. As perverse as it sounds, many people consider sleeping as little as possible a badge of honor—especially in high-octane male-dominated fields. When I was in my ultracompetitive business school and Wall Street environments, getting seven or eight hours of sleep meant that I wasn't working hard enough. So dumb. I remember feeling down when I read that Martha Stewart slept only four hours each night so she could be more productive. I remember thinking I too could train myself to succeed with minimal sleep, that I could evolve to this ability with some commitment and fortitude. I tried, but *devolve* is a more apt term to describe what happened. I got by on minimal sleep for many years, but it exacted such an enormous toll. Now I do a much better job prioritizing sleep!

We need to sleep more, got it. *Easier said than done*, you may be thinking. There are a million techniques that can make going to bed easier. Most experts recommend shutting the computer down an hour before bedtime—that means no more working, you workaholics out there! The blue light that emanates from electronic displays can really screw with your sleep-inducing melatonin production, so avoid as many screens as possible shortly before bedtime. Making your room cool and dark helps. If you can't make your room dark and the sun wakes you up too early in the morning, try wearing a soft, comfortable eye mask. If you are easily awoken by various noises (from honking outside to honking—er—snoring inside!), try turning on white noise. This works wonders for me. Interestingly, a Swiss study[53] published in the journal *Nature* found that keeping your extremities warm is the best way to facilitate sleep, so wear those socks to bed! There is no shortage of methods ranging from the ultrascientific to the downright wacky, but find one that works for you.

In step 3 we talked briefly about Stan Tatkin's research into rituals. Stan says that one of the best ways to increase trust and intimacy in a relationship is by cultivating specific routines right before bed. These include reading together, listening to an audiobook together, or simply holding each other close. In addition to relieving stress and bringing you closer with your partner, bedtime routines also facilitate better sleep.

GET THE BLOOD FLOWING!

Of course there are other ways to make yourself strong, healthy, attractive, and feeling great. I swear by yoga; vinyasa is my preferred form. I used to belong to an amazing Upper West Side yoga studio, but as I continued to get busier with family and work I had a tough time getting to a class with any regularity. Now I do yoga at home to very upbeat music (and it's free). I can only squeeze it in once or twice a week for twenty or thirty minutes, but it makes a huge difference. It's such an incredible mood booster. Once again, take it over, science! A German study from 2005[54] followed two dozen women who described themselves as "emotionally distressed." They were given two ninety-minute yoga classes every week for three months. At the end of the study, the women's depression scores improved by 50 percent, anxiety scores improved by 30 percent, and overall well-being scores jumped by 65 percent. Moreover, the women reported fewer symptoms of headaches, back pain, and insomnia.

I also try to take a short run or brisk walk during the week in Central Park, usually managing to get my sons or husband to join me, and when I'm lucky I'll squeeze a karate class in on Sunday morning. Plus, as a New Yorker, I put on miles each week walking my kids to school, to the subway, the Bronx Zoo, museums, and so on. I do push-ups or sit-ups every morning while listening to NPR. (Okay, a little nerdy, but thanks to *Morning Edition* and twenty years of doing push-ups I finally have muscle tone in my arms!)

If you hate exercise, just commit yourself to a fifteen-to-twenty-minute brisk walk every day, or at least a few times a week. Grab a friend or find a Spotify mix or a super-awesome podcast and you might even learn to love this routine. If the weather isn't cooperating, there are plenty of yoga or Pilates videos out there, not to mention all of those intense seven-minute daily workout routines. Sanjay and I sometimes put on our favorite music and have dance parties with our boys on weekends. *SO. FUN.* (Florence and the Machine! Adele! Joan Jett! Pharrell! And my personal favorite: the Beach Boys!) Some people I know swear by five to ten minutes of daily jump rope. It's inexpensive, you can do it anywhere, and with some rocking music you may not want to stop!

There are endless ways for you to shake your bootie and get exercise, which keeps your mind sharp, mitigates stress, and helps you age gracefully, among countless other benefits. Whether it's running, power walking, cycling, hitting the gym, jumping rope, or yoga, find something that boosts both your heart rate and your happiness. Plus, if it helps you shed a few pounds and you feel better because you look better, that's a bonus.

PAMPER YOURSELF. YOU DESERVE IT!

What feels like an indulgence? What can you do a little more frequently to make yourself feel relaxed, strong, beautiful, and pampered? I encourage you to think of gifts you can grant yourself. Treat yourself well, regularly. You deserve it. These indulgences don't have to be expensive or difficult. By taking good care of yourself, and by giving yourself the occasional reward, you'll feel happier and more relaxed, and you're also likely to give off the vibe that you're worthy of love and care. For example, I recently indulged in one of those ten-minute minimassages after getting a pedicure. It was kind of weird to be massaged in the middle of the spa, but what the hell. It felt *so* good.

I have seen women make so many sacrifices for other people that they have nothing left for themselves. These noble martyrs are often left depleted, angry, tired, stressed, and lonely. As they suffer, their relationships often suffer, too. They incur greater health risks. I know these women have others' best interests at heart, but I can't help but feel that by treating themselves or pampering themselves occasionally, they'll have more to offer their loved ones.

By recharging your batteries and taking steps to feel good, you will have more goodness to share. Sure, there are some Mother Teresas out there who sacrifice themselves and still manage to radiate joy, love, and peace. I admire them greatly. For the rest of us, I say invest in your well-being and do not feel guilty about it. Feel great that you care enough about yourself to treat yourself and occasionally indulge. Yes, some of these require coin and can be a little tougher to do with regularity if you're on a tight budget. But there are always hacks that the budget conscious and time constrained can avail themselves of. Perhaps indul-gence will eventually become more like required maintenance than an infrequent guilty pleasure!

Whether it's a mani-pedi, a facial, a massage, a new lipstick, taking time off to meet a friend for coffee, a great bottle of wine, a new pair of shoes, a weekend getaway, private tennis lessons, a kid-free weekend, reading a delicious novel, a chance to sleep in, new pajamas, or wear-ing pretty lingerie every day even though you're the only one who will see it—it took me a long time to figure this one out, sadly—you deserve to be treated. That little glow that comes from within you may even be contagious.

CULTIVATE A SENSE OF FEMININITY AND MYSTERY

"It isn't always the lack of closeness that stifles desire, but too much closeness. And while love seeks closeness, desire needs space to thrive. That's because love is about having, and desire is about wanting."

—ESTHER PEREL

Sometimes a relationship can be a little too close. *Huh?* you're thinking. *Isn't this book all about growing closer to him, not further away?*

Yes, of course, for the most part. By learning how to radically accept his unlovable parts, you will undeniably grow closer with your partner. I'm not advocating that you grow apart; rather, it's worth creating a little bit of mysterious space to keep things interesting. Esther Perel, the phe-nomenal author of *Mating in Captivity*, is a psychotherapist and popu-lar TED speaker known for exploring the relationship between security and freedom in human relationships. She writes that,[55] "Eroticism occurs in the space between self and other," meaning that in order to keep a relationship fresh and supple, you need to have a little bit of independence to spark desire.

Let's explore what Esther means by "other." Have you ever gone to a party with your partner and watched him talk with people you don't know, and then think to yourself: *Hmm. I'm seeing a whole different side to him*? Maybe it's watching him interact with children, or maybe it's seeing him in a whole new element. Seeing an entirely new side to a person you've known for a long time can be very fun—and very sexy.

I have two friends, Diana and Jason, who have been in a long-term relationship for years. They love each other dearly, but things were getting a little stale. They had successfully built safety and trust in their relationship, but there wasn't much of that old excitement anymore. Diana remembered the first few weeks after she met Jason, how they were both so excited to learn about each other. She then decided to mix things up a bit. She started coming home later from work, each time with vaguely mysterious reasons. "Oh, I was out with friends," she'd say, or "Oh, I just went for a nice long walk." In truth, she was taking intense salsa lessons! She and Jason were attending a wedding later that summer and she wanted to surprise him. The night of the wedding came, and Diana hit the dance floor and knocked everyone's socks off with her moves. Jason was astounded—and super turned on! Just when he thought he knew Diana, here was an entirely new, fun, sexy side to her.

Don't believe the myth that you need to know everything about your partner and that he needs to know every last nugget about you. If he does, then create some new ones like Diana did! Esther recommends that you have a few of your own friends whom you occasionally hang out with independently (more on this below). Develop a new interest. Invite him to unusual new events. Shake up your look. Finding new ways to capture his attention and exhibit some unpredictability is a wonderful way to inject some spice and eroticism into your relationship. This is also a fun way to build your confidence and tap into parts of yourself that may even be unfamiliar to you! Remember, self-confidence is the most magnetizing trait out there.

WITH A LITTLE HELP FROM YOUR FRIENDS

Spend time with your best girlfriends. If you want to feel validated and supported, some quality time with your gal pals is invaluable. Close friends are important and therapeutic—and often abandoned when you're super busy with a job, marriage, and kids.

A UCLA study[56] found that for women, spending time with friends counteracts stress. Traditionally, we believed that stress causes an ancient survival mechanism called the fight-or-flight response. But among women, stress can stimulate the production of one hormone in particular, oxytocin. One of the authors, Laura Cousin Klein, PhD, assistant professor of biobehavioral health at Penn State University, explains that instead of preparing the body for fight or flight, oxytocin encourages a dramatically different behavioral response: tending to children and gathering with other women. When a woman "tends and befriends," her body creates a virtuous cycle whereby more oxytocin is released, calming and counteracting the stress. It makes sense when you think about it. Have you ever had a truly horrible day at work and impulsively texted your best friends to grab a drink? Did you feel a lot better after hanging out with them? The study found that simply being among other women can release more oxytocin, which has a calming effect on stress.

"Study after study has found that social ties reduce our risk of disease by lowering blood pressure, heart rate, and cholesterol. There's no doubt," says Dr. Klein, "that friends are helping us live longer." And plenty of scientific evidence indicates that friends are also helping us live better!

Meanwhile, Dr. John Gray told me[57] that in addition to oxytocin, estrogen and progesterone are also powerful stress-reducing hormones. Both hormones are released during any activity in which women are together and supporting one another. "Friendships are so important in a woman's life," John agrees. "They free her from the needs of pair-bonding and allow her to balance her stress through social caring." By spending time with your girlfriends, all sorts of good-for-you, feel-good hormones flood into your brain, washing away all sorts of stress.

ME-TIME

John's daughter, Lauren, has embraced her father's research and has become a fantastic relationship counselor in her own right. She stresses the importance of "me-time." As Lauren says, "The danger lies in becoming overly dependent on your partner to make you happy." To avoid this trap, it's crucial to plan "me-time" for yourself and your friends. A small amount of healthy detachment is good, and it will help make the time you spend alone with your partner that much more special. Lauren lists five counterintuitive ways that me-time actually brings you closer to your partner. Here are some paraphrased excerpts from her course:

ABOLISH "NEEDY." *You don't want to fall into a trap where you depend on your partner for love and self-worth. Me-time allows you to become more self-confident and self-sufficient.*

IGNITE ATTRACTION. *You don't want your relationship to suffer from "cabin fever." Spending too much time with your partner can make you feel allergic to him, and vice versa. As Lauren says, "By taking me-time, you ensure that you're balancing time together with time apart so that you're actively igniting attraction rather than letting it fade."*

END BICKERING. *Sometimes it seems like every conversation ends up in an argument. Without enough me-time, it's harder to see yourself and your partner as individuals, and everything becomes "my way or the highway."*

PROMOTE ACCEPTANCE. *All couples dread growing apart. These feelings arise when one or both partner does not feel that he or she is being fully seen and accepted. Me-time allows you to develop your own individuality. Your partner can't accept you unconditionally unless you can accept yourself unconditionally!*

MOTIVATE HIM TO CONTRIBUTE MORE TO THE RELATIONSHIP. *If your partner feels he cannot make you happy, he will stop contributing to the relationship. You can make things easier for him if he knows that you have many ways to be happy— both with him and without him. This way he can focus on the special things he does best.*

For some great tips on how to cultivate "me-time," visit John and Lauren's website at www.marsvenus.com.

Maintaining these friendships doesn't just help you deal with stress and create a healthy level of space in your relationship. The Harvard Nurse's Health Study[58] followed hundreds of thousands of women over decades. One of the more significant findings was that women who had the most friends were less likely to develop physical ailments and more likely to report feeling joy in life—so much so that not having close friends was considered just as detrimental as smoking. Meanwhile, a decade-long investigation in Australia of nearly fifteen hundred seniors found that people with more close friends were 22 percent less likely to die during the study compared with seniors with fewer friends.

Never forget your besties! When you're dealing with the stress from work and family, it's easy to push friends to the back burner. While you should make your partner a priority, don't forget about the people who are by your side during the best and worst of times.

"Rare as is true love, true friendship is rarer."

—JEAN DE LA FONTAINE

BE BOLD! BE BRAVE!

I'd like to wrap up this chapter with some simple advice: Be bold! Be brave!

How? Well, for starters, I ask myself from time to time, "What would I do if I weren't afraid of looking foolish?" I try hard to honor the answer and not be deterred by fear. I try super hard not to beat myself up and ruminate forever on mistakes I have made. I learn from them and move on.

I regularly encourage my team at YourTango (who are mostly women) to try new things and not be deterred by failure. I remind them that you cannot innovate without taking risks—and that not all risks will turn out positively. Rather than avoiding the possibility of failure, I encourage them to embrace it. I know they'll use their sound judgment and not be careless or reckless. They know I trust them and feel empowered by this latitude and support they have earned.

In your own life, you can start by taking moderate risks. Maybe it's writing something deeply personal and sharing it on Tumblr. Maybe it's telling someone an uncomfortable truth in a way that is empowering and constructive. Maybe it's something simple—like wearing a bright shade of lipstick or nail polish or some other change of appearance or apparel that you secretly would love to do. All of the little things add up. But I hope you'll embrace some of the bigger risks that make life an adventure, that give you the chance to realize your full potential and to be fully seen. Maybe it's having a vision for something that seems impossible and then going for it, or having the courage to share your unbridled passion about something with friends and strangers alike. Maybe it is summoning up the courage to mend fences with someone important to you with whom there's been a deep hurt or long-held grudge.

If you are ever looking for inspiration on being a brave, bold female, head to MAKERS.com and get ready for a big treat. The vast body of stories and videos assembled there will knock your socks off. See and hear from female astronauts such as Mae Jemison and Julie Payette; a female US Navy fighter pilot, Lea Gabrielle; plus, the likes of Oprah, Gloria Steinem, Ruth Bader Ginsburg, Abby Wambach, Rosie Rios (the first female treasurer of the United States!), and hundreds of other truly extraordinary, strong women. You will walk away feeling energized and inspired to put your dent in the universe and to be your best self.

There are zillions of small and large ways to be brave and to be bold. But the most significant is to have the courage to take off your mask and express yourself as you really are. Be bold, be brave—be you!

- Focus on the three qualities that you'd love to project, those that make you attractive, admirable, unique, and strong. Regardless of whether you're in a relationship or single, find ways to show off the qualities that will make you feel your best.
- Carve out time with your gal pals. You offer each other an important source of health and well-being.
- Don't fall prey to the female confidence gap nor let the quest for perfection undermine what makes you good or great. Remember that some of the most powerful women on the planet have been willing to share their vulnerabilities. Spend time with strong women who keep it real!
- Take steps to be bold and brave and to get out of your comfort zone. Trying new things and taking risks are powerful ways to build confidence and reveal new parts of yourself.

MAKING IT LAST (AND MAKING IT MORE FUN!)

RADICAL ACCEPTANCE WILL take root and beautifully transform your relationship with practice, practice, and more practice. The five steps of Radical Acceptance are habit forming; they're skills and behaviors that become easier and more reflexive the more you do them. But unless you're the most accepting person in the world or the next incarnation of the Dalai Lama, there will be plenty of hiccups along the way. The key is to be patient with yourself when you slip up, forget, or fly off the handle. This will all happen. Just like you try to extend empathy to your partner when he slips up, extend it to yourself when you slip up. Remember that Radical Acceptance is a journey, one that can help you in the short run and be transformative over the long run.

It's going to be a lot of work, but you're going to be amazed by what emerges. Remember, do not expect instant reciprocation. Delight in how great it feels to have so much love for your partner, and feel the sweet sense of liberation when you release yourself from the (illusory) shackles of control.

I am excited to share the proverbial icing on the cake! By having made it this far, you've tackled the hard work and laid the foundation for Radical Acceptance. Now it's time to have a lot of fun together and to create many more wonderful memories. In this chapter we will build further upon the idea that love is an action word. We'll explore how using nonsexual touch enhances attachment and strengthens your bond. We will discuss how incorporating large and small surprises can add a wonderful sense of mystery and zest to your relationship. We'll also see how doing new things together is one of the most powerful ways to keep your relationship strong and romantic.

Finally, I'll introduce you to a strategy I find really helpful: Harville Hendrix and Helen LaKelly Hunt's Zero Negativity movement, which can prevent needless fights from ever happening. Sprinkle on a little more sex, a bit more fun, and voilà—you're that much closer to happy, lasting love!

· · ·

There are many things you can do to ensure Radical Acceptance takes root and succeeds in your life. The first is, of course, to commit to it. We've covered this tirelessly, I know, but the more you tell yourself you are going to love him right here, right now—not some idealized future version of him—the more likely you are to actually do it.

Second, when you're in a rut and find practicing Radical Acceptance especially laborious, remember this Socrates quote from the film *Peaceful Warrior*: "Those who are the hardest to love need it most." This doesn't justify abuse or plain old bullshit bad behavior, but it does help us understand that so many loved ones out there could use a little more compassion—especially when they make it especially hard for us to provide it.

The third component required to make Radical Acceptance last in your life is to—you guessed it—regularly practice it. You don't learn to cook by reading cookbooks. You learn to cook by reading cookbooks and *then* getting your hands dirty in the kitchen.

Before we dive in, I want to share a story that has touched my heart deeply. I know that this book is written in way that speaks specifically to female readers, but it's crucial to understand that *anyone* can take this message to heart.

Some time ago, I reconnected with an old friend of mine. We were friends on Facebook but hadn't spoken in nearly twenty years. Kevin had read an article I had written about Radical Acceptance on YourTango. He was intrigued by the concept and managed to use Radical Acceptance to navigate some extraordinarily difficult situations that would have left most people bitter and hopeless.

Kevin's first marriage was to a woman with whom he knew he was not compatible. She could be a bully and she could be extremely negative, but worst of all, Kevin thought he deserved it. When the relationship ended, Kevin's confidence was shattered and he sought out the first person who would be kind to him. He found her—and then married her—but there was zero connection. They divorced amicably after eight years, and Kevin was disillusioned. He was still struggling with his confidence and didn't think a relationship with a genuine connection was in the cards for him. Then, believing he had finally found the perfect match, Kevin married for a third time to a woman who on the surface fit the bill. She was beautiful and smart and was seemingly in love with him. In a story fit for a Hollywood script, it turns out she was a con artist who eventually stole Kevin's life savings and wreaked extreme emotional havoc upon him. He was just the latest in a long string of victims.

Such a horrendous series of events would be enough to crush most people, to make them bitter and resentful. Yet Kevin kept going, taking steps to rebuild his life, becoming a minimalist and vegetarian in the process. He read my article on Radical Acceptance and realized that he had to come to terms with his own vulnerabilities and shortcomings. He had to accept that he was a good person who deserved happiness. He deserved to be with a good person whom he truly loved.

Around the same time, Kevin reconnected with an old friend from middle school, Karen—the first girl he had ever fallen in love with, though she never knew it. She was going through a separation and he was coming back from hell. It eventually became clear that they were falling in love. Kevin was determined to make it work, but things were tricky. As she still had children living at home—and feelings for her husband of twenty-six years—she was loath to call it quits. She was scared, and reluctant to be honest with Kevin. She would lie to him, saying she was with her parents when she was actually with her husband or home with her family. Kevin initially felt resentful and angry toward Karen—after all the emotional abuse he had endured over the years, who wouldn't? Was she just another person taking advantage of him?

But Kevin decided to practice Radical Acceptance. He forced himself to empathize with her situation, to understand that she was scared and vulnerable. "Even though she had lied to me, I accepted her going back and forth about choosing her husband or me. I knew there was a very good chance that she was going to go back and stay with him and that I would lose her forever. I told her, 'You have to spend the time to figure this out.'" Karen needed to be unsure, she needed time, and though it took everything out of him, Kevin accepted that.

After Kevin confronted her about the lies and told her he loved her no matter what, Karen broke down in tears. "Oh, my God," she told him. "That's the most amazing thing anybody's ever done for me." A short period later, she made her decision: she wanted to be with Kevin. Karen realized she could take off her mask. She knew it was safe to be truly honest and open with him. Here was a man who had been so abused and beaten down by bad relationships, yet he managed to open his heart and offer compassion, empathy, and acceptance to her. "If I hadn't radically accepted the position she was in," Kevin told me, "she wouldn't feel the way she does about me. We wouldn't be together. I've never been with a person in my life who I felt honestly knew who I was and loved me for it. She knows who I am and she knows I'm a good man. Words can't describe how happy that makes me."

OBSERVE OTHER COUPLES

One helpful way that you can improve your relationship is to observe couples you know who appear to be in safe, secure relationships. How do they treat each other? How do they have fun together? How often do they hold hands, touch, or stay close together? Are they supportive of each other? How do they manage when one slips up and says something negative or hurtful? What can you learn from them? Try to pick up on the subtle cues that may not be so evident at first.

Be careful, though, because many relationships seem beautiful and happy on the surface only to be disguising terrible dysfunction underneath. Have you ever opened your Facebook feed only to see lovey, gushy, kissy photos from Julie and Penny's latest globe-trotting vacation, or the wonderful bouquet of flowers Dave bought Linda for the third time this week? You know the type. Try not to become bitter or envious; the strength of a couple is not reflected in curated appearances on social media. Indeed, according to a Northwestern University study,[59] people who are feeling romantically insecure are often *more* likely to share cutesy photos and posts with or about their partners. In my experience, the strongest couples are the ones who don't need to prove to everyone else that they're strong.

YourTango covers this topic at length. We have a popular article[60] that's been shared hundreds of thousands of times entitled "The Best Sign of a Healthy Relationship Is No Sign of It on Facebook" by Bob Alaburda. The article references NFL legend Walter Payton, who once said, "When you're good at something, you'll tell everyone. When you're great at something, they'll tell you."

Great couples know "that there's value in secret little moments that no one else gets to know about," Bob's article explains. "They know that showing your love through a third party lessens its sincerity because when you have an audience, everything feels like a performance. They don't spend time on Facebook; they spend it with each other."

Instead of judging couples by how many presents and kissy-face posts they adorn each other with, look for the small things. Do couples you admire make eye contact when they speak? Are they tuned in to one another? Do they take steps to really, actively *care* for one another and look out for each other? Do they cut each other slack when one of them slips up?

Among your couple friends, try to notice the small (and large) ways in which they undermine and disparage each other. Sure, it can feel fun and entertaining to tease your partner in social gatherings, except for when small (and large) often thinly veiled resentments emerge. As for me, I am pretty self-effacing and don't mind being the subject of teasing as long as it's all in good fun. Sanjay also has a good sense of humor and a thick skin, so we are quick to tease each other among friends. This is a fairly common social pattern among many of our friends and family members, especially among those with big egos and big personalities. It's a bit of a badge of honor to be able to both dish it out *and* take it.

However, from observing our friends, I realize that sometimes I behave in ways—unintentionally, of course—that might push the fun too far and may actually be hurtful to Sanjay. Ack! It's also tough to see friends whom I know are deeply in love yet still undermine each other in front of others. Often it's after a drink or two. It's also more often (but not exclusively) my female friends putting their husbands down. I can't help but wonder if this is because these women don't feel heard or validated by their husbands in private so they, essentially, rebel in public? There are plenty of couples who dish it back and forth with a deeply unpleasant undertone. Be aware of this behavior, and learn from it.

I remember one evening we were out with a very powerful, successful couple. The guy, call him Sam, was really putting his wife, Kay, down because she didn't cook enough for him. This woman is among the most brilliant, successful, and kick-ass women I know. She is very warm, thoughtful, and generous. Given how much she has going on in her life and that they have ample domestic help, I can understand why cooking actual food for him isn't what she focuses on.

By observing other couples, you can emulate the behavior you admire while avoiding the ways in which they subtly and not so subtly put each other down. You can also use this time together to listen to what message your partner may be trying to communicate to you. In the example above, I am convinced that Sam was effectively saying "Kay, you don't love me enough" when he criticized her for not cooking. Sam is also very successful, funny, and hard-working. But he has a huge ego, and I can see how Kay might feel that pouring ever more love onto him could be like feeding the abyss. Though it might seem superfluous to her, cooking slightly more often might well be something Kay could do to help Sam feel more loved. Home-cooked meals may be his primary love language. However, Sam needs to understand that criticizing her publicly is not cool and is not likely to achieve what he really desires. It's hard to ask for what you want but that's what he (and all of us!) should do.

HAVE MORE SEX!

We have already mentioned sex in this book, but we're going talk about it again because it's so crucial and so fraught with challenges. And that's not just my opinion: there is *SO* much amazing data out there about the benefits of sex and how to achieve a fulfilling sex life.

First, variety is the spice of life—and in the bedroom! I always counsel people to broaden their sexual horizons. These can include obvious techniques like trying different positions; sharing fantasies (even the embarrassing ones. *Especially* the embarrassing ones!); new toys; role-playing; reading erotic stories aloud to each other or watching sexy movies together; or even giving him a striptease or a super sexy lap dance. (In the spirit of gender parity, he too can give you a striptease or a super-sexy lap dance! Remember, gender parity is meant to apply to every page of this book!)

There's a viral YourTango article,[61] "The 9-Step Guide to Giving Your Man a Crazy-Hot Lap Dance," by a duo of sex educators who call themselves the Pleasure Mechanics. They write,

> *Choosing to give your lover a lap dance is a very powerful step toward more sexual confidence, in and out of the bedroom. When you can accept that fact that you are gorgeous and a worthy object of his attention, you start to forget to care about the little imperfections and instead focus on the incredible pleasure your body can feel. Lap dancing is a gift for both of you. Your lover gets the joy and arousal of watching you dance, and you get all of the pleasure of feeling like a powerful seductress. Remember, start the journey by setting aside time to dance in private and bring your awareness to how much pleasure you can feel just by moving to one of your favorite songs.*

Talk about being seen! Giving this kind of lap dance or striptease would be vulnerability on steroids for so many of us; it's a powerful way to create emotional intimacy. Do you have the guts to give it a try?

While quality of sex is important, of course, *quantity* is also important. In other words, more sex means a happier relationship—up to a point. More on this shortly. Here is what you need to know, unequivocally: Without a sufficient amount of physical intimacy in a marriage or long-term relationship, it will eventually die. You will eventually fail to exist as a happily married couple.

There's an abundance of research that proves a sufficient amount of sex is directly correlated to the satisfaction in a long-term relationship. A crack team[62] at the University of Toronto Mississauga studied a whopping 25,510 Americans, two-thirds of whom were married or in an established relationship. According to Amy Muise, the lead researcher, there is "a linear association between sex and happiness." Translation: more sex, more joy!

Well, maybe you're thinking that it's just *men* who are more fulfilled by more sex. There's a famous scene in *Annie Hall* when Alvy's therapist asks him how often he has sex with Annie. "Hardly ever," he responds. "Maybe three times a week." When Annie's therapist poses the same question, Annie responds: "*Constantly*. I'd say three times a week." So does more sex just mean happiness for him? Well, good news, ladies. The research shows that the correlation between increased sex and overall happiness remains the same regardless of gender or even age.

I know what you're thinking now: *Is there a limit?* Will all of life's problems magically go away if you have sex every day and night? As fun as that may sound to some of the twenty-five-year-old readers without children out there . . . no. Unfortunately, the research demonstrates a pretty consistent ceiling. It turns out that relationship happiness peaks after having sex around once per week. While you won't likely see huge psychological benefits from having sex every day—but by all means, go for it!—you can definitely see a boost if until now you've been doing it infrequently.

Of course, what if there are issues in your relationship that are adversely affecting your sex life? Or what if you simply can't "get in the mood"? That's okay, but I urge you to try and separate your sex life from other issues that may be occurring in your relationship. As Ian Kerner, the fantastic sex counselor[63] and bestselling author, told me, "When sex is working, it's 20 percent of the relationship. When it's not working, sex is 80 percent." A bad sex life is not always the cause of broader relationship problems, but lack of sex can severely magnify these problems.

Do you have sex at least once a week with your partner? If you do not, aside from any obvious geographical or physical hurdles, how come?

The most common response is something along the lines of: "I'm not going to have sex unless I want to. Sex should happen spontaneously, not part of some schedule." And then a litany of excuses emerges: "I'm too tired," "I'm too stressed," "We're not alone in the house," "I'm angry with him," "I don't feel turned on by him right now," "My sex drive is low," or "I'd just rather read a book or watch TV." Hollywood hasn't exactly helped us here—watch enough rom-coms and you're likely to believe that all sex should be the impassioned, tear-each-other's-clothes-off variety. If you're not in the mood, why should you have sex?

I advised previously that you should sometimes have sex even when you don't necessarily feel like it. Do I mean that you need to be ready to have sex on command? Decisively not.

This is not so much about whether you don't feel like having sex today—no biggie if you're too tired or whatever once in a while. It's a much bigger issue if you rarely or never feel like it.

If you don't feel like having sex pretty much most of the time, just like you might not feel like exercising or going to the grocery store or flossing your teeth, I say do it anyway with some regularity. It's not just good for you, but it's also crucial for your relationship over the long run. Note: if you're completely repelled by your partner sexually, you may need therapy and/or to use Radical Acceptance out of the bedroom to re-establish an emotional bond before becoming sexually active again.

Ian says that humans have two sexual systems: excitement and inhibition. Excitement is like the gas pedal in a car: the more you push it, the more excited you feel about your body and your partner's body. Maybe it's that look he gives you or the way he's dressed. The higher that excitation system is revved, the more you positively anticipate, and sometimes even thirst for, the sex you are going to have. Inhibition, meanwhile, is the brake pedal. Inhibitions are those little nagging thoughts in the back of your mind that turn you off from sex. *What if I don't get enough sleep? What if the kids walk in on us? What if my pre-*

sentation next week doesn't go over well at work? What if the dishes aren't washed? What if we miss Game of Thrones*?* In every relationship, sex drive is a combination of excitation and inhibition—how much we're on the gas, how much we're on the brakes.

Intimacy issues can be very serious and may require professional help, but eliminating as many potential inhibitors can go a long way toward facilitating a healthy, satisfying sex life. While you're in bed, you want to be thinking about *him* after all, not everything else. If you're worried about the kids, send them over for a sleepover or to stay with your parents. If you're worried about work, put in a few late nights earlier in the week to make room for personal time. And the hell with those dishes; they'll still be there when you get around to them.

As unsexy as this sounds, you do sometimes have to schedule sex. As an expert in sex therapy, time and again Ian has seen couples who suddenly realized how much they missed having sex only after Ian had them actually schedule it into their calendars. As I like to say, the most important sex organ is your brain. Think about what turns you on and go for it. Is it acting out an actual fantasy? Or maybe visualizing one? Is it dirty talk? Sexy stories and images? Props and toys? We have all heard how men vacuuming or doing dishes is one of the greatest forms of foreplay. If housework is preventing you from having an active sex life, lovingly let your partner know this. Ask him to help with X, Y, or Z and then together plan for some sexy us-time, posthaste! Nothing is more of a libido-killer than resentment and criticism. By practicing Radical Acceptance, you are paving the way to a better sex life.

There are a million more data points about the benefits of sex. Regular sex also contributes to better health, better skin, better immunity, better sleep, pain relief, reduced stress, better moods, and so much more. What else can I say but "Quit making excuses and just do it!"

Here's a story from Carolyn, a friend whom I have counseled about the importance of sex in her marriage. Her experiences may resonate with you, especially if you're middle-aged with kids and have a demanding job, a husband, and seemingly endless things to do.

> *My husband and I have different needs in this area. I want to talk and share, which, to me, fosters emotional closeness. My husband likes the physical closeness of making love. Over the history of our relationship, I have found that when I'm stressed, my desire for lovemaking goes down. When my husband is stressed, his desire for lovemaking goes up.*
>
> *It's been a challenge for us! However, with Radical Acceptance, I have altered my perception of sex. I recognize that making love is a way to show my care for my husband and for him to show his care for me. Additionally, when I get out of my head and shift my attention from my worries (which cause me to feel stressed) to being in the moment and enjoying the physical sensation of kissing my dear husband, being embraced by him, and getting turned on by one another, we both benefit. I experience physiological relaxation, even though my initial thoughts—I'm too tired, I don't have time, I'm not interested—usually conspire to deter me. I have learned to just overcome my own resistance because it's so good for both of us. After the fact, my husband and I are more likely to talk to each other, to laugh together, and to act and feel closer.*

It's been said that men talk with women so they'll have sex with them, whereas women have sex with men so that they'll talk with them. I know this is a sweeping generalization, but when I think about Carolyn's experience, and innumerable other couples' experiences, it's clear that sex is a powerful common means for both men and women to get the intimacy they need out of a relationship.

Did I say *just do it, already*? All righty, then.

ATTACHMENT

Love can be strengthened through nonsexual physical touch. In this book, we have talked about the "cuddle hormone," oxytocin. Oxytocin makes us feel warm and happy when we're with loved ones, close friends, or even pets. In one University of North Carolina at Chapel Hill study,[64] researchers asked long-term couples to hold hands and reminisce about happy memories. After drawing blood and having participants fill out questionnaires, the researchers determined that the happiest couples also had the highest levels of oxytocin circulating in their blood.

Meanwhile, recent studies have shown that oxytocin makes all of us, male and female, more sympathetic, supportive, and feel more secure in our relationships. One analysis found that couples with the highest levels of oxytocin were more likely to remain together six months later. Moreover, these couples were more attuned to each other: they finished each other's sentences, they laughed more, and—most notably— touched each other more.

Simple, everyday touching has greatly enhanced my own marriage. I make a very deliberate effort to touch Sanjay regularly, starting with hugs. Hugs are super important, friends! Health-wise, a Carnegie Mellon University study[65] of about four hundred adults found that people who felt the most social support in the form of stress-reducing hugs were less likely to get sick after being exposed to the cold virus, and even those who did get sick were more likely to recover faster. The more you hug your partner, the more oxytocin is released into your system. You will be happier and healthier!

I regularly hug Sanjay, especially after coming home from work. He'll often loosely put his arms around me and then instinctively pull away after a moment. Not so fast! I squeeze him even tighter, hold it for several seconds, and say something funny or loving to him. I am very conscious about finding other ways to touch him and vice versa, whether it's sitting next to each other on the couch, holding hands while watching a movie or while walking or driving, touching our feet while we eat or sit at a table, et cetera.

It's amazing how Mother Nature causes oxytocin levels to rise when two people touch in loving ways. Helen Fisher, also a passionate advocate for maintaining and strengthening attachment through touch, wholeheartedly agrees! She told me, "To sustain feelings of attachment, you need to stay in touch. And by *in touch* I don't mean by phone. A hug. A kiss. Hold hands. Put your foot on top of his during lunch. Learn to sleep in his arms. Put your leg over his leg. Sit side by side in the restaurant. Put your hand on this thigh. All of this drives up the oxytocin system and gives you feelings of deep attachment."

These tiny gestures, ideally repeated several times a day, truly add up. Be sure not to keep score and don't get angry if he doesn't touch you as often as you touch him. We're all different.

A joint survey[66] conducted by the renowned Kinsey Institute for Research in Sex, Gender, and Reproduction and K-Y (yes, the makers of the lubricant. My brother Tom likes to quip, "Lubri-can't? Oh, I say lubri-*CAN!*" Touché, Tommy!) found that 87 percent of both men and women agree that touch is extremely important to intimacy, but sadly more than a third admitted they don't get enough of it in their relationship. Numerous studies have found that engaging in cuddling after sex for at least fifteen minutes has positive effects on your body and relationship. If you have the time to extend that fifteen minutes even longer, go for it! Sure, you may have a million things to do, but try to remember how beneficial this time together is for you both.

ROMANCE: THE VALUE OF NEW EXPERIENCES

Attachment keeps you connected in a deep, loving way. But let's face it: what's most exciting about romantic love is, well, the romance! As we all know, that's what is celebrated and trumpeted in endless books, epic movie romances, and TV shows. The chemistry behind romantic love is potent. Who hasn't experienced the high of being head over heels for someone? Your brain chemistry is altered during the phase of intense infatuation. Needless to say, these feelings of lust and magnetic romantic attraction almost always fade as time goes on, even for couples that still love each other deeply. As Helen LaKelly Hunt says, "After the ecstasy comes the laundry." I'm not sure whether to laugh or cry at her assessment, but what's certain is that I wholeheartedly agree.

We all crave these feelings of excitement and chemistry, and we all want them to last. Cheer up, folks. I have some good news for you! There is a relatively easy and fun way to maintain or rekindle those early exciting romantic feelings: experience new things together.

I can attest to how adding novel activities and experiences has kindled romance and excitement in my marriage. But the real "aha!" came to me through research I conducted. A few years back, YourTango surveyed 584 people about their relationships. We asked, "What's the number one way for couples to avoid becoming lazy or complacent in their relationship?"

The overwhelming answer? More than 52 percent of respondents answered, "Try new things together." A distant second, at only 20 percent, was, "Do small gestures like writing love notes and doing the other's 'chores,'" followed by "Go on dates on a regular basis" clocking in third place with only 16 percent of the vote. I gotta hand it to the wisdom of the crowds here!

I shared this insight with Helen Fisher who enthusiastically agreed and corroborated my research findings as brain science. To paraphrase her response: Your brain lights up when doing new things, much like it lights up when experiencing the early stages of romantic love. In both cases, dopamine and norepinephrine give you a nice little buzz.

Guess what this means?! You gotta add novelty to your relationship, including shaking up your date night routine!

I was excited to see how Tara Parker-Pope, one of my favorite *New*

York Times columnists, further corroborates my insights: "Using laboratory studies, real-world experiments and even brain-scan data," Tara wrote in a column, "scientists can now offer long-married couples a simple prescription for rekindling the romantic love that brought them together in the first place. The solution? Reinventing date night." She added that "Several experiments show that novelty—simply doing new things together as a couple—may help bring the butterflies back, recreating the chemical surges of early courtship."

Prioritize planning a date at least two to three times per month. (A date should not be limited to what you'd typically do on a Saturday night. A date is anything you do that's meant to give you and your partner quality time together.) Weekly is better, but do what you can. Commit yourself to trying different things and hanging out with different people as a way to add some zing to your relationship, especially if you have been together for a long time. In other words, going to your favorite restaurant followed by a movie week after week will no longer cut it. New experiences stimulate your brain's reward system by flooding it with dopamine and norepinephrine. *Ding, ding, ding!* Remember my conversation with Helen Fisher above? Dopamine and norepinephrine are those beautiful neurotransmitters that make you feel happy and high when you are in the early, exciting stages of romantic love.

"We don't really know what's going on in the brain," Helen admitted about this phenomenon. "But as you trigger and amp up this reward system in the brain that is associated with romantic love, it's reasonable to suggest that it's enabling you to feel more romantic love. You're altering your brain chemistry." Indeed, Arthur Aron, a professor of social psychology at the State University of New York at Stony Brook, studied fifty-three long-term couples and found that those who tried ten weeks of exciting new activities scored much higher on marital-satisfaction surveys compared with couples who merely did the same old thing week after week.

There are so many ways to shake up date night: going dancing for the first time in a million years, taking a cooking class, seeing a new exhibit in a nearby museum, attending a live sporting event, or going to a new bar in a different part of town. In most cities, there are so many options: improv or stand-up at a comedy club, concerts, musicals, plays. The list goes on and on. Sometimes they are even free! In New York City, every summer throughout parks in the five boroughs, the New York Philharmonic plays for free. This is one of my absolute favorite things to do.

While planning will be required some of the time, spontaneity can also pay off. If the weather is nice and the sky is clear, you can go out to stargaze. So many cool apps make stargazing easier and more rewarding, no telescope required. You can go for an evening walk, drive, or if you live near water, go for a boat ride. Stop for a decadent dessert or two or a glass of wine at that hole-in-the-wall wine bar on your way home. Many museums, universities, and cultural centers offer lectures, concerts, and other events. Put on perfume and something to wear that makes you feel attractive. Or go in a different direction. Try Tough Mudder or even hashing (yes, I mean to refer to the more formal name of Hash House Harriers. Not familiar? Google it. You're in for a treat!)

By the way, this isn't exclusively relegated to date night! There are a million more ways to infuse your relationship with novelty. You can try going on a road trip to someplace new, discovering a new (or old) TV show on Netflix that you both love and look forward to watching together, exploring a new neighborhood after Sunday brunch, or taking up a new sport that you can both play—the possibilities are truly endless. You will find that with a little initiative, you will have a blast and stay closer than ever!

Whatever you choose, force yourself not to think about work or things causing you stress, but instead enjoy this time to relax, have fun, and experience some novelty together.

One of the things I love most about doing new things together is how it creates lasting memories. Just think about it: Do you remember going to the same restaurant again and again or watching TV reruns together night after night? No! You are more likely to remember the special occasions, when something was different, and hopefully fun and somehow impactful. Moreover, by venturing out of your comfort zone, even just a little, you can count on different emotions bubbling up to make these experiences more meaningful and memorable. Whether you feel apprehensive, happy, amused, or challenged, these emotions are likely to stick with you and facilitate bonding. Emotions are the ink with which your brain records lasting memories.

What's also cool about doing new things together is the sense of anticipation that often builds in advance. When Sanjay and I plan to do something new, I love the simple joy of looking forward to trying something different together and then having a special, funny, or challenging experience to reflect upon after the fact. It becomes part of our shared history.

Another reliable way to add novelty to your relationship is through surprises. Studies have shown that surprises—even simple ones like chocolate or flowers—trigger the reward centers of our brains by supplying a healthy dose of dopamine, which adds a sense of mystery to a secure and stable relationship. The key is to make them unpredictable. Once someone starts to expect a certain behavior, while still thoughtful and appreciated, it ceases to be a surprise.

When I had first moved to New York, Sanjay sent me a bouquet of roses for Valentine's Day that could have been a centerpiece at the Four Seasons or Ritz-Carlton. They were so beautiful. Three dozen enormous, four-foot-high roses with towering stems and bursting red petals. God only knows how much he spent on them! Even after all these years I remember that surprise so vividly.

Some of the wonderful surprises that I have sprung on Sanjay include concert tickets for some of his favorite bands—yes, even though some of them are far from my favorites—and Broadway shows such as *The Book of Mormon*. I planned an elaborate surprise birthday party with some of his best friends where we all enjoyed a cooking lesson in a darling little restaurant in the East Village. Sanjay had always wanted to learn how to make a perfect spaghetti Bolognese. Now he knows! Years later, our friends still talk about that night.

Once we were on vacation when we came across a jewelry store. I'm not someone to fuss over jewelry, but I fell in love with a silver David Yurman necklace with a gorgeous blue topaz pendant. It was stunning, but just not practical for wearing day to day. I ended up picking a different necklace with a pretty silver pendant that was much more functional, one that I could wear every day. But when we returned to the hotel, Sanjay told me that he and our one-year-old son, Nicolas, had a surprise for me. There was the blue topaz pendant! I was shocked and so touched by this loving, generous, and unexpected gesture.

While jewelry and flowers are always a treat, what's even better is when Sanjay comes home early from a long trip as a surprise to the kids and me. Another sweet, surprise gesture is when he'll call or text me around the time I typically leave my office in Chelsea to tell me he is waiting outside in an Uber to escort me home. Hah! Take that, C train!

One of my favorite surprise stories comes from a couple we know at my kids' school, Maria and Jason, who have three young boys. In a truly made-for-the-movies gesture, Jason made arrangements for his in-laws to look after the boys so that he could whisk Maria off for an extended, romantic weekend. He had made all of the arrangements in secret, and on the day of the trip he simply told Maria to pack a bag. He wouldn't tell her where they were going until they reached the airport. Maria almost died when she saw her boarding pass—Paris! Of course, any trip to Paris is a dream come true, but for a hands-on mom with three young boys, Maria was especially deserving of such a loving, over-the-top surprise.

Another one of my favorite stories is when my dear friend Brian engineered a surprise fortieth-birthday party for his wife and one of my besties, Meredith. What makes this story especially cool is that Brian and Meredith live in Houston and the party was in New York!

Brian managed to get a bunch of Meredith's closest far-flung friends from Texas, Raleigh, Atlanta, and beyond to all converge in the Big Apple for an epic girls' weekend. Meredith initially thought Brian was sending her up to merely spend the weekend with me, but she started becoming suspicious when another of her close friends was "coincidentally" on the same flight from Houston. After they landed, they picked up our friend Jaime from Atlanta at a different terminal at La-Guardia Airport, and within eighteen hours Brian had managed to get ten of her best gal pals together for one of the best weekends ever. He stayed home to watch the kids, but he made sure we were all well fed, sufficiently "watered," and otherwise entertained! It took a lot of planning and coordinating, but it truly meant the world to Meredith. We all had a blast being part of an ingenious surprise for someone we all love and admire.

I could go on and on and on. While it's wonderful to be on the receiving end, it's also hard to beat the fun and excitement of planning and keeping a secret for your partner that you know he'll love. And remember: a wonderful surprise doesn't have to involve elaborate plans or exorbitant sums of money. A handwritten, heartfelt letter; a surprise day-date together to some unexpected nearby place or perhaps the beach; tickets for two to a movie he's been talking about; or getting up early to grab his favorite fresh doughnuts or bagels from the local bakery. Just pay attention to what interests him and be ready to seize the moment!

What small surprise can you pull off this week? Is there a big one that you can get in motion? Have fun!

PRIORITIZE FUN AND LAUGHTER

As Charlie Chaplin once said, "A day without laughter is a day wasted." That goes doubly so for relationships. Study after study demonstrates that the couples who laugh together the most are also the happiest. In one study conducted by researchers at the University of North Carolina,[67] seventy-seven couples were videotaped together as they recalled how they first met. The researchers noted how often these couples laughed together and how long the moment lasted. Then the participants filled out surveys to judge their overall relationship satisfaction. Sure enough, the research team concluded that "In general, couples who laugh more together tend to have higher-quality relationships. We can refer to shared laughter as an indicator of greater relationship quality."

Fun is part and parcel with trying new experiences and surprises, which we talked about in the previous section. But even when you're not on some new adventure, laughter and fun also deserve to be a daily experience. Sanjay and I share a quirky sense of humor, which allows us to have a lot of fun together. I like to tease him a lot, lovingly of course. Sanjay has a healthy ego, but he knows how to laugh at himself, too. A little humor goes a long way to keeping egos in check—both yours and his!

Sanjay is also the ultimate audience. He will offer up a hearty laugh even at my lame attempts at humor. He is a very good sport and we are able to have fun even during the more mundane aspects of our life. We have quite a few inside jokes that ebb and flow, but over the years we have brought a lot of fun and laughter into our home and our relationship.

Take vacations together as much as you can reasonably afford. It wasn't until Sanjay and I had kids that we really started prioritizing vacations. And I now take this time away together much more seriously. I would rather forgo material items any day to spend quality time with Sanjay and our friends and family.

When Nicolas, our oldest son, was two, Sanjay and I took an incredibly memorable bike trip through Burgundy with some friends. The combination of entertaining company, delicious food, and long days of riding through beautiful scenery (oh! And a ton of uh-mazing wine), was a real splurge for us. But totally worth it. It was the trip of a lifetime.

Too tight on time or money to do a vacation? Even a two- or three-day weekend to a destination an hour or two away can do wonders. Airbnb has revolutionized tourism, making it much more affordable to travel. I am also a huge fan of camping. One of the most spectacularly smart decisions this great nation of ours implemented was to create so many fantastic national parks, and there are many campgrounds that accommodate budget-conscious travel. Plus, there's nothing like being in the great outdoors to lift your soul, and nothing more romantic than marveling at the magic of Mother Nature with someone you love.

If you cannot afford to take the time off to travel now, that's okay. But if it's mostly a matter of inertia that is preventing you from shaking up your routine and launching off on a bit of an adventure together, I say do it!

Besides, I am pretty sure there is scientific evidence that proves hotel sex is, in fact, the best sex.

LEARNING TO SAY YES!

We talked at length about how leaving the comfort zone and saying yes to new experiences and people can led to beautiful outcomes for singles.

Learning to say yes works very well in existing relationships, too—especially those that have become a bit calcified, where each partner knows his or her role and they play it to a T. Do you often find yourself saying no to your partner? If so, really examine why this is. I bet you'll find there are some grubby, menacing control issues at work that are preventing you from saying yes to a potentially awesome experience, or at least to something that really shouldn't be automatically ruled out. Raise your hand if you're guilty of doing this to your partner, if you're guilty of reflexively saying no without a solid reason to something he wants to do. Yes, I admit it: my hand is high in the air. Hard to type with one hand of course, but I have to be honest.

Try to be conscious of when you are automatically saying no. Too much work. Too little sleep. I know—there is always so much work to do. If you have young kids, they have to eat, learn how to read, eventually take a bath, and a spontaneous dinner out or road trip to a nearby amusement park hasn't been scheduled into your calendar. You know—all the crappy reasons we give for saying no to our partners. Unless his suggestion is likely to inflict bodily harm, or if it's illegal (and even then at least consider it!), really try to say yes as often and as wholeheartedly as you can.

This is a beautiful story from a woman named Cynthia who finally said yes about something that powerfully improved her marriage and entire family life. She wrote to me,

I consider myself to be a spiritual person rather than a religious one. While raised Catholic, I became disenchanted with the more mainstream religious outlets in my area. I have long sought to awaken, evolve, and find meaning through spirituality. My husband, Jake, isn't religious or spiritual, but he has always been a good sport about my spiritual studies and interests.

When our oldest child, William, turned seven, I wanted him and our six-year-old daughter, Hanna, to grow up in a community tuned into the "bigger picture," e.g., to God, or consciousness, or the Source of Life. I felt frustrated that we were not finding a strong moral message and a tradition that had legs beneath it. Furthermore, I knew that if my children were to look to me as the primary example of living a spiritually directed life, I would fall short, like, every day.

I felt stuck. It was really important for me to have our family join a strong, spiritually centered community, but so far, no luck. One day Jake said, "Let's try the Orthodox Church." He was raised going to an Orthodox Church by his parents, but he hadn't been a member on

his own accord. Invoking Radical Acceptance, I set aside all my hang-ups about traditional Christian churches. I agreed to try it.

    Our family went to a local Orthodox Church and we were thrilled by what we discovered. We found that the leadership and church community was remarkably open-minded and the tradition itself was rich with philosophy, scholarship, and depth. Questions and doubt are actually embraced here! I was also really encouraged by the priest, who is super smart, kind, and humble. I finally felt that I had landed upon a mystical path that would allow me to become closer to God and share this important experience with my family. Attending church together and participating in this community as a family have become an important part of our lives, something that my kids enjoy and something that has greatly strengthened my marriage.

    The love and wisdom of Radical Acceptance enabled me to put my preconceived notions aside. By saying yes to something that, in fact, I had incorrectly judged, I finally found something that I have sought my entire life—in the most unexpected place. I feel deeply blessed that I get to share this treasure with my family.

Can I get an Amen!? I truly love this story. Often, the most powerful action you can take is to open your heart and mind, especially to your partner. In this case, Cynthia did both by saying yes to something she was convinced was not for her. Her experience reminds me of *Green Eggs and Ham*. Dr. Seuss was seriously on to something. Sure, we think of it as a fun-to-read kids' book, but hooey! It's downright prophetic. The moral of the story: even if you're convinced you know what you're talking about, sometimes it's worth laying aside your preconceptions to say, "Okay, I will try it."

    And say! Like this new thing, you may! Try it, try it, I say! Preconceptions be damned, you may like it anyway! You may like this new thing here or there, you may like this new thing, anywhere! (Don't worry, I have not summoned Thing One or Thing Two to assist with any further writing of this book.)

ZERO NEGATIVITY

I want to mention a simple but powerful strategy from Harville Hendrix and Helen LaKelly Hunt that works to minimize put-downs and slights. Remember the concept of symbiotic consciousness? We tend to assume that everyone around us sees the world more or less the same way we do. If another person disrupts that narrative—especially a loved one—it throws our brain chemistry out of whack. This is particularly prevalent during disagreements. Harville notes that during fights you don't have two selves interacting; you have two *defenses* interacting. Why? Because we can't accept, from a neurobiological standpoint, that this other person can possibly see things differently.

In step 3, we talked about positive and productive ways to fight, but that doesn't necessarily mean that fighting is inherently good. Conflict arises when we can't accept another person's point of view. But for all you third-degree Radical Acceptance black belts out there, you might be thinking: "If I can always radically accept him, why should we ever fight?" Good question!

Difference is a defining feature of nature, and we're always going to have varying opinions. No couple is perfect, and it's nearly impossible to have a conflict-free relationship, but through practice and an abundance of reliable, predictable safety in your relationship, you can become closer with a technique known as Zero Negativity. Note: this is not a justification to avoid conflict for all of you out there who identify as conflict avoiders! Additionally, you don't want to avoid conflict before you have the tools to deal with it safely and productively. If you avoid conflict because you are afraid of dealing with his temper, or if you are afraid that he'll put you down, then you are not in a healthy, safe place.

I urge you to master the Imago framework we talked about in step 3 before you tackle Zero Negativity. When you are at peace with conflict, then you can work on putting it to bed.

Harville and Helen realized that most relationship fights arise because one partner puts the other down—often times inadvertently. When you are negative toward your partner you are chipping away at the safety in your relationship. Harville and Helen told me about a nightly practice they stumbled upon: every evening for five minutes they discuss when they each felt put down by the other, no matter how trivial it seemed. For example, one time they were in a taxi together and Harville said, "Helen, look! They're putting up a new building on that corner." Helen, who was busy on her iPhone, mumbled, "Oh, that's great," without looking up from the screen. Later that night Harville mentioned that he had felt slightly rejected. "Nothing is as important as feeling honored in a relationship," Helen says now. "Even if I'm not in the mood, I always make sure to look up when he says, 'Hey, look at that!'"

Reserving a five-minute window every day like this is a fantastic way to build trust in your relationship, though it's a good idea to establish some ground rules first. Before you begin, both you and your partner must agree not to be defensive, not to reject what the other person has to say. Zero judgment, zero negativity—only acceptance is allowed. It might be a bit awkward and scary at first, but this exercise can rapidly become a mainstay of your routine. You can even pair this with Stop, Reflect, Introspect! If he is negative toward you earlier in the day, use Stop, Reflect, Introspect to avoid an outburst. Then, later at night, you can calmly bring it up in a safe space.

Try challenging yourselves by seeing how long you can go without being negative! At first, Harville and Helen tried going twenty-four hours without being negative toward each other. Then they began filling out a calendar and marking each successful day with a smiley face. It took them quite a long time to be able to make it a day without putting each other down. But they stuck with it and now they practically glow when they're together. Harville and Helen have started a Zero Negativity movement to teach others what they know to be very difficult, but ultimately extremely rewarding and transformative. Don't expect results overnight—it was hard for even the foremost relationship experts in the world to master—but it can be done!

You can even make a contest out of it (this is especially great if your partner has a very competitive spirit). The more you can relax and enjoy yourself, the more comfortable you will feel being vulnerable. And you'll quickly find how incredibly contagious kindness can be!

THE GRASS IS ALWAYS GREENER WHERE YOU WATER IT

I am happy to save some of my favorite, best advice for last. It flows largely from Zero Negativity, but it's also super simple and distilled: compliment and express your appreciation to your partner. Helen Fisher described to me research she stumbled across revealing that couples who compliment each other three times per day lower their levels of cortisol, which is the body's principal stress hormone. Moreover, these couples also lower their overall cholesterol levels through this mutual admiration activity. Expressing gratitude and sincere appreciation to each other makes you happier *and* healthier! It's easy to complain that the grass is always greener on the other side. I prefer to say that the grass is greener where you water it! Regularly dispensing gratitude and appreciation is a great way to water your relationship.

Offering three genuine compliments or expressions of gratitude every day to your partner also helps feed the positive-illusions effect, which we talked about during step 4. To recap, positive illusions are ways in which we can accentuate the positives in someone while overlooking the negatives. By complimenting or expressing appreciation to him regularly you aren't just making him feel better about himself; you're training your brain to seek out the best in him.

Make sure you do it sincerely. Don't phone it in. After all, he won't believe you really love his haircut if you're actually answering emails when you deliver the compliment. In addition, make sure not to repeat the same three compliments every day. By delivering three specific compliments every day, you are enabling yourself to see your partner in the best way possible. I used to not notice or think about as many positive, specific things about Sanjay over the course of my day. And if I did, I would not necessarily verbalize it to him. The three-compliments method has opened up yet another sweet communication channel between us. Sometimes I'll tease, and say something that is very gratuitous and we both laugh. He'll say something that's semijudgmental but cloaked as a compliment and we laugh—it is so much more of a positive, effective way for him to communicate critical feedback to me.

Dr. John Gray agreed with me about how consistent positive reinforcement is incredibly important:

> *The two most important things that a man needs from his partner to bring out the best of him and to lower his stress are unconditional acceptance of who he is, and appreciating the efforts he puts forth.*
>
> *When your partner is talking, if you say something like, "Wow, that makes sense," you've suddenly given him the message that you appreciate and trust him. Immediately he'll puff up and feel better. A practical takeaway is to remember these phrases: "That makes sense," "good idea," "you're right," or "that's so helpful." Any of those expressions coming from a woman's heart will brighten a man's day.*
>
> *When your partner doesn't feel accepted the way he is, he may begin to lose his confidence, which triggers the fight-or-flight response.*

That's why simple kindness and affirmation can go such a long way toward reducing his stress levels. Feed his ego and have fun spoiling him with three bits of daily praise. It's good for your body and your heart—and his, too.

Add in plenty of "thank you's" for good measure. If he does the dishes or takes out the trash, say thank you. Gratitude is incredibly contagious. Especially if you have kids in the house, find reasons to say, "You rock!" or "Thank you! You're amazing!" even for small things. It feels so good to be appreciated.

Finally! My last suggestion is the simplest: manage your relationship for the long run. You want to be happily together with him for years and years? Then take the long-term view and behave accordingly. I swear it works and becomes easier the more you do it! Sanjay and I do this much more readily for one another and our marriage has benefitted greatly as a result.

Rather than being reactive and operating in the immediate moment, simply remind yourself that what you do and say (or don't do and say) is paving the way for your future as a couple. How will that loving gesture or knee-jerk negative response help or hinder your long-term success? You are on the same team, *and you want to remain on the same team.*

Even when you feel like lashing out, hitting back, defending your point of view, withdrawing, proving you were right, or doing anything that will be perceived as hurtful or a put down, please, please, pause. Instead, lead your relationship where you really want to go, *together*: up the high road, and for the long run. This is the path that leads you to happy, lasting love.

- Watch couples that you admire. Notice the subtle things: when they look out for each other, when they apologize, when they cut each other slack.
- Have more sex! A relationship will eventually wither without sufficient physical intimacy. Aim for having sex at least once per week.
- Surprise him from time to time with something sweet, small or large. Whatever it is, make it thoughtful and unexpected. Savor the fun you have in being sneaky in such a loving way.

- The grass is always greener where you water it! Give your partner three genuine compliments or phrases of praise or thanks every day. Make them specific and real. Conversely, try to eliminate negativity toward your partner. Most fights happen when one of you puts the other down, oftentimes carelessly and inadvertently.

- Open your heart and mind to the person you love. Practice saying *yes!* as much as possible—even if you have doubts or something isn't your first choice. The key is that you're on the same team and you have each other's backs for the long run.

Whew!

We have concluded this phase of your Radical Acceptance journey. I hope you are inspired and energized, and that you have already started taking steps to love your best! You have accomplished a great deal by reading through to the end of this book and hopefully taking time to go through the various exercises.

I want to underscore that this is a process. I know I have said that many times, but please take it to heart, and as you continue this journey, give yourself all the credit and praise you deserve. There is no way to practice Radical Acceptance perfectly. In an ideal world, each person's approach to Radical Acceptance, pursued with a full heart, will be perfectly imperfect. And, of course, please also give yourself plenty of kindness and understanding along the way, especially when you fall short.

Radical Acceptance is truly a way of life. While I have written this book to assist with dating, marriage, and other forms of romantic relationships, I hope that you have found that Radical Acceptance is a framework that empowers you and has started to positively impact your other relationships, too. I use Radical Acceptance not just in my marriage, but with friends, family members, and business associates.

I hope you will return to this book periodically and find something valuable each time you pick it up. At different stages in your life, certain insights are likely to resonate more than others. Finally, I hope you share your Radical Acceptance experiences with others you love . . . as well as with me! You can reach me at andrea@radicalacceptance.love, as well as on Facebook, Twitter, www.YourTango.com/RadicalAcceptance, and www.radicalacceptance.love. I am also encouraging users to share their Radical Acceptance triumphs and experiences via social media using the hashtag #RadicalAcceptance.

I am always over the moon to hear what's working and when Radical Acceptance makes a powerful, positive impact on people's lives. I also appreciate when people share their challenges and concerns about Radical Acceptance. It is a living, actively evolving practice, one that I am eager to continue to improve upon, so please do share any feedback you may have with me.

I would love it if you were motivated to share your favorite Radical Acceptance highlights with your friends and family, too. With enough of us practicing Radical Acceptance and talking about our experiences, we stand a real shot at sparking a powerful, positive social movement. As I think of it, when we love ourselves and our significant others without judgment, we positively impact who we are as individuals and how we interact with virtually everyone in our lives.

Whether you spread the news or keep Radical Acceptance more of a private thing, I am so grateful to you for being on this journey with me. Thank you. I wish you an abundance of love and happiness.

ACKNOWLEDGMENTS

THANK YOU TO many generous, wonderful people who have been crucial to the birth of this book. Some directly, in a very hands-on way. Others of you have been key to helping me build YourTango and/or helping me get closer to achieving my full potential as an author, entrepreneur, business leader, and person who has learned to be brave and to love deeply without judgment. I am so very grateful to you.

Starting with my parents, Mike and Judi Miller; Sanjay Bhatnagar and his parents, Ram and Krishna Bhatnagar; our beautiful children, Nicolas and Alexander; my spectacular agent from ICM, Kristyn Keene, and my brilliant editor from Simon & Schuster, Sarah Cantin: thank you for being passionate champions of *Radical Acceptance*. An extra special shout-out goes to Nick Bromley for the incredible help you provided in assisting with editing, writing, and researching *Radical Acceptance* along with Gene Stone. David Bell: this book would have never been written had it not been for your encouragement.

My deep, endless gratitude goes to Tom Miller, Maria Miller, Sadhna Bhatnagar, Melanie Gorman, Sabrina James, Helen Fisher, Barry Fingerhut, Phil and Tammy Murphy, Joe and Suzanne Sutton, Mike Perlis, Wenda Harris Millard, Paul Woolmington, Janet Hanson, Phiroze Nagarvala, Mary Elise Miller, Joe and Patsy Shuster, Jimmy Garland, Jacqueline Lundquist, Mark Gatlin, Harville Hendrix and

Helen LaKelly Hunt, Hanna and Wally Miller, Cy and Therese Hennes, and Tom Dechman.

To the YourTango team—thank you! High-fives and hugs all around, as always! Love you all! And to the broader YourTango community: our Expert members, contributors, investors, and partners: huge thanks for your contributions and helping us achieve our mission! You rock! Steve Carlis, Hank Norman, Terri Trespicio, and Jani Moon: thank you for helping get this ball rolling.

Thank you so very much to Judith Curr, Suzanne Donahue, Albert Tang, Lisa Sciambra, Jackie Jou, Tory Lowy, Lisa Keim, and the many other talented, incredible people at Atria who have been crucial to bringing *Radical Acceptance* to the world.

Lots of love and thanks to all of my amazing friends and family members—especially to my super awesome cousins—as well as to the leadership, instructors, and my fellow karateka at JKA NYC. Osu!

Infinite thanks to those of you who allowed me to interview you for this book and who shared your stories with me. And finally, huge, heartfelt thanks to the wonderful researchers, authors, and thought leaders whose research and insights I reference in this book.

I am so grateful and indebted to you all. Namaste.

NOTES

1 *Helen has discovered compelling insights:* Dr. Helen Fisher (biological anthropologist), interview with the author, February 20, 2016. See also, Helen E. Fisher, *Anatomy of Love: A Natural History of Mating, Marriage, and Why We Stray.* (New York: W.W. Norton, 2016), 306–8.

2 *There is no safe investment:* C. S. Lewis, *The Four Loves.* (New York: Harcourt Brace Jovanovich, 1991), 121.

3 *Rather than relationships shaping people:* Dr. Dan Siegel (clinical professor of psychiatry), UCLA School of Medicine, interview with the author, June 2, 2016.

4 *There was a famous antidrug PSA:* Johann Hari, "The Likely Cause of Addiction Has Been Discovered, and It Is Not What You Think," *Huffington Post,* January 20, 2015, http://www.huffingtonpost.com/johann-hari/the-real-cause-of-addicti_b _6506936.html?

5 *Nine out of ten laboratory rats:* "Cocaine Rat—Drug-Free America," YouTube video, posted by "Video Disorder," August 21, 2011, https://www.youtube.com /watch?v=7kS72J5Nlm8.

6 *From a mystical perspective:* Lorell Frysh (interfaith spiritual counselor and PhD), interview with the author, April 5, 2016.

7 *The ability to trust another person:* Dr. Stan Tatkin (clinician), interview with the author, February 10, 2016.

8 *Ideally, all babies have a parent:* Stan Tatkin, *Wired for Love: How Understanding Your Partner's Brain and Attachment Style Can Help You Defuse Conflict and Build a Secure Relationship* (Oakland, CA: New Harbinger Publications, 2011), 16.

9 *As Helen explained:* Helen LaKelly Hunt (author and relationship counselor), interview with the author. April 28, 2016.

10 *Go and love someone:* Project Happiness. Accessed May 5, 2016. https://project happiness.com/challenge-go-and-love-someone-exactly-as-they-are-and-then -watch-how-quickly-they-transform-into-the-greatest-truest-version-of-them selves-when-one-feels-seen-and-appreciated-in-their-own-essence.

11 *When I told the illustrious professor:* Dr. Pat Love (author and relationship counselor), interview with the author, March 15, 2016.

12 *In one of her brilliant TED Talks:* Helen Fisher, "Why We Love, Why We Cheat," TED, posted September 2006, transcript, https://www.ted.com/talks/helen _fisher_tells_us_why_we_love_cheat/transcript?language=en.

13 *To better understand how this works:* Ian Kerner (psychotherapist and sexuality counselor, PhD, LMFT), interview with the author, April 14, 2016.

14 *An interesting set of studies:* Judith Gere, Geoff MacDonald, Samantha Joel, Stephanie S. Spielmann, Emily A. Impett. "The Independent Contributions of Social Reward and Threat Perceptions to Romantic Commitment, *Journal of Personality and Social Psychology* 105, no. 6 (2013): 961.

15 *You are the problem with you!* "The Price of Admission," YouTube video, posted by "Kemamam222," August 21, 2011, https://www.youtube.com/watch?v=r1tCAX VsClw.

16 *In 2012, the Harvard University social scientist Amy Cuddy:* Amy Cuddy, "Your Body Language Shapes Who You Are," TED, filmed June 2012, transcript, https:// www.ted.com/talks/amy_cuddy_your_body_language_shapes_who_you_are /transcript?language=en.

17 *A University of California, Berkeley study:* Tanya Vacharkulksemsuk, Emily Reit, Poruz Khambatta, Paul W. Eastwick, Eli J. Finkel, and Dana R. Carney. "Dominant, Open Nonverbal Displays Are Attractive at Zero-Acquaintance. *PNAS* 113, no. 15 (2016), 4009–14.

18 *My advice is this: Settle!* Lori Gottlieb, "Marry Him! The Case for Settling for Mr. Good Enough," *The Atlantic*, March 2008, http://www.theatlantic.com/mag azine/archive/2008/03/marry-him/306651.

19 *A Harvard professor:* Paul Bentley, "Why an Arranged Marriage 'Is More Likely to Develop into Lasting Love,'" *Daily Mail*, March 4, 2011, http://www.dailymail .co.uk/news/article-1363176/Why-arranged-marriage-likely-develop-lasting -love.html.

20 *When you hear a Flo Rida song:* Aziz Ansari and Eric Klinenberg, *Modern Romance* (New York: Penguin, 2015), 247.

21 *As the psychology professor Barry Schwartz famously points out:* Barry Schwartz, *The Paradox of Choice* (New York: HarperCollins, 2009).

22 *The hilarious Aziz Ansari recounts:* Ansari and Klinenberg, *Modern Romance*, 90.

23 *Just think of reasons to say yes:* Dr. Helen Fisher (biological anthropologist), interview with the author, February 20, 2016.

24 *In a lecture for the Royal Society for the Arts:* "The Power of Vulnerability—Brené Brown." YouTube video, posted by "The RSA," August 15, 2013, https://www.you tube.com/watch?v=sXSjc-pbXk4.

25 *One variable she found was courage:* Brené Brown, "The Power of Vulnerability," TED, posted December 2010, transcript, https://www.ted.com/talks/brene _brown_on_vulnerability/transcript?language=en.

26 *I ran into this unnamed thing.* Brené Brown, "The Power of Vulnerability" TED,

posted December 2010, transcript, https://www.ted.com/talks/brene_brown_on
_vulnerability/transcript?language=en

27 *Recently,* Time *magazine ran a fascinating article:* Alexandra Sifferlin, "The Healing Power of Nature," *Time,* July 14, 2016, http://time.com/4405827/the-healing
-power-of-nature.

28 *In one amazing study:* James A. Coan, Hillary S. Schaefer, and Richard J. David-
son, "Lending a Hand: Social Regulation of the Neural Response to Threat," *Psychological Science,* December 2006.

29 *Most people live in a symbiotic consciousness:* Harville Hendrix (author and relationship counselor), interview with the author, April 28, 2016.

30 *Safety is nonnegotiable:* Harville Hendrix (author and relationship counselor), interview with the author, April 28, 2016.

31 *In an interview, Dr. Porges explained:* Dr. Stephen Porges (professor in the Department of Psychiatry, University of North Carolina at Chapel Hill) interview
with the author, June 30, 2016.

32 *Neil Sattin, who interviewed Dr. Porges:* Neil Sattin, "34: The Science of Safety
with Stephen Porges," April 11, 2016, http://www.neilsattin.com/blog/2016/04
/34-the-science-of-safety-with-stephen-porges.

33 *The experiments were popularized*: Emily Esfahani Smith, "Masters of Love," *The
Atlantic,* June 12, 2014, http://www.theatlantic.com/health/archive/2014/06
/happily-ever-after/372573.

34 *John Gray, author of the mega-bestseller:* Dr. John Gray (author and relationship
counselor), interview with the author, May 16, 2016.

35 *Stan writes in his book:* Stan Tatkin, *Wired for Love: How Understanding Your
Partner's Brain and Attachment Style Can Help You Defuse Conflict and Build a
Secure Relationship* (Oakland, CA: New Harbinger Publications, 2011), 93.

36 *For example, a study conducted by psychologists*: Patricia Donovan, "Study Finds
That Curiosity Is Key to Personal Growth in Many Spheres, Including Intimate
Relationships," the State University of New York at Buffalo, December 16, 2002,
http://www.buffalo.edu/news/releases/2002/12/5996.html.

37 *Dr. Pat Love, the preeminent relationship expert:* Dr. Pat Love (author and relationship counselor) interview with the author, March 15, 2016.

38 *One of Helen's colleagues:* Fisher, *Anatomy of Love,* 307.

39 *We'd go to the Metropolitan Museum:* Dr. Helen Fisher (biological anthropologist), interview with the author, Feb. 20, 2016.

40 *John Gray agrees:* Dr. John Gray (author and relationship counselor) interview
with the author, May 16, 2016.

41 *For example, an Institute of Leadership and Management study*: Katty Kay and
Claire Shipman, "The Confidence Gap," *The Atlantic,* May 2014, http://www.the
atlantic.com/magazine/archive/2014/05/the-confidence-gap/359815.

42 *In another fascinating study:* Katty Kay and Claire Shipman, "The Confidence
Gap," *The Atlantic,* May 2014, http://www.theatlantic.com/magazine/archive
/2014/05/the-confidence-gap/359815.

43 In *studies, men overestimate their abilities:* Katty Kay and Claire Shipman, "The Confidence Gap," *The Atlantic,* May 2014, http://www.theatlantic.com/magazine /archive/2014/05/the-confidence-gap/359815.

44 *In an interview with the* Huffington Post: Laura Dunn, "Women in Business Q&A: Shelley Zalis, Founder of The Girls' Lounge," *Huffington Post,* July 05, 2014, http:// www.huffingtonpost.com/laura-dunn/women-in-business-qa-shel_b_5559460 .html.

45 *A Harvard University study:* Britta K. Hölzel, James Carmody, Mark Vangel, Christina Congleton, Sita M. Yerramsetti, Tim Gard, and Sara W. Lazara, "Mindfulness Practice Leads to Increases in Regional Brain Gray Matter Density," *Psychiatry Research* 191, no. 1 (2011): 36–43.

46 *Finally, a UCLA study:* Eileen Luders, Nicolas Cherbuin, and Florian Kurth, "Forever Young(er): Potential Age-Defying Effects of Long-Term Meditation on Gray Matter Atrophy," *Frontiers in Psychology* 5 (January 21, 2015):1551.

47 *For women, sitting still:* Dr. John Gray (author and relationship counselor), interview with the author, May 16, 2016.

48 *For example, a study conducted jointly by the Wharton School:* A. C. Hafenbrack, Z. Kinias, S. G. Barsade, "Debiasing the Mind through Meditation: Mindfulness and the Sunk-Cost Bias," *Psychological Science* 25, no. 2 (2013): 369.

49 *A 2013 study of more than six hundred heart-disease patients:* Rachael Rettner, "Heart Disease: Why Positive Attitude May Bring Longer Life," *LiveScience.* September 10, 2013, http://www.livescience.com/39550-heart-disease-positive -attitude-exercise.html.

50 *Numerous studies following medical students:* Roger Collier, "Imagined Illnesses Can Cause Real Problems for Medical Students," *Canadian Medical Association Journal* 178, no. 7 (2008): 820.

51 *I love this quote from Arianna Huffington:* Arianna Huffington, "How to Succeed? Get More Sleep," TED posted January 2011, transcript, https://www.ted.com /talks/arianna_huffington_how_to_succeed_get_more_sleep/transcript?lan guage=en.

52 *Arianna makes a cogent, extremely compelling case:* Arianna Huffington, *The Sleep Revolution: Transforming Tour Life, One Night at a Time* (New York: Harmony, 2016).

53 *Interestingly, a Swiss study:* Kurt Kräuchi, Christian Cajochen, Esther Werth, and Anna Wirz-Justice, "Warm Feet Promote the Rapid Onset of Sleep," *Nature* 401 (September 2, 1999): 36–37.

54 *A German study from 2005:* A. Michalsen, P. Grossman, A. Acil, J. Langhorst, R. Lüdtke, T. Esch, et al.. "Rapid Stress Reduction and Anxiolysis among Distressed Women as a Consequence of a Three-Month Intensive Yoga Program," *Medical Science Monitor* 11, no. 12 (2005): CR555–61.

55 *She writes that:* Esther Perel, "How to Put a Healthy Dose of Space and Mystery into Your Relationship," Esther Perel, March 8, 2015, http://www.estherperel.com /how-to-put-a-healthy-dose-of-space-and-mystery-into-your-relationship.

56 *A UCLA study:* Harlan Lebo, "UCLA Researchers Identify Key Biobehavioral

Pattern Used by Women to Manage Stress." UCLA Newsroom, May 17, 2000, http://newsroom.ucla.edu/releases/UCLA-Researchers-Identify-Key-Biobehav ioral-1478.

57 *Dr. John Gray told me:* Dr. John Gray (author and relationship counselor), interview with the author, May 16, 2016.

58 *The Harvard Nurse's Health Study:* Dr. Randy Kamen, "A Compelling Argument About Why Women Need Friendships." *Huffington Post*, November 29, 2012, http://www.huffingtonpost.com/randy-kamen-gredinger-edd/female-friendship _b_2193062.html.

59 *Indeed, according to a Northwestern University study:* L. F. Emery, A. Muise, E. L. Dix, and B. Le, "Can You Tell That I'm in a Relationship? Attachment and Relationship Visibility on Facebook," *Personality and Social Psychology Bulletin* 40, no. 11 (2014):1466–79.

60 *We have a popular article:* Bob Alaburda, "The Best Sign of a Healthy Relationship Is No Sign of It on Facebook." YourTango. November 10, 2015. http://www .yourtango.com/2015282659/best-sign-healthy-relationship-no-facebook.

61 *There's a viral YourTango article:* Pleasure Mechanics, "The 9-Step Guide to Giving Your Man a Crazy-Hot Lap Dance," YourTango, January 9, 2016, http://www .yourtango.com/experts/pleasure-mechanics/give-him-a-lap-dance.

62 *A crack team:* Amy Muise, Ulrich Schimmack, and Emily A. Impett, "Sexual Frequency Predicts Greater Well-Being, but More is Not Always Better." *Social Psychological and Personality Science*, November 18, 2015. June 1, 2016 27:836-847.

63 *As Ian Kerner, the fantastic sex counselor:* Ian Kerner, PhD, LMFT (psychotherapist and sexuality counselor), interview with the author, April 14, 2016.

64 *In one University of North Carolina at Chapel Hill study:* "News in Health, February 2007—National Institutes of Health (NIH)," *NIH News in Health*, February, 2007, https://newsinhealth.nih.gov/2007/february/docs/01features_01.htm.

65 *Health-wise, a Carnegie Mellon University study:* Sheldon Cohen, Denise Janicki-Deverts, Ronald B. Turner, and William J. Doyle, "Does Hugging Provide Stress-Buffering Social Support? A Study of Susceptibility to Upper Respiratory Infection and Illness." *Psychological Science* 26, no 2 (2015):135–47.

66 *A joint survey:* Jordan Gray, "The ONE Thing Missing from Your Bedroom That'll CHANGE Your Sex Life," YourTango, February 26, 2016, http://www.yourtango .com/2016285871/one-thing-missing-your-sex-life-isnt-sex?utm_source=self.

67 *In one study conducted by researchers at the University of North Carolina:* L. E. Kurtz and S. B. Algoe, "Putting Laughter in Context: Shared Laughter as Behavioral Indicator of Relationship Well-Being." *Personal Relationships* 22, no. 4 (2015): 573–90.

INDEX